Mastering Discourse

......

Mastering Discourse

The

Politics

of

Intellectual

Culture

Paul A. Bové

Duke University Press

Durham and London

1992

A number of chapters or parts of chapters in this book have appeared in previous publications, sometimes in an earlier form.
Chapter 1: 1990, "Discourse," in *Critical Terms for Literary Study*, ed. Frank Lentricchia and Thomas McLaughlin (Chicago: University of Chicago Press), 50–65.
Chapter 2: 1980, "The Penitentiary of Reflection: Søren Kierkegaard's Critical Activity," *boundary 2*, 9 (1980), 233–58.
Chapter 3: 1983, "Variations on Authority: Some Deconstructive Transformations of the American New Criticism," in *The Yale Critics*, eds. Jonathan Arac, Wlad Godzich, and Wallace Martin (Minneapolis: University of Minnesota Press), 3–20.
Chapter 4: 1984, "The Metaphysics of Textuality: Nietzsche's *Use and Abuse of History* and Marx's *Eighteenth Brumaire of Louis Bonaparte*," in *After Theory*, a special issue of *The Dalhousie Review*, 64 (Summer 1984), 401–22.
Chapter 5: 1986, "The Ineluctability of Difference: Scientific Pluralism and the Critical Intelligence," in *Postmodernism and Politics*, ed. Jonathan Arac (Minneapolis: University of Minnesota Press), 3–25.
Chapter 6: 1986, "Agriculture and Academe: America's Southern Question," in *The Legacy of Antonio Gramsci*, ed. Joseph Buttigieg, a special issue of *boundary 2*, 14 (Spring), 169–96.
Chapter 7: 1988, "The Rationality of Disciplines: The Abstract Understanding of Stephen Toulmin," in *After Foucault*, ed. Jonathan Arac (New Brunswick: Rutgers University Press), 42–70.
Chapter 9: 1990, "Paul de Man: Some Notes on the Critic's Search for Authority Against Consensus," *Criticism* 32, 2 (Spring), 149–61.
Chapter 10: 1992, "Madness, Medicine, and the State," in *Rewriting the History of Madness*, eds. Irving Velody and Arthur Still (London: Routledge).

For my mother

Contents

......

Preface

......

Hegel's *Phenomenology of Spirit* establishes that the universe of modernity is a universe of discourse;[1] it has been literary theory's task in the last thirty years or so to deal with the authority of Hegel's claim and the factuality of what it represents about life in the modern and post-modern world.[2] Anyone even remotely familiar with theory, even by way of *Newsweek* and the *New York Times*, realizes that theoreticians, especially poststructuralists, are said to believe such things as "there is nothing except language" or "reality is constructed by words." These misrepresentations have a bit of truth about them; certainly theoreticians repeatedly come up against the givenness of modernity as a world of discourse and have treated it as itself a human, cultural, and political artifact, a sign of the presence of self-consciousness, as it were. From Derrida commenting on Bataille on Hegel through Foucault writing on madness, discipline, and sexuality to Kristeva or Irigaray on the chora or the speculum, "discourse" has been both an operator and object of criticism—one given special force in Gayatri Spivak's consideration of "decolonization."[3]

The essays collected in this book, beginning with chapter one, all belong to the critical determinations and instabilities that exist when discourse problematizes itself, even if, as in these pieces, only partially and incompletely. I contend throughout this volume that critics who rush to extend their work through the many senses that discourse has taken on within the academic institutions should not too easily cele-brate their discovery of this intellectual tool, this intellectual, insti-

tutional reality. Repeatedly, and the pattern is too interesting to be accidental, contemporary oppositional critics, empowered with new de-
vices and concepts associated with notions of discursivity, become too
confident in their stance or position, too sure of their place "beyond" or
"post" the objects of their critique; as a result, they work and so remain
within discourse itself, untroubled even by the status of intellectual
"work" carried out as critique, as a form of negation essential to discourse. In the very process of critique, then, their "work," as such, draws
them up against the limits discourse imposes upon intellectual freedom
when it is detached from efforts to slip around, as it were, the determinations of discursive history. These limits often appear, as the following
essays try to show, as what within discourse we call contradictions,
especially between the naive facts that "oppositional" practices always
and unavoidably begin in very important ways as supports for the discourse that enables the very critique they carry out.

"Discourse," which becomes uniquely modern around the end of
the eighteenth and beginning of the nineteenth century, poses itself as
the form assumed by subjectivity, knowledge, the state, and their cor-
ollaries within society. As I try to indicate by the final essay in this book,
Foucault's early studies of madness, medicine, and the structures of
knowledge in the classical and modern periods suggest as much. These
writings, especially those on medicine, show that the praxical and
institutional embodiments of discourse are—in a familiar formula—
already inscribed across the highest linguistic embodiments of cultural
expression of the time, namely, philosophy and literature. In other
words, despite all that has been written by Foucault himself as well as
others about his revolutionary challenge to the history of philosophy
and history of ideas through the writing of archaeologies and genealogies of "anonymous" and "impersonal" forces or power structures, his
stories about discourse matter insofar as they rewrite, not to disprove
or even displace—perhaps only to evade—what were the then emergent modern formations which, as in Hegel, construct an identity of
"reason," "discourse," "subject," "history," and "the state." Kojève's
reading of Hegel, which underpins the problematics of poststructuralism, decodes the *Phenomenology* as the text that specifically creates the
universalizing identification of all these other terms with "discourse."

"Discourse" has taken on an important but diminished sense in literary criticism in which it refers to an organized, consistent, professional,
institutionalized language used to produce and reproduce knowledge.

Conceived in this way, critics understand neither "discourse's" existence as the enabling given for intellectual production—especially in the act of liberatory negation which critics interested in recounting either the "genealogy" of some empirical reality or sociological concept take as their basic task—nor the consequences that follow upon its redeployment as a device of critique, of negation. Hegel's central contribution to the establishment of "discourse's" identities rests upon making negation do its work. Academics in the United States, often confronted with this difficulty and with the serious efforts of some poststructuralists to deal with it, typically either evade it—through various anti-theory, neo-historicist programs—or simplify it beyond recognition (the term is apropos here) by appealing to popular science or philosophy of science: they talk about "double-binds" or unavoidable contradictions—thereby doing the work of the negative while resting within it. As Derrida says of Bataille on Hegel, "In discourse (the unity of process and system), negativity is always the underside and accomplice of positivity."[4]

Discourse has come to refer to not only an assemblage of statements (énoncés) with a common object of reference, but also the ability to think in an orderly way, an endowment identical with "reason," itself. It is a representational potential of this kind that establishes the identity of meaning with history through their mutual recollected embodiment in the system of concepts that makes up not only the history of philosophy, but also, as we might say with reference to Hegel's preface to the *Phenomenology*, the structure of Being working patiently to manifest itself in historicized culture. This manifestation pre-empts the movements of critique as negation carried out after the rediscovery of discourse as the given of social and intellectual modern human existence. Following Nietzsche's and Heidegger's directions and after the best of French Hegel, Foucault, like Derrida and other poststructuralists, finds what that cunning German had hidden in the open, and he specifically tries to make the term *discourse* work to unwind the system. He struggles to turn it into the operator of critique—an understandable but nonetheless strange and perhaps impossible move for an avowed anti-Hegelian and anti-dialectician. Foucault tries to pass through the moments of identity constitution that takes place in discourse—a fact that perhaps explains his lifelong attempt to understand the nature of subject formation in a manner he felt would obviate Hegel's story and disclose some of what historicized dialectics occluded.[5]

The critique of discourse cannot bring the mastery of discourse which contemporary criticism seems to feel it can accomplish in its neo-historicist manifestation—with its concerns for representative systems of power—or in its avowedly more "political" concern with supposedly concrete material institutions. "Mastery" is, we might say, the device that slides critics back within the servility that discourse has planned for them. Masters, we recall, depend upon struggle and the willingness to risk their lives in a battle for recognition.[6] Slaves are either afraid of death or lack the strength to succeed in struggle. And so it is from within the resources of cowardice, diminishment, and defeat—especially after the 1980s—that critics alone can hope to overcome both their fear of struggle and their place within discourse that defines the range of their possibilities in advance.

It is, of course, a post-Hegelian answer to this problem to suggest that acting to change the world in line with more rational, just, and rewarding ideals will alter the world and consciousness, thereby overcoming the dilemma from within it. And indeed such an argument begins to transcend the limits of servility; however the argument needs to see itself as already an important part of the story told to establish that history is a struggle for mastery and recognition. Its "transcendence" derives, so to speak, from a hope to become masters. (It is to avoid the structure of repetition that Bataille and Derrida pose the "sovereign" as an alternative to the "master.") It is, as it were, a predictable move of negation with a fatal consequence: "masters" recognition depends upon the subjugation of others, the production of slaves unless and until the entire structure is transcended in its own fulfillment—the emergence of a wise philosopher. (We should recall that in its fulfillment, the structure assigns criticism to the immature phase of unhappy consciousness and its success to a strong statist regime.)

Of course, academic critics can simply assert that none of this matters, that the daily empirical work of the academy, the disciplines, and their reform is all that is available and cannot help but proceed, and better that it proceed for reform than not. Of course, such an attitude is at best liberalism and at worst skepticism. But it cannot avoid the truth of the relations discourse determines as it masters its would-be conquerors.

And yet the weakness of discourse lies just in its seriousness, in its demand for and efforts to impose universal recognition. This means that the work of critics always stands within it, that discourse always masters critics as they become what they are. Yet as mastery discourse cannot be complete in itself; its partiality, its weak strength, its frustrated insistence that nothing can happen that it does not contain—all this must be made the object of derision, but from within the diminished, subaltern position alone left to those who might try to deride it. As Nietzsche knew, mockery can be dangerous to the mocker, marginalizing the effort, but potentially freeing in its capacity to let the intelligence know its circumstances, recognize its very pre-emptions, and devise tactics for its moment-by-moment struggle to evade the fearful position of the Other's Other.

The essays that follow, written over a more than ten-year period, touch on these problems as thematics. Mostly they explore the difficulty that powerful and wise critics have confronting their circumstances at a very bad political and intellectual time. At times they try to evade the problems discourse poses for writing; at other times they attempt the route of discursive and institutional critique that also now seems so failed despite its ongoing success in telling us much about our history and the places in which we work. They represent something of the history in which various critical efforts were taken up and celebrated with varying degrees of enthusiasm. They record as well the growing temptation to stoicism and skepticism the events of the period encourage. Finally, perhaps, they suggest some despair or at least the impatient question, "What would you have us do?" Surely they are vulnerable to the charge that they are neither complete nor representative. I make no claim for either quality. I claim only to record some part of an effort to understand and deal with a limited set of problems as they presented themselves during a certain period of time. They need to be read—and welcomed or rejected—on those terms.

With the exception of chapter 8, all of these essays appeared in previous publications, sometimes in slightly different form. I would like to thank the editors and publishers involved: The University of Chicago Press; The University of Minnesota Press; boundary 2; The Dalhousie Review; Rutgers University Press; The Minnesota Review; Criticism; Rethinking Marxism; and Routledge.

I wish also to thank again my colleagues on boundary 2, Jonathan Arac, Joseph Buttigieg, Margaret Ferguson, Nancy Fraser, Michael Hays, Daniel O'Hara, Donald E. Pease, William Spanos, and Cornel West, for providing that rarest of intellectual qualities, a community of different and debating scholars. I want also to thank my Pittsburgh colleagues for their patience and help. I acknowledge too the generous support of the University of Pittsburgh Research Office in completing this manuscript.

I owe a special debt to Joanne Ferguson of Duke University Press, who encouraged me to assemble this book and to Reynolds Smith who, with great patience, took on the task upon Joanne's retirement.

Carol M. Bové provided support and encouragement all during the years when this book was being written, sometimes at the expense of time given to her own writing. Always, however, working along with her has made the life of academia lose all of its sometimes regrettable qualities. Our daughter, Laura, has added immensely to life just precisely as she gives time to us to take us away from our desks and our secondhand knowledge.

When I was a child, my mother, Carmella Caspanello Bové, never let me be satisfied with what came easily and taught me always to try harder and to be independent. Her teaching has always been there even when I have not always kept to it. Hence, I dedicate this book to her.

Paul A. Bové
Wexford, August 9, 1991

Mastering Discourse

......

I

......

Introduction:
Discourse

"Discourse" has been a key concept in modern literary criticism. The New Critics, for example, would speak of the "discourse of the novel" as opposed to "poetic discourse" as a way of identifying and separating genre. And, of course, for the New Critics, this distinction implied a hierarchy: poetry was always superior to prose, despite T. S. Eliot's description of the latter as "an unspeakably difficult art." Even the New Critics who wrote fiction and poetry called themselves primarily "poet-critics." Allen Tate, for example, thought of his fine novel, *The Fathers*, as a diversion, an experiment, and considered himself a poet.

To look, then, at the New Critics' use of "discourse" might be a good beginning to an understanding of certain changes that have taken place recently in this key critical term. For the New Critics, "discourse" marked differences and established identities. For example, it helped them set the limits of certain kinds of language use; and the New Critics and their heirs (including, in this case, Northrop Frye) tried to discover whatever it was that made for the identity of one sort of language as opposed to another. These are the sorts of distinctions critics came to think of as "genre differences." In other words, each "discourse," in itself, from this point of view, has an identity to be discovered, defined, and understood; in addition, each discourse established the limits of a particular genre: Tate, for example, could approve moments of *Finnegans Wake* because they were "poetic"; but he could not praise the entire novel, precisely because it exceeded the limits of any genre— that is, it was neither this nor that, neither purely poetry nor purely prose. Joyce's book, for Tate, was off the grid made up by the categories of discourse which, for him and many other modern critics, defined the identity of genre and marked the differences of one genre from another. Not incidentally, this categorization of "genre" was essentially ahistorical and resulted in the consideration of literature apart from the specifics of history and culture (many important contemporary critics have since tried to reverse this result).[1] Indeed, one might say that the New Criticism's conservative political and cultural character appears most fully in its notion of genre: in opposition to what they saw as an unchanging "present" of capitalistic excess and the scientific dominance of culture, they counterposed the "memory" or "myth" of an equally unchanging agrarian or pastoral past. Only from this stable community of class relations, they believed, could there re-emerge the relatively fixed benevolent forms of tradition that capitalism destroyed (during the Civil War in the United States and globally in World War I) and that modern literature and criticism would fruitfully modify, replace, or restore.

Quite consciously, then, the New Critics (particularly the Southerners among them who passed through agrarian and regionalist moments in their development) linked these essentialist—and, thus, timeless—"genres" to specific modes of social existence, and they saw them as "expressive" of stable relations in a particular kind of rural or classical community. But paradoxically, they thought these genres still existed and that their recreation and use might help reestablish, in our world, the cultural values that had belonged to the societies that produced them. However, we should not forget that these idealistic and ahistorical notions developed in highly charged and specific political contexts.[2] Another way to put this would be to say—with some contemporary poststructuralists like Michel Foucault and Gilles Deleuze—that the New Critics' idea of genre masked a specific link to power and desire. It obscured the New Critics' own historical needs and wants. It helped transform their real historical experiences of concrete political and cultural deprivation into a conservative expression of their mythic desire to recover a lost origin, a supposed premodern state of innocence best named by T. S. Eliot as "an undissociated sensibility."

It is worth pointing out, then, that, in effect, the New Critics put to use this term "discourse." Indeed, their case illustrates exactly how key terms are finally more important for their function, for their place within intellectual practices, than they are for what they may be said to "mean" in the abstract. In other words, we must try to see that while the

New Critics were carrying on the post-Renaissance business of making distinctions and marking identities about such things as genre, their use of the term "discourse" powerfully shaped the field of literary critical understanding and contained an entire range of aesthetic, moral, and political value judgments which were often unacknowledged as such— although they were sometimes quite clearly understood.

To be more specific, we might say that "discourse," used in this New Critical sense, is itself an example of how we might now delineate the functioning of "discourse" as a category within contemporary critical practice: it helped to constitute and organize an entire field of knowledge about language; it helped discipline the judgment, and thereby the response, of students and teachers; and, in so doing, it revealed its links to forms of power—such as teaching—that have effects upon the actions of others. And in the case of New Criticism, we can, if we choose, easily trace this pattern, in which an intellectually specialized language of a professional discipline is constellated and made functional; we can see it extended both into a broader coherence with other discourses constituting other fields and into the processes which institutionalize discourses. When their "discourse" about language and criticism became institutionalized, it effectively produced the language of professional literary criticism and, accordingly, helped make up an academic discipline by giving it some of the characteristics of other intellectual fields already professionally organized. As a result, criticism joined in the general disciplinary project of producing and regulating the movement of knowledge, the forms of language, and the training of minds and bodies. Professionalized academic literary criticism came into being.

But a reader might ask: How can we arrive at such a far-flung set of conclusions? He or she might argue, for example, that Tate simply inherits the apparently self-evident distinction between "poetry" and "prose." It is part of "his discourse" as a man of letters, a literary critic, and poet-novelist; this traditional opposition makes possible, for example, Tate's quite remarkable discussions of Faulkner and Eliot. In other words, such a reader might say, this opposition is merely an accepted critical "tool" that allows Tate to produce essays and that makes possible the debate that surrounds them. Perhaps we would best respond to this respectable line of thought by saying that it is the very utility of the discourse that must be seen as functional and regulative. It hierarchizes not only poetry and prose but, implicitly, identity and difference, authority and subservience, taste and vulgarity, and continuity and discontinuity as well—that is, we might say, it shares in the operation of the generalized discourse of our society that constitutes its most basic categories of understanding and thought.

We might continue to answer this question by saying that *of course* this kind of "genre discourse" speaks through Tate and, indeed, from our point of view the very fact allows us to say that in *these terms* he too is a "function," that in doing his work, he helps maintain and extend the very hierarchies and disciplines we have already mentioned. The final poststructuralist attempt to convince such a questioner that these conclusions are legitimate (even if not fully demonstrated here) would be a quite simple argument: above all, what is noticeable about the way "discourse" functions in the New Criticism is that it draws attention away from itself, from its disciplinary operations and effects—with their promises of reward and assistance—and focuses the attention of the New Critics' apprentices on the need "to get the job done," to understand the "meaning" of texts and produce "new readings" of them. Like all successful discursive categories, in other words, the New Criticism became, for a time, transparent, naturalized, and self-evident. Its effects within the field of knowledge established by the discourse to which it belongs were not noticed or examined by those operating within—that is, producing knowledge defined by—that field.

II

The work of Michel Foucault has given a special prominence to the concept of "discourse" in contemporary intellectual and political analysis. He used the term throughout most of his significant writing, but with *L'ordre du discours*, his inaugural lecture at the College de France (1970), and his methodological book *The Archaeology of Knowledge*, the idea gained a new rigor and a new significance that, one might say, has effectively changed the way in which we think of language and its relation to social institutions, systems of power, and the role of intellectuals in our society.

It must be said that in light of the new tenor given to "discourse," we can no longer easily ask such questions as, What is discourse? or, What does discourse mean? In other words, an essay like the present one not only does not but *cannot* provide definitions, nor can it answer what comes down to essentializing questions about the "meaning" or "identity" of some "concept" named "discourse." To attempt to do so would be to contradict the logic of the structure of thought in which the term "discourse" now has a newly powerful critical function.

Of course, the reader of a book like this one may wonder why these questions about meaning cannot be answered and perhaps cannot even be asked. Do I not overstate my case? Do I not really mean that poststructuralists don't speak clearly and so cannot answer such commonsensical questions? To such remarks as these, I must reply that the original statement was correct: these essentialist, defining questions quite precisely *cannot* be asked of "discourse." But why not? Because to ask them and to force an answer would be, in advance, hopelessly to prejudice the case against understanding the function of "discourse" either in its poststructuralist context or in its existence as an institutionalized system for the production of knowledge in regulated language. To be more precise, poststructuralists hold that these essentializing questions emerge from the very interpretive models of thought which the new focus on "discourse" as a material practice aims to examine and trace.

Yet, without a doubt, these questions that I label illegitimate are absolutely "commonsensical" and "normal" within our disciplines' systems of knowledge and inquiry; but poststructuralists would argue that their very "normalcy" gives them a troubling power to shape thought and to hinder the posing of other questions. Indeed, poststructuralists would, I am sure, follow Gramsci in saying that it is their very place within the realm of "common sense" that should be questioned so that their effects—their "values" or "ideologies," if you prefer—can be brought into focus.[3] Put yet another way, we can say that these questions imply a norm of judgment: meaning and essence are better and more important than a discussion of "how things work" or "where they come from." That is, within the normal procedures of our disciplines and the knowledge-producing system they make up, these "commonsensical" questions are more important than genealogical and functional questions. Such questions are "self-evident" because they are part of a particular network of powerful intellectual and disciplinary expectations. They are asked in all innocence, but their "anonymous" effect is directed and power-laden: to make a theory which "chooses" not to answer them appear to be naive, obfuscating, needlessly difficult, or simply wrong and confused. By obliging all to answer the "same" questions, the "discourse" of "truth" and "definition," of

"understanding" and "meaning," to which these questions belong ho-
mogenizes critical practice and declares "invalid" whatever does not
and *cannot* operate on its political and intellectual terrain. In other
words, in this little exemplum, we can see something of what the new
sense of "discourse" allows us to describe: the "self-evident" and "commonsensical" are what have the privilege of unnoticed power, and this
power produces instruments of control. This matter of control is rather
difficult; it does not mean, as it might in certain Freudian or Marxist
theories, control by repression or by exclusion. It means, rather, control by the power of positive production: that is, a kind of power that
generates certain kinds of questions, placed within systems that legitimate, support, and answer those questions; a kind of power that, in the
process, includes within its systems all those it produces as agents
capable of acting within them. For example, it produces psychiatrists
who let people talk—"confess," as Foucault puts it[4]—and so come to
constitute themselves as a certain kind of subject who believes sexuality alone defines his or her identity. Indeed, from Foucault's point of
view, all intellectuals, all teachers and students within the disciplines,
are to some extent incorporated within these systems of control based
upon the mode of knowledge and truth production that defines much
of our social world. There is, in other words, no place for any of us to
stand outside of it.

We should, then, ask another set of questions: How does discourse
function? Where is it to be found? How does it get produced and
regulated? What are its social effects? How does it exist—as, say, a set of
isolated events hierarchically related or as a seemingly enduring flow of
linguistic and institutional transformations? In effect, then, to understand the new sense of "discourse," one must try to position it, to see it
in its own terms, to describe its place within a network of other analytic
and theoretical concepts which are "weapons" for grappling with contemporary society and its history. For example, Foucault gives us a
strong sense of discourse as an enduring flow by tracing the genealogy
of "discipline" as a series of events existing as transformations of one
another.[5]

"Discourse" provides a privileged entry into the poststructuralist
mode of analysis precisely because it is the organized and regulated, as
well as the regulating and constituting functions of language that it
studies: its aim is to describe the surface linkages between power,
knowledge, institutions, intellectuals, the control of populations, and

the modern state as these intersect in the functions of systems of thought.

There is a broad political purpose to this project that develops out of a radical skepticism about "truth" and the correspondence of fact and concept. It is worth pointing out, however, that this skepticism is not nostalgic; that is, it does not regret the passing idealistic philosophies or empirical scientific certainties. On the contrary, it celebrates, if you will, the increasing impossibility of defending "truth" in any metaphysical way and welcomes the political possibilities for self-determination inherent in a recognition that "truth" is made by humans as the result of very specific material practices. A general source for this kind of thinking is in the writings of Giambattista Vico, who insisted upon seeing history and society as human productions. For poststructuralists, however, who are not historicists, a more important and immediate source for the development of this project is the philosophy and history of science developed in France, most notably by Gaston Bachelard and Georges Canguilhem—two important influences on Foucault (another is Georges Dumézil's study of ritual, while a fourth would be Kojève's, Koyré's, and Jean Hyppolite's critiques of Hegel).[6]

Canguilhem's influence was particularly important. His work showed that the history of systems of thought, of disciplines, and of sciences was not merely the chronology of concepts, ideas, and individual discoveries. He did at least two things that helped make possible certain characteristic poststructuralist efforts to rethink the functions of knowledge and truth in modern and postmodern societies. In a sense, he de-personalized science; that is, he showed that it did not have to be understood in terms of individual genius, even of individuals finding solutions and posing problems; he outlined the history of science as the workings of a number of material practices that make up a society. He traced how some of these practices and sciences extended—like "vectors," as it were—throughout a culture, and he showed how they opened new spaces for new forms of knowledge production. By so doing, Canguilhem also showed that science(s) "cohere"; this is a difficult notion. By saying that different sciences and systems of thought "cohere," he claimed that they share what Edward W. Said has called "adjacency,"[7] or what Wittgenstein and Chomsky let us call loosely "family resemblances." The order of business for the historian and philosopher of science, then, was to become a historian and philosopher of entire "systems of thought." This approach created unique problems as well as opportunities. Most important, it obliged Canguilhem and others after him to consider how, within the "systems of thought" they constituted, various "sciences" might be institutionally and even conceptually discontinuous; how they might be practiced, as it were, at disparate points within a culture and yet, given their "adjacencies," make up a coherent system of thought spread across a range of institutions and discourses whose family resemblances can be traced by the genealogist interested in their multiple origins, transformations, and their value for the present. (A similar problem for the literary critic might involve tracing the adjacencies between the rise of the realistic novel and, say, such pertinent discourses as anthropology or psychology.)

These three lines of inquiry intersect in poststructuralism and, joined with a certain understanding of Nietzsche,[8] make possible a skeptical and relativistic, or perspectival, view of the authority of scientific disciplines and, indeed, of all humanistic discourses. In effect, for poststructuralism, all "truths" are relative to the frame of reference which contains them; more radically, "truths" are a function of these frames; and even more radically, these discourses "constitute" the truths they claim to discover and transmit. In its thinking about discourse, then, poststructuralism offers us a kind of nominalism: all that exists are discrete historical events, and the propositions or concepts which claim to tell the truth about them have no reality beyond that acquired by being consistent within the logic of the system that makes them possible. This would seem to be a radical perspectivism, except as poststructuralism develops this idea, it has no psychologistic element; no given perspective depends upon the viewpoint of any actually existing person or even group of persons. The function of discourse and the realities it constructs are fundamentally anonymous. This does not mean that no individuals hold these perspectives nor that no individuals affect them. It means, rather, that their effective realities depend upon no particular subject in history. In opposition to certain kinds of Marxism, for example, this understanding of discourse does not make discourse the product of a particular class or set of class conflicts and conjunctions. There is no natural or necessary identity to the dispersed coherence of discourse; nonetheless, in their randomness the events form a coherence.

But how can this skepticism have a politics? A poststructuralist response would go something like this: Discourses produce knowledge about humans and their society. But since the "truths" of these discourses are relative to the disciplinary structures, the logical framework in which they are institutionalized, they can have no claim upon us except that derived from the authority and legitimacy, the power, granted to or acquired by the institutionalized discourses in question. This large fact turns us to an analysis of the history of discourses, or, more precisely, to their genealogies.

"Genealogy" complements the critical dimension of poststructuralism's radical skepticism. It aims to grasp the formative power of discourses and disciplines. This involves a double analysis, but one in which the two parts are not really separate. First, genealogy tracks down the ways in which discourses constitute "objects" and "classes of objects" which are available for study. Second, and more important, genealogy traces the way in which discourses constitute these objects as subjects of statements which can themselves be judged as "true" or "false" according to the logic, syntax, and semantics of the empowered discourse. Not unless a statement is about an "object" and can be judged in its truthfulness does it enter into a discourse; but once it does, it furthers the dispersal of that discourse and enlarges the realm of objects and statements which produce knowledge that can be judged legitimate or illegitimate. There is a relationship of constitutive reciprocity, then, between the "objects" and "statements" within any discourse. Neither can be studied without seeing it in its relation to the other.

For example (and this is a privileged example in poststructuralism), how did the human subject come to be that about which entire sets of psychological statements can be uttered that, in turn, as propositions, can be judged true or false? In effect what this kind of questioning supposes is that both the object of disciplinary study, in this case the subject as psyche, and the discipline which forms authenticated statements about the object are functions of discourses "about" the subject they constitute: for only within these discourses and the practices that grow from and depend upon them does the "psyche" exist as an object of a certain kind of knowledge ("a certain kind" is a necessary part of this formulation in light of Foucault's work in the second and third volumes of his history of sexuality; he showed there that sex can be and has been the "object" of many different kinds of knowledge and practice).[9] Genealogy tries to get hold of this power that crosses discourses and to show that it is, among other things, the power that makes possible and legitimate certain kinds of questions and statements. It is, in other words, the power to produce statements which alone can be judged "true" or "false" within the knowledge/power system that produces "truth" and its criteria within a culture. It is, in effect, recognizing that "truth" is produced in just this way as the "effect," so to speak, of systems-in-place to which are reserved the authorities of judgment—it is by recognizing this effect of power that genealogy does its work. Indeed, genealogy lets us confront how power constructs truth-producing systems in which propositions, concepts, and representations generally assign value and meaning to the objects of the various disciplines that treat them. Value, we might say, circulates along the paths or vectors these disciplines sketch. Within literary studies, for example, we might say that this power shapes the language that lets us speak about such creations of the discipline as "the author," while not easily letting us see the workings by which "the author" has come to be constituted by and for us when we "discourse" about literature and writing.[10]

But how, then, is "discourse" key to more than a politics of abstract language games? The answer lies in the materiality of discourse. That is, "discourse" makes possible disciplines and institutions which, in turn, sustain and distribute those discourses. Foucault has shown how this works in the case of prisons and medical clinics. In other words, these discourses are linked to social institutions which "have power" in the very ordinary sense we mean when we use that phrase: such institutions can control bodies and actions. But there is more to them than "having power" in the sense of being able to dominate others. And this is more slippery and strange as an idea, but it is central to grasping the utility of discourse for political intellectual analysis.

Discourses and their related disciplines and institutions are functions of power: they distribute the effects of power. They are power's relays throughout the modern social system. One of Foucault's late meditations usefully gets at this idea:

> In effect, what defines a relationship of power is that it is a mode of action which does not act directly and immediately on others. Instead it acts upon their actions: an action upon an action, on existing actions or on those which may arise in the present or the future. . . . A power relationship can only be articulated on the basis of two elements which are each indispensable if it is really to

be a power relationship: that "the other" (the one over whom power is exercised) be thoroughly recognized and maintained to the very end as a person who acts; and that, faced with a relationship of power, a whole field of responses, reactions, results, and possible inventions may open up.[11]

Power must not be thought of as negative, as repression, domination, or inhibition. On the contrary, it must always be seen as "a making possible," as an opening up of fields in which certain kinds of action and production are brought about. As power disperses itself, it opens up specific fields of possibility; it constitutes entire domains of action, knowledge, and social being by shaping the institutions and disciplines in which, for the most part, we largely make ourselves. In these domains we become the individuals, the subjects, that they make us. This phrasing, of course, makes things sound more deterministic than they are in fact, for there is no subject there to be determined in advance: the subject comes to be whatever or whoever he or she is only within this set of discursive and nondiscursive fields. What Foucault means when he says that power acts upon actions is precisely that it regulates our forming of ourselves. "Individuation," then, is the space in which we are most regulated by the ruling disciplines of language, sexuality, economics, culture, and psychology.

"Discourse" is one of the most empowered ways in modern and postmodern societies for the forming and shaping of humans as "subjects." In a now-famous play on words, we might say that "power" through its discursive and institutional relays "subjects" us: that is, it makes us into "subjects," and it "subjects" us to the rule of the dominant disciplines which are empowered in our society and which regulate its possibilities for human freedom—that is, it "subjugates" us. (The French have a set of words that gives them some punning insights into this whole matter: the poststructuralists have made much of the word *assujettir*, which means to subject and to subjugate.) Indeed, we must even hypothesize that power affects the forms which our resistance to power can take. In other words, according to this notion there is no essential self somewhere else within power; consequently, resistance to any particular form of power—resistance to any discursive "truth"— depends upon power and not some abstract category of freedom or the self.

How does this happen? Recall that "true statements" are always relative to the authority of empowered discourses; recall, in addition, that what is constituted as "real" are only those objects of which statements can be judged true or false. As humans, we are the "subject" of these discourses and their crossings; if we are professional critics, literary criticism would be prominent among them. But before we had received our professional training, we would already have been the subject of other disciplines which criticism might enforce or, in part, subvert. Surely sexuality, law, and the psyche, embedded in fundamental institutions and discourses, would be the earliest means to "subject" us all within this culture. We would become, then, in very large measure, the objects who are the subjects of these (our own) discourses: readers and writers, subjects assessed by statistics, bodies available to punishment regulated by the helping services, psyches to be normalized, bodies to be "engendered," and so forth. A genealogical study of "discourse" would be a study of how these things have come about; even more, it would be a history of how the present has come about in part by virtue of the increasing ability of the power which forms such disciplines to arrange social and individual life.

The study of "discourse," then, leads inevitably to a study of institutions, disciplines, and intellectuals: poststructuralists like Foucault would argue that the research areas opened up by this concept of "discourse" are inherently restricted to matters of the local; other thinkers, especially those who might try to align some of these poststructuralist notions with certain forms of recent Marxist thinking— much of it derived from Gramsci—would argue that such study cannot stop at the local level but must be expanded to outline the relationship of these discursive institutions to the largest forms of power—civil society and the state.[12] In both cases, though, there seems to be a common concern: to understand how these material discursive realities act upon the actions of others, that is, of all of us, no matter where and how differently placed we are in the grid of identity and privilege these realities constitute.

Foucault argues that power is deeply rooted in social relations but that this fact should not be taken fatalistically:

> For to say that there cannot be a society without power relations is not to say either that those which are established are necessary, or, in any case, that power constitutes a fatality at the heart of societies, such that it cannot be undermined. Instead I would say that the

analysis, elaboration, and bringing into question of power relations and the "agonism" between power relations and intran-
sitivity of freedom is a permanent political task inherent in all
social relations.[13]

"Genealogy" provides unique access to these relations and struggles:
unlike Marxism and whiggism, two major forms of historical explanation which it opposes, genealogy separates itself within the "will to
truth" by trying to unmask discourse's associations with power and
materialities; also, it is not reductive, that is, it alone allows for a full
description of the complexly determined discursive practices it studies; and, finally, it describes and criticizes these practices with an eye to
revealing their "subjugating" effects in the present—it means always to
resist disciplining and speaking for others in their own struggles.[14]

"Genealogy" aims not to trace causal influences among events, nor to
follow the evolution of the "Spirit of History"; it does not adhere to
strict historical laws, nor does it believe in the power of subjects, great
or small, to act "originally," that is, to "change history." Rather it describes events as transformations of other events which, from the
vantage point of the present and its needs, seem to be related by a
family resemblance. It shows how these transformations have no
causal or historical necessity; they are not "natural." It shows how the
adjacency of events, that is, their simultaneity within ostensibly different fields, can transform entire domains of knowledge production:
the rise of statistics and the development of discipline within massed
armies helped transform punishment from torture to imprisonment
with its rationale of rehabilitation. It also shows that this new penal
discipline makes the body's punishment the space wherein the modern soul, the psyche, comes into being and is made available to the
"helping" (that is, the disciplining) professions of social work, teaching,
and medicine.

In the process of this description and criticism, genealogy also en-
gages in intellectual struggle with the major forms of explanatory discourse in modernity, with what are sometimes totalizing oppositional
discourses—such as psychoanalysis and Marxism—which, from the
point of view of poststructuralism, are inescapably caught up in the
same disciplining formations as penology, medicine, and law. This is
not to say that genealogical work is simply "anti-Marxist" or "anti-
Freudian"; rather, it is interested in describing how these grand opposi-

tional discourses have become authoritative and productive within the larger field of humanistic discourse which defines modernity—and in trying to pose other questions. Foucault would have it, for example, that everyone is a Marxist: how can one not be? What this means, of course, is not just that the fundamental Marxist analysis of class domination and struggle, as well as other basic Marxist concepts, are uncontestable but also that we are all inscribed within the larger realm of discourse of subjectivity and struggle of which Marxism is, for certain intellectuals, a privileged part. Nevertheless, the centrality of discourse to poststructuralism requires understanding something more about its relation to Marxism, especially in France. In France, poststructuralism's questioning of Marxism has much to do with the student revolt of May 1968 and the so-called new politics that grew out of it. This questioning also grows out of a concern for socialism's weaknesses, of that kind now broadly (if wrongly) associated with Gorbachev's policy of *glasnost*. Intellectually, this concern has found its best voice in certain dissidents' objections to what one of their number calls "actually existing socialism."[15] It implies a conflict with Marxism's dialectical materialism and the principles of elite political leadership contained within it; for example, Foucault's experience of the events in Paris in 1968 led to his criticism of established forms of political leadership and representative institutions.[16] Just as genealogy can produce a critique of how liberal disciplines create the subjugated subjects differentiated, as such, within the regulated space of discourse, so Marxism—from this point of view—with its understanding of the proletariat as the subject of history, appears as a relay of power which acts upon the actions of the class it "constitutes" and the individuals disciplined by its institutions.

Foucault grew increasingly interested in what the rise of the modern disciplines had to do with modern state power—with what he called "governability"—and how it displaced sovereignty as the hegemonic figure of power and authority. A genealogical analysis of the discourses and practices that made for this transformation does not suggest that dialectics stands outside it. For example, a study of governability in an era of constitutive and regulative disciplines shows that actions always follow upon actions acting upon agents at a distance: liberal and Marxist discourses, by contrast, always think of the actors as metaphysically constitutive subjects (for an example of how complex this notion can be, see George Lukács's discussion of "putative class consciousness"[17]).

Politically, then, politics and democracy are the issues in poststructuralism's attempt to theorize power, action, agency, and resistance. In disciplinary societies, self-determination is nearly impossible, and political opposition must take the form of resistance to the systems of knowledge and their institutions that regulate the population into "individualities" who, as such, make themselves available for more discipline, to be actors acted upon. In this understanding of governability, truth produced by these knowledge systems blocks the possibility of sapping power; it speaks for—or, as we say in Western republics, it "represents"—others. But for poststructuralism, it is not self-evident, for example, that notions of oppositional leadership, such as Gramsci's conception of the "organic intellectual,"[18] will be significant alternatives to the regulating ideal of "speaking for." Having emerged out of the events of 1968, poststructuralism remains politically suspicious of all rhetorics of leadership and all representational institutions. It gives priority to the politics of local struggles against defining forms of power and for marginalized identities; and it speaks for the difficulty (not the impossibility!) human beings face in trying to make their own "subjectivities" within the given sets of power relations.

The genealogical analysis of discourse, then, sets out with an eye on the present to criticize and trace the systems of power which have come to constitute being human in our world. It does this to stand in opposition to them and to provide the results of its work to whomever would like to use them in their struggles against the forms of power they are trying to resist.

III

The contemporary use of "discourse" turns literary critics away from questions of meaning; it also turns us from questions of "method" to the description of function. It suggests that a new set of questions should replace the interpretive ones that have come to constitute criticism and the normal practice of teachers and scholars. We might ask such things as, How does language work to produce knowledge? How is language organized in disciplines? Which institutions perform and which regulative principles direct this organization? With these questions and the turn from a discourse of "meaning," from hermeneutics, or from interpretive criticism as the grand humanistic practice, we turn to the question of the subject. We turn especially to the question of how the subject is produced within social discourses and institutions and how, also, the subject becomes the "subject-function." Within literary critical studies, this requires that we consider the function of the "author" in critical discourse and in the larger formation of the subject and the discourses of subjectivity within the modern and postmodern worlds.

Now with the question of the author, we come to an area heatedly debated and much misunderstood in recent criticism. Barthes, Derrida, and Foucault have variously proposed an apparently scandalous idea: the author is "dead"; language speaks, not the poet; the author is irrelevant. For the humanistic critic raised in the tradition of *belles lettres* or of American common sense or profitably invested in the defense of "traditional values," this sort of notion is either nonsensical, or, rather neurotically, taken to be a "threat to civilization," or not taken seriously, or, perhaps most commonly, simply dismissed as just too hard to understand.

One must try to clear up some of the confusion by recalling Foucault's assertion that no one is interested in denying the existence of the writer as a cause in the production of literature or any other form of written discourse. However, what Foucault and others interested in the material effect of writing intend to argue is that there are different ways to organize our considerations of writing—that, indeed, we need first of all to describe and criticize the already institutionalized ways in which writing is conceptualized if we are to picture the principles which regulate the organization and which enable not only what we can *say* about writing but writing (and discourse) itself. In other words, when viewed as an element in a historical system of institutionalized discourse, the traditional idea of the "author," and the privileged value accorded to it in literary scholarship and criticism, is one of the two or three key concepts by means of which the critical disciplines organize their knowledge around questions of subjectivity and discipline both their practitioners and those they "teach."

The Foucauldian notion of discourse requires that we skeptically ask the question How did the category of "the author" become so central to critical thinking about literature? This means "central" not only in theory but in practice: in the way single-figure studies dominate criticism; in the organization of texts in "complete editions"; in biographies; and, above all, in the idea of style, of a marked writing characteristically the "expression" of a person's "mind" or "psyche" whose essential identity scrawls across a page and declares its imaginative "ownership" of these self-revealing and self-constituting lines. (Even critics, after all, aspire to their own "style.") Carrying out this genealogy is beyond the scope of this essay. The attempt to do so, however, would in itself move critical analysis into a different realm and—if carried out in a nonreductive manner, one which did not simplify the complexities of discourse, one which did not newly reify certain "genealogical" categories—would exemplify a valuable new direction for literary criticism. In the process, it suggests the privileged place "lit. crit." has held in the construction of modern subjectivity—though it is by now a rapidly retreating privilege. It also suggests to some, however, that literary criticism might assume a powerful oppositional political position within our society or that it might be of assistance to some people in their own forms of struggle elsewhere in the system. Were this possible, it would be very important. Since ours is a society which increasingly tries to ensure its political order through discursive systems that discipline our language and culture, any successful resistance to that order would seem to require strong weapons aimed to weaken that discipline. Hence the value of the poststructuralist idea that genealogical, discursive analysis can be politically valuable to others struggling against the established forms of power wherever they might be.

In other words, literary criticism, presumably always especially sensitive to the functions of language, and newly sensitive to its relationship to power on the site of institutionalized disciplines, can turn its tools to the critical examination of how, in relation to the state and its largest institutions, power operates in discourse and how discourse disciplines a population. How, in particular, discourse helps to maintain a population as a set of actors always available for discipline, to act to ends announced by agents themselves responding to (or even resisting) the distributed effects of power in this society.

In sum, then, discourse can turn literary studies into a full criticism, one which is skeptical, critical, oppositional, and—when appropriate—sustentative. It can help us to avoid reduction, either of the historical context of an event or of the rhetorically complex display of power within a textualized discourse or institutionalized discipline.

Of course, it is, in itself, no panacea of critical opposition; it is no talisman—although many newer critics chant its terms as if they were a magical charm. It, too, can become a new disciplinary technique—some would argue it already has—within our regulated society, one that enables the production of new texts, new discourses, whose "contents" may be different and whose politics may be oppositional but whose effects on given power relations may be either minimal or unpredictable and undesired. Criticism must always watchfully resist the promotional powers of the disciplined discourse in which it is placed. It can exploit the possibilities of that discourse to produce what Foucault calls a "counter-memory," but it needs to be careful not to assume the right of speaking for others in forming that memory. Above all, it needs to avoid becoming what R. P. Blackmur would have called a "new orthodoxy."

In his turn away from the very New Criticism that he had helped to establish, Blackmur explained that he was motivated by a commitment to criticism, to a process and position that Edward W. Said sums up as "critical negation,"[19] and that I am calling here "skepticism." When the tools of opposition, useful to a point and in a specific local struggle against a particular form of power, lose their negative edge—when their critical effect makes no difference and they simply permit the creation of new texts, new documents recording the successful placement of the previously "oppositional" within the considerably unchanged institutional structures of the discipline—at that point criticism must turn skeptical again and genealogically recall how the heretical became orthodox (perhaps the most powerful example of just this move is Blackmur's critique of Kenneth Burke).[20] This is a difficult chore of critical renewal: a perpetual measure of criticism's task in our society, one that must transcend both professional enticements and critical egoism. As Foucault says of Hegel's (that is, of philosophy's) encounters with his twentieth-century readers: it commits us to a task of "continuous recommencement, given over to the forms and paradoxes of repetition."[21]

2

......

The Penitentiary
of Reflection:
Søren Kierkegaard
and
Critical Activity

The appearance in English of Søren Kierkegaard's collected letters and of the complete text of *Two Ages* does not, of course, offer English language students of the Danish philosopher's work any radically new perspective on his thought or the relation of his life to his work. The latter is well-known from biographies and critical studies and his thought remains an especially rich body of material nourishing fields as important—and sometimes as distant—as philosophy, psychology, criticism, theology, and hermeneutics. Yet, the appearance of these translations does allow us to see some of the different formulations Kierkegaard has given to central aspects of his amazingly self-consistent project; they make available to us some of the most interesting versions of the lived-experience of his thought and in *Two Ages* we have his most sustained piece of literary criticism, a "review" almost as long as Thomasine Gyllembourg's novel, *Two Ages*, is in itself. At the same time, Mark Taylor's fine book, *Kierkegaard's Pseudonymous Authorship: A Study of Time and the Self*, examines how the pseudonymous writings form a consistent body of work directed by Kierkegaard's teleological vision of individual faith. Taken together these three texts provide a useful opportunity for a reconsideration of Kierkegaard, not for a "revision" of the importance and merit of his writing and its major concerns, but for a more modest repetition of *some* of his interests and purposes to see what value they might hold for the contemporary critical intellectual.[1] Mark Taylor rightly stresses that Kierkegaard's works demand a dialogic rather than a neutral or objective response because they are maieutic works, almost Socratic exercises, intended to become part of and the entry to their readers' lived-experience. Furthermore, Kierkegaard himself repeatedly emphasizes that one has the right to effect or to penetrate the existence of the other only if one understands oneself in the context of an idea or intention in the service of which one decides upon a certain disturbance of the other. Kierkegaard's works seem, in this context, to authorize a hermeneutic response to this steady querying which sees them in the light of a particularly troubled human activity, literary criticism, which needs now to be open to a variety of models of intellectual activities of which it can then judge their individual relevance and possibility in the present and for the future.

Kierkegaard's works have been recently of comparatively small value to literary critics. With the exception of a series of essays on repetition and irony, contemporary critics seem to find Kierkegaard's theocentricism and attention to the self incompatible with formalist, structuralist, poststructuralist, or neo-Marxian methodologies which, in various ways, deconstruct or demythologize the ideologies of religion and selfhood. Of course this was not always the case. Not only existentialist critics but impeccably sophisticated critics of poetry like W. K. Wimsatt turned at times to Kierkegaard's authorship in an attempt to locate value or truth and to try to understand that important modernist question of the relationship of literature and belief.[2] Postmodern criticism, however, has different questions for the most part and different projects—deconstruction, archeology, semiotics, Lacanian analysis—to which Kierkegaard speaks indirectly, if at all. I have tried to suggest elsewhere that there is a conjunction between Kierkegaard on irony and the deconstructive interests of Jacques Derrida and Paul de Man.[3] And, in different ways, William V. Spanos and Edward W. Said have treated Kierkegaard's ideas of repetition and authority at some length to relate them to modern and postmodern narrative and poetic stylistic and hermeneutic charges.[4] But apart from these various thematic connections to postmodern critical concerns, Kierkegaard's general project remains largely untested even in outline as a "model" for critical activity. The significance of his intellectual procedures, in fact, the image of the critical intellectual which appears throughout his writings, has as yet had no real influence inside the academy of critical letters. While more and better studies of Kierkegaard's themes and historical context are certainly needed, what is shamefully lacking is a steady, full-scale discussion of the intellectual processes and interests of Kierkegaard in his social-cultural context. This is needed so that we can see the problems he confronted, the methods he adopted to attempt to solve them, the nature of critical-intellectual activity he not only advocated but practiced in his life and writing, and so we can have a sense of the successes and failures, the insights and blindnesses, the fine results and poor effects of his way of living the intellectual life. Such a study would, in itself, suggest an alternative image of the life of the critical intellectual to that we have now, for the most part, of the academic critic. While Kierkegaard's philosophical project is not unquestionably internally coherent, the mutual reflection of his lived-experience in his work and vice-versa is a coherence never once threatened. And so to attempt to understand a thinker whose most profound works call for the interrelationship of action and reason in willful decision by merely interpreting his themes is an injustice. Kierkegaard, above all, senses the need for understanding how the intellectual life is lived to see how to evaluate the ideas of the intellect alone. Put in language perhaps more suited to our time, Kierkegaard sees meaning as resident not only in production, but in the symbolic living of that meaning; in other words, from his own perspective, Kierkegaard attempts to minimize in his own lived-intellectual activity the separation of meaning-production-symbol which capitalism brings about. His success is, of course, only partial and it is always "guaranteed" by a special relationship to truth, to divinity. Nevertheless, he experiences and describes the socio-cultural forces reducing intellectual activity to a mere commodity. His theoretical discussions of these matters arise out of his perception of the contradictions in Danish society he describes and not merely out of solipsistic meditation. His work is such a fine early testament to alienation's perniciousness because it reflects the disjunctions in culture between symbol and meaning and because in his own life and work he became a locus classicus in the battle between those forces which attempted to maintain the identity of symbol and meaning and those which succeeded, largely, in transforming the work of the intellectual into a fetishized, often comic commodity.

Mark Taylor's book provides a fine starting point for this reconsideration of Kierkegaard's figuring of intellectual processes and possibilities. Taylor focuses almost entirely on the "pseudonymous" works from Either/Or to Concluding Unscientific Postscript. He deliberately sets his study apart from those which have followed the line of biographical/ psychological analysis of Kierkegaard because such analyses too often take the Journals and Papers as their point of departure and ignore the specific problems of writing implicit in the "authorship" and because they fail to locate the essential continuity of the project. Although he is influenced by Stephen Crites's important work on Kierkegaard and Hegel, Taylor rejects Crites's historico-comparative method claiming that, despite its profound virtues, "it frequently forces the writer to abstract Kierkegaard's ideas, or the meaning of his concepts, from the totality of the works.... If one is to arrive at an adequate understanding of Kierkegaard, one's inquiry must be conducted in light of the various stages of existence and of the different meanings that terms have at these stages" (KPA, 33).[5]

Taylor's wariness of abstraction is methodologically significant and is in keeping with Kierkegaard's own concern. Precisely, Taylor suggests that the comparative-historical approach loses contact with the specificity of the temporal structure of Kierkegaard's writing, a temporal structure which in its contextualism assigns different meanings and values to the same (literal) figure in his texts. As Taylor shows in "time," the "eternal," etc., all change in relation to the evolving stages of life and consciousness which Kierkegaard's works represent. The "self," for example, is a fluid sign in Kierkegaard, changing from a designation of an almost foetal sense of immediacy without any reflection to the complex double-reflection of Christianity. The comparative-historical method takes a global view in relation to the works and systematizes them irresistibly, that is, regardless of the commentator's intention.

To an even greater degree, the descriptive-thematic approach compounds the merging of specific differences into a homogenous image. Paul Sponheim, for example, because he contends that Kierkegaard is "systematic," is forced by his methodology to find elements of unity, the strands weaving the tapestry: "he organizes his study according to what he regards as the most important systematic problems in Kierkegaard's works rather than organizing his analysis according to the writings themselves."[6] Of course, Sponheim's method of close reading on a global model is familiar to literary critics as perhaps the most powerful way to discover meaning in an author's work. It is a hermeneutic model which has been authorized by the New Critics, Geneva-style phenomenologists, and structuralists as well. Taylor points to a practical danger in applying this forcefully penetrating procedure in this case: "Statements from all of the works are treated in the same manner without regard for the pseudonym through whom they are spoken, and hence without regard for the point of view they represent. This oversight finally proves to be the undoing of Sponheim's analysis" (KPA, 35). This global approach levels the only distinctions which give meaning to Kierkegaard's figures; only the various pseudonymic stages inscribe his words with dramatic authority. This leveling abstraction not only mistakes the *sense* of Kierkegaard's symbols, but mistakes the nature of the process by which symbols are given meaning in the dramatic enfiguring and querying of the various intellectual- and life-styles represented by the pseudonyms: "Sponheim's 'systematic' analysis cannot comprehend the intention that leads Kierkegaard to employ the pseudonymous method" (KPA, 36). Forgetful of the time-structure of Kierkegaard's form, the global method "spatializes time" and, of course, obscures insight into the "intention" of the authorship since "intentionality" is by nature temporal and can appear only to an interpretive procedure open to the *projective*, futural possibilities of writing as an activity in time. The various "symbols" central to Kierkegaard's project have no set abstract sense because only in their immediate temporal context of the dramatic enfigurement of types—the aesthete, the ethical man, the Knight of Infinite Resignation, etc.—can they combine their status as "products" with a sharable communal "meaning," only, in this projective context can they, in other words, be symbols connecting the public and private worlds.

Taylor's discussion of "spatialized time" makes clear that Kierkegaard has considered—and rejected—the global hermeneutic procedure of some of his best critics: "Kierkegaard holds the understanding of time presented in much of the philosophical tradition to be inadequate for explaining human existence. . . . The conception of time of which Kierkegaard is critical can be called spatialized time. The term 'spatialized time' is intended to indicate that time so understood refers primarily to *objects*. This is to be distinguished from 'life-time,' which Kierkegaard thinks is a more appropriate way of conceptualizing time in relation to *subjects or selves*." After insisting that the difference between these two ideas of time does not correspond "to the difference between externality (objective time) and inwardness (subjective time)," Taylor indicates that Kierkegaard conceives of spatial time as an identification of time with space which subsumes the former to the latter. However, of most importance to Kierkegaard is the fact that the spatialization of time is a visualization of time and experience which abstracts, alienates, and in the act of leveling each to each inhibits the association of community and bifurcates symbol and meaning.

The traditional metaphysical conception of time represents it as the measure of the movement of an object along a line in space. This space permits the conceptualization of "before" and "after" by identifying an infinite number of points, all of which "are homogeneous and equivalent" (KPA, 83). This leveling understanding of time identifies each moment with a point in space and facilitates the quantification of time and motion. And it is this quantifying measure which Kierkegaard strongly identifies with reification and visualization. Several consequences follow from this: it allows for the "placing" of events in spatial relation but does not allow for judgment of their value—intention and purpose are made irrelevant in this objective view; it reduces the complexity of time to an external series of "presents" each of which is ultimately "free" from any of the consequences or claims or effects of the others; it reduces each particular "present" to what Kierkegaard calls in *The Concept of Dread* (76) " 'a silent atomistic abstraction' " (KPA, 85).[7]

Mark Taylor is alert to the fact that Kierkegaard's distrust of the power of abstraction as a *cause* of "atomism" emerges not from an equally abstract formal or logical objection to a metaphysical formulation, but rather from his sense that this idea conflicts with purposeful activity, that is, with events the importance of which are experienced by those who intend them and who associate lived-historical meaning with them. "Atomism" not only levels the value of moments as lived by disregarding their significance until they can be abstractly placed in patterns an understanding of which presents power to those who know how to use it, but it denies the fullness of a moment's action in which the "product" and its "meaning" are one. It is impossible to speak of the past or of the future in this spatialization of time and so it becomes an important cultural tool justifying the status quo as an "eternal present." While "lived-time" reflects the desire to restore value to time as an ideological location for association of groups in common action, for reestablishing history by revealing the coherence of past, present, and future, spatialized time denies to consciousness all these senses. Instead, it actually reenforces the ideological value of the present moment by legitimating "objectivity" as "visualization." The freezing of time in the present makes it difficult to "become aware of the past and of the future. But the only way for such a recognition to take place would seem to be from a standpoint outside of the time continuum. . . ." (KPA, 86). "Knowledge" becomes the "objectification" of history in space—something of which

Kierkegaard accuses Hegel. While the historical predominance of "spatialized time" in Kierkegaard's lifetime indicates the dominant ideology of centralized power and authority, it also provides those who hold that power with a weapon to secure their position culturally. The "objective" figure standing outside time is not only the emblem of a declining feudal order's theocentrism and oppressive authority, however; it is also the representation of the tool adopted by a capitalist science and culture to extend its own authority. For the global perspective on society and history this tool provides is the philosophical equivalent to the panoptical nature of the disciplinary apparatus which Michel Foucault elaborates in *Discipline and Punish*.[8]

It is not an accident that the dominance of panopticism—a disciplinary technique of timeless, disembodied surveillance—appears in the work of Jeremy Bentham and in the architecture of cities and public buildings at about the same time as "speculative philosophy." The connection between the panopticon and "speculative philosophy" is not limited simply to the common metaphor of "oversight." Rather, "speculative philosophy," especially as it appears in Hegel, while representing perhaps the final attempt to legitimate the ancient regime in its *aeterno modo*, is primarily the philosophy of the bourgeois. For as a cultural instrument, it not only suggests that the end of history corresponds with the society of the bourgeois, but it effectively turns all intellectual attention away from lived-history to a realm of reflection and ideality which, of course, empties "reality" of all its materiality, that is, it so rarefies "meaning" that it is no longer attached to the symbols of men in association in everyday life.

Mark Taylor's discussion of Kierkegaard's critique of Hegel isolates the former's analysis of Hegelian alienation: "In speculation, as the etymology of the word suggests, the individual is related to the world in a way similar to a spectator in a drama. The attention of the observer is directed away from himself and toward an object (or objects) that manifests itself to him. The aim of speculation is not self-knowledge, but a clear knowledge of the object being examined. In order to attain this goal, one's idiosyncratic interests must, as far as possible, be overcome. For Kierkegaard, however, such speculation prevents one from coming to terms with one's individual existence. . . ." (KPA, 178). Kierkegaard's analysis of "speculative philosophy" is not a matter of merely cerebral metaphysics. On the contrary, it takes actual social life as its point of departure. It is not simply the dominant authority of Hegelian metaphysics that obsesses Kierkegaard from 1841–55, but rather the nature of social life among the rising bourgeoisie in Denmark which is conveniently represented by "speculative philosophy."

Because of this concern for the *actuality* symbolized by "reflection," "speculative philosophy," "spatialized time," etc., Mark Taylor's fine thematic study tends somewhat to misrepresent Kierkegaard by stressing from the beginning that the guiding teleology of the pseudonymous works is the integrated, harmonious self in an isolated, private relationship to God. There is no doubt that for Kierkegaard the self finds itself in God and that the stages of existence—aesthetic, ethical, religiousness "A," and Christianity—represent *formal* moments in the evolution of the self toward itself and God. And, as Mark Taylor argues convincingly, these stages have general psychological validity for Kierkegaard and can be seen to correspond to developmental phases in Freudian and post-Freudian psychology. The argument can also be made that to some extent they parallel periods of Kierkegaard's life while, on the basis of an analogy to Hegel's idea of the evolution of Spirit in History, one could also claim the stages correspond to ages in Western history.

While Taylor demonstrates the formal and thematic coherence of the pseudonymous works quite clearly, his decision to understand these texts solely on the basis of the individual self's attempt to reintegrate itself in and through individual actions leading to God does create some problems. As already suggested, the "genesis" of Kierkegaard's sense of alienation is not merely an individualistic matter, but emerges from an understanding of a social condition of behavior in the intellectual and bourgeois classes. Furthermore, although Taylor, intelligently developing an insight from Crites, eloquently establishes the dialogic dimension of Kierkegaard's pseudonyms, he does not seem to have considered fully that each pseudonym's representation of a particular individual and cultural type is meant not only to lead the reader through an experience of each type or stage, but that, in fact, each type is an accurate dramatized reflection of a social actuality standing somewhere between individual figures and automatic emblems of the "age." Mark Taylor makes a convincing case that Kierkegaard views each "phase" or "stage" represented by his pseudonyms as forms of alienation and despair which are visible as such because of the "dis-relationship" in which the "self" stands to the ideal of a fully integrated "self," a harmonious "self" immediately present to the Incarnation. Taylor sees the pseudonyms fundamentally as psychological projections of stages of consciousness as the "self" moves in time toward the perfect relationship with God. While this is correct, it is inadequate because the "types" are social representations of alienated individuals as well, that is, they signify various concrete actualities for life among the intellectual and bourgeois classes. They are judged to be "alienated" and "in despair" from the point of view of an *ideal* Christian relationship to truth.

Taylor very precisely identifies the movement from "religiousness A," or "infinite resignation," to Christianity as "the movement of one who recognizes that humanly speaking he has exhausted his possibilities, and [who knows that] if further possibilities . . . are to be reestablished, it must be through God himself" (KPA, 317). The relationship of faith has curious social consequences. Kierkegaard repeatedly stresses that the Knight of Faith is "unrecognizable," indistinguishable by all appearances from the bourgeois of Christendom. Kierkegaard furthermore repeatedly insists, in opposition to Hegel, that the "inner" and the "outer" are not the same. This cluster of ideas is at the nub of Taylor's reservations about Kierkegaard. Since Kierkegaard often claims the priority of "inwardness," of states of consciousness, over all other relationships, Taylor concludes ultimately that in the Kierkegaardian perspective not only is intention or inwardness more important than action and social relations, but also "one can never be certain that another person's outward actions are congruent with his inward intentions" (KPA, 305). It is certainly true that for Kierkegaard, Faith is a matter of "inwardness" and that his Socratic probings of the disease of his age rest on that pure inwardness. But there are other elements to be considered here which temper two of Taylor's major reservations about Kierkegaard:

> Kierkegaard's view of faith as inward entails the conviction that there is no definite *outward* distinction among selves at different stages of existence. . . . If faith is inwardness, as Kierkegaard argues, there would seem to be no way for him to know that the lives of the apparent Christians in nineteenth-century Denmark were actually aesthetic. Whether or not one is faithful cannot be discerned by another person, and can be believed only by the faithful individual himself. . . . The result of Kierkegaard's argument is the establishment of two fully discrete identities of the individual self—an inward one and an outward one. Furthermore, these

identities bear no necessary relationship to one another. One's inner and outer identities can be either consistent or at odds with each other. (KPA, 345-48)

While acknowledging that Kierkegaard does arrive "at a sophisticated comprehension of the nature of the self's individuality," Taylor charges in conclusion that "he does not proceed to reintegrate the self into the social and natural whole from which it has been distinguished" (KPA, 354).

First of all, to make outwardly clear the nature of inner faith would be to so validate "objectivity" that it would threaten the man of faith with the loss of mystery and paradox. The mystery of faith cannot be adduced directly into an alienated world without sacrilegiously transgressing against the fullness of the integrated self. Put differently, one might say that the public symbols of faith have been so co-opted by the alienated age of reflection in Christendom that, whenever they are put directly into play in a social context, they are immediately emptied of any significance which would legitimately typify the achieved selfhood of an individual or group of individuals. In other words, Kierkegaard's rhetorical restriction of faith to the inner realm of personality is a defensive stance against the hegemony of an abstracted "public" caught in "speculation." Yet Kierkegaard's response is not to abandon the possibility of community and association. He attempts to form a "counter-ideology" through his method of indirect communications. Kierkegaard never removes the individual from social actuality. On the contrary, the project is to find a method of signifying the lived-experience of all "stages" in such a way that its symbolic processes can effectively contact "the other." As a good historical thinker, Kierkegaard knows this cannot be done in abstracto so, in his indirect communications, he adopts the various figures or "symbols" of "Christendom" and "speculative philosophy" current in his age and re-contextualizes them. More precisely, he makes explicit in his "existential dialectic," by parody, satire, example, and fable, the actualities present in current modes of self-conception, but actualities of which those who in fact embody them are often unaware. It is as always the problem of interpersonal relations which dominate Kierkegaard's pseudonymous works—obviously in the aesthetic and ethical stages and their concern for love and marriage, and indirectly in the religious phases. In the latter, even at its most abstract and individualistic, Kierkegaard is concerned with the problem of intersubjectivity achieved through the mediation of Christ *and* the way in which the Knight of Faith, even though often unrecognizable can indirectly "give witness."

Although Taylor's work implicitly recognizes that Kierkegaard's use of the "temporal structure" in the pseudonymous works is an attempt to reidentify history and time as the ideological location for a victory over alienation, his focus on the *subjective* importance of "indirect communication" obscures Kierkegaard's social intention. Works produced in this "indirect" mode reflect Kierkegaard's sense that certain "truths" cannot be communicated directly because the means of direct communication have been assumed into the "public" sphere of bourgeois reflection. But Kierkegaard's defensive ironies not only *protect* his "witness" from those who cannot recognize it, but make it available to those who themselves sense their alienation. In this way, the maieutic functions of indirection help to form a *style* in which the impotent culturally enabled to associate and to form a "counter-ideology" or "counter-practice" to the hegemonic power of the capitalist culture.

In *What is Literature?*, Sartre outlines the generally accepted thesis that the middle of the nineteenth century in France sees the turn of the bourgeois artist away from any connection with the values and rhetoric of his class. Saving art means sacrificing society.[9] Edward Said and Eugenio Donato claim also that in Flaubert's writing one sees the paradigm of the bourgeois author alienated from the powerful scientific and empirical discourse of his time creating a competing, ironic, deconstructive discourse designed to disclose the emptiness of the sign-systems of bourgeois representation. Kierkegaard's situation is parallel, a concern with and a desire to overcome the dominance of the bourgeois and intellectual classes by their own self-destructive lifestyles and discourse.[10] Perhaps because capitalism is not as advanced in Denmark as in France, Kierkegaard does not author a deconstructive discourse, but a *competing* discourse, based on Christ, whom he saw as the only alternative to the will to power of capitalism's repressive objectification. He had a strong sense of the cultural power of representations to control the lived-experience of the intellectuals especially and he was adept at discovering the nature of this experience mediated in their writings.

Taylor's objection that there is no way to come to know the inwardness of others would seem to minimize the possibilities of even indirect association. But his objection does not take into consideration the figures of Abraham from *Fear and Trembling*, the *Book of Job*, and the young man in *Repetition*. In each of these texts, Kierkegaard would have us realize the mystery of the Knight of Faith's return to the social world. Specifically in the case of *Fear and Trembling*, Johannes de Silentio, the narrator, is a Knight of Infinite Resignation who cannot understand the mystery of Abraham's faith: the paradoxical belief that by killing Isaac he will keep him alive as his son. The Abraham parable indicates how difficult it is to know what faith is and it also shows how the Knight of Faith always returns to the World; he does not hover above it like the man of reflection. Yet, how is the Knight of Faith to be known since he is silent and his inwardness a mystery? The maieutic function of the pseudonymous works is not only to lead the reader through an emotional experience to a point of decision, but it is also to educate the reader in the skills of decoding the age's major types. As *Repetition* suggests, the Kierkegaardian goal is to find a reader for this reflection of an age so self-alienated that it cannot recognize its own alienation. Those readers who are adept at decoding the typical characters of their age can, for example, tell the difference between the aesthetic monster of immediacy who is the seducer and Kierkegaard when he abandons Regine. It is true, as the letters to Emil Boesen suggest, that Kierkegaard willfully deceived Regine and their acquaintances so that he would appear to be "an egotistical and vain man, an ironist in the worst sense" (LD, 90). He confided his complete motives to no one and this has been the subject of extreme psychological speculation since, and will no doubt continue to be with the appearance of the symbolically charged letters to Regine in English (LD, 61–88). Kierkegaard comes nearest to explaining himself to Emil Boesen, his one confidante, when he writes from Berlin: "To allow her to sense my enormously tempestuous life and its pains and then to say to her, 'Because of this I leave you,' that would have been to crush her. It would have been contemptible to introduce her to my griefs and then not be willing to help her bear the impact of them" (LD, 115).

Yet, the evidence that Kierkegaard is neither the seducer (the monster of immediacy, the type of the solipsistic aesthete) nor the young man of *Repetition* (the poet, the reflective aesthete) is clear from the other signs in his life and work. Traces of his relationship to Regine can be found throughout his work. In *Two Ages*, for example, in his discussion of Mariane's love for Bergland—a love denied passion by being lived in an age of reflection—Kierkegaard remarks:

Instead of being a source of confident, invincible courage that in matters of love dares to ask anything of actuality, convinced in its inspired ignorance that actuality is the world where love has its home, being in love is for her a source of sadness. The inwardness may be just the same . . . but the difference is essential. Instead of perceiving her being in love as a vocation tendered by a world that wants to indulge it in everything, she is inwardly accustomed to resigning herself to renunciation: in the split second she falls in love she secretly realizes that this, too, will be forced back into her inward being, will be a secret life others know nothing of, and will simultaneously be improved health and yet, humanly speaking, an infirmity. (LD, 50)

Of course, the Mariane/Bergland—Regine/Kierkegaard ratio undergoes a series of inversions with Mariane alternately Regine and Kierkegaard, himself. Moments of this sort are not only testimony to the truth of Kierkegaard's remark "I serve her" (LD, 93), but of the possibility of decoding actions and writing to distinguish between "faith" and "seduction."

In Two Ages, Kierkegaard gives an example of how one "reads" inwardness from external signs. While Taylor is correct in saying that for Kierkegaard there is no "necessary" connection between inner and outer, or sign and sense, he is wrong in concluding that one cannot read signs to discover the inwardness of the character reflected in their "meaning." Kierkegaard "reads" the technique and mode of presentation of Mrs. Waller, the housewife of Part II of Two Ages, to discover a correspondence between behavior and character: The novel is "continually illuminating Mrs. Waller's lack of character in the momentary mirror of reflection. . . . The art lies in the repetition of the psychological conception in the presentation itself, and as philandering is the unstable emptiness, so throughout the whole novel Mrs. W. is an unstable flurry of busyness, represented in her transitory relations to the older and younger men. . . ." (TA, 54). It is an axiom of Two Ages that character must be understood as the type of the age. The age reflects itself mediated in the domesticity—this is, after all, a bourgeois domestic novel Kierkegaard is reviewing—of the individual. Dialectically reading the character reflected in the age and the age illuminated by the character's choices produces a critical figure, a "type," located somewhere between the "age" and the "individual," as the way a group of readers can understand themselves in their society and join together in an associated rhetoric and method. The characters of the age and of the individual always present themselves to a critical understanding willing to decode the signs and to produce a new set to mediate this critical understanding in a group.

It is precisely in this method of understanding which Kierkegaard's indirection demands in the face of a capitalistic hegemony alienating one from the others and self from product that one can see the peculiar nature of his intellectual life. It requires a willingness to see and understand the connections between life and writing, to see that the works of alienated people are reflections of that alienation and microscopic tools in its extension. It requires a recognition that the text is not ever a detached product; for, while the author may feel detached from the product as commodity, there is an attachment which reflects the alienated, often self-deluded state of the author.

In the introduction to *Two Ages*, Kierkegaard addresses himself to the killing of the father which occurs when each generation establishes its own modernity and "authority." He remarks that this patricide reflects an impatience, egotism, and lack of care which prohibits education:

> Zealousness to learn from life is seldom found, but all the more frequently a desire, inclination, and reciprocal haste to be deceived by life. Undaunted, people do not seem to have a Socratic fear of being deceived. . . . Even less do people seem to have above all a Socratic fear of being deceived by themselves, do not seem to be the least aware that if the self-deceived are the most miserable of all, then among these, again, the most miserable are those who are presumptuously deceived by themselves in contrast to those who are piously deceived. (TA, 10)

In the moment of self-definition, the cultural parricide relegates the past to the junk-heap of history and, thus, furthers his own demise. Youth's violence destroys its innocence and inserts it in history. The loss of innocence is the loss of "the happy days of youth when we ourselves were the demand of the time" (TA, 10). As Mark Taylor suggests in his discussion of atonement (KPA, 307ff.), and as this passage indicates, Kierkegaard always warns of "consequences"—the results of birth in a certain family and time, the effects of past actions, the inescapability of "character" formed by environment and one's own decisions. Even forgiveness of sins is, for Kierkegaard, essentially a remembrance of consequences. The act of parricide is endlessly repeated and generates the eternal drama of children becoming "father" and then being killed.

This pattern constitutes not only one example of the way in which classes and individuals are self-deluded, but it is the paradigm of such self-delusion because it contains the fundamental images of "original" alienation, ignorance, and self-destruction. It also marks the historical rebellion of the bourgeoisie against the patriarchal authority of the king, and suggests that, at the origin of the bourgeois revolution, is the seed of its own self-destruction—a seed full-grown, as Marx indicates in The Eighteenth Brumaire,[11] when capital sacrifices bourgeois civil liberties to Louis Bonaparte, and in late capitalism, when capital sacrifices the family and other stabilities of bourgeois culture to isolate and repress the workers in mass culture: "faithlessness is the mutual likeness of the antagonists" (TA, 11). In opposition to this self-delusion, Kierkegaard offers his own practice as a counter-example. In his Journals and Papers (v, 5891) he writes: "Given the conditions in the world as it is, to be an author should be the extraordinary employment in life. . . . Therefore not only should the author's production be a testimony to the idea, but the author's life ought to correspond to the idea" (TA, 141).

II

Two Ages is, of course, Kierkegaard's most political text. And the third part, "Conclusions from a Consideration of the Two Ages," especially gathers together many of his central themes and gives them authoritative formulation. There are three parts to Two Ages following its introduction discussed above. In the first, "Survey of Contents," Kierkegaard provides a plot summary with a general sketch of the characters outlined against the background of the "two ages," the "Age of Revolution"—the French Revolution—and "The Present Age"—Denmark in the period of transition to a constitutional monarchy with an elected assembly. The second section, "An Esthetic Interpretation," examines Gyllembourg's novel as an attempt to reflect the particularity of each age. But this is not meant to suggest that Kierkegaard looks to the novel for the immediate "realistic" presentation of the "age" and its individuals; on the contrary, Kierkegaard's idea of art's "reflection" of social order and psychological structure depends upon a recognition of the mediating processes of the novel's art: "The novel has as its premise the distinctive totality of [each] age, and the production is the reflexion of this in domestic life; the mind turns from the production back again to the totality of the age that has been so clearly revealed in this reflexion. But . . . the author did not intend to describe the age itself; his novel lies somewhere between the presupposed distinctive character of the age and the age in reflexion as illustrated by this work" (TA, 32). As critic, Kierkegaard is not interested in the question of the uniqueness of the characterization: is Claudine or Mariane "believable" and "possible"? "No, the critic's question is: may a girl like Claudine appear as *typical* in this particular age" (TA, 33).

Kierkegaard continues his discussion in the second section with a detailed psychological analysis of the central characters of both parts of the novel. His aim is not merely to understand each figure, but to indicate how each is a "reflexion" of the age. Kierkegaard's hermeneutics involves moving into the text and the specific analyses with a "presupposition" regarding the external age and its "effects," and then back out again from the characters to the age. The aim is always to understand one in terms of the other since it is impossible to understand either alone. His interest lies in decoding the signs Gyllembourg's novel has inscribed to mediate between the domestic level of representation, of the "plot" and "character," and the general nature of history and society which the novel not only "reflexs" but out of which it very self-consciously emerges.

Kierkegaard's fullest statement on the "double vision" of his technique stresses not only its correspondence to the technique of the "author," but also its efficacy in accounting historically for psychological forms of action:

> The critic is obliged to assume the double approach by which the story has made its task so difficult. The author does not dare to present the age as having automatic consequences in the individuals, for then he would transgress his task as novelist and merely describe the age and *illustrate it by examples*, instead of viewing the reflexion in domestic life and through it illuminating the age. Action must always occur through the psychological middle term of the individual. . . . The relation between the age and an individual's action must be psychologically motivated, and only then can there be any mention of the special character of the age as influencing or permitting this manifestation. (TA, 41)

Kierkegaard's analyses in the rest of section two provide the terms in which his discussion of the present age will develop in the third section.

Kierkegaard concludes the second section with a disclaimer that although the "superficial reader" might mistakenly believe that he has found more in the novel during his review than is "really" there, he has only been exposing what lies beneath the "unpretentious" surface of the text: "Yet I cannot accept a compliment from the reader but must convey it to the proper person, the author, who, even if I did understand all of it, is, after all, first the creator and is also the one who had the art to conceal that fact and, finally, perhaps knows and puts into the novel much that I have not been able to discover" (TA, 58). What Kierkegaard is addressing here is the central problem of indirect communication. In a typically offhand and parenthetical way, he represents the precise hermeneutic situation which forms an association of individuals for whom there is always a connection between the subject and society. The "superficial reader" who *consumes* texts and reviews not only will mistake this novel's complex reflexion of the entanglement of the intellectual and bourgeois class with their "age," but he "will be startled" (TA, 58) by the revelations of Kierkegaard's "review." It is typical of Kierkegaard always to keep the complete cycle of writer-reader-critic-reader in view in his discussion. Hermeneutic activity exists in every relationship between each of the figures in this cycle. The "superficial reader" is not just the careless reader, but, in the context of Kierkegaard's later discussions of the "public," must be seen as the typical reader who in the "age of reflection" is so alienated from his own intellectual and emotional processes that he *does not have available to him directly and immediately* the interpretive techniques to realign symbol and meaning in his understanding of the text. Symbolically, Kierkegaard's figure here represents the reading public's divorce from the conscious process of associating the inwardness of the "character" or "author" from the "outwardness" of the age. In fact, we see clearly that the "age" produces a reading public unable to mediate between the subject and history; the "age" *herds* the self-deceived intellectual bourgeoisie into a "public" which, under the guise of "association," so abstracts interpersonal relations that, individually and as a group, they are not aware of their own alienation.

Yet at the same time, Kierkegaard's figure in this passage represents not merely an abstract wished-for counter-possibility. It offers, rather, a true association between Gyllembourg, himself, and their understanding readers. Even the "superficial reader" is shocked by the results of Kierkegaard's hermeneutic action, and while he attempts to deny its results, is drawn up, momentarily, into the counter-discourse of indirection. The novel *Two Ages* is itself indirect because its simplicity masks the social and psychological complexity Kierkegaard excavates. And Kierkegaard's own task is indirect; for while it seems to be merely an interpretation of the "meaning" of the novel, its "reduplication" in name and strategy, it gives witness to the efficacy of the indirect method in preserving unified symbolic processes from abstraction and in reenforcing the association of those trying to form a counter-discourse to capitalism's "reflective public." And "to give witness" is to attempt to extend this "counter-discourse" subversively, throughout the intellectual classes. Kierkegaard and Gyllembourg, of course, in this prefigure both the later nineteenth century's alienation of literature from the bourgeoisie and those displaced bourgeois authors' attempts to establish a "religion of the word" as an alternative to the social world of capitalism.

In part three, "Conclusion," the longest part of the "review," Kierkegaard emphasizes the difference between the type of association he advocates, indirectly, and the type of "association" which his age enforces through a variety of "leveling" processes. Toward the opening of this section, in a lyrical, but satiric passage, Kierkegaard figures three different social orders in musical images. His topic is "the measure of essential culture" (TA, 61). Romantically, he suggests that an uneducated maidservant, passionately in love, is ". . . essentially cultured. Whereas there is only affectation, the pretense of form, in the external piecemeal training correlative with an interior emptiness, the flamboyant colors of swaggering weeds in contrast to the humble bowing of the blessed grain, the mechanical counting of the beat correlative with the lacklustre of the dance, the painstaking decoration of the bookbinding correlative with the deficiency of the book" (TA, 62). The temptation is, of course, to dismiss this comparison as obvious, Rousseauistic, and naive. But what Kierkegaard reflects here are the very processes of self-alienation resulting from a social order which *trains* its individuals in various disciplines which are concerned with success ("flamboyant colors of swaggering weeds"), order ("the mechanical counting of the beat"), and the consumption of products answering to no lived need ("the painstaking correlative of the bookbinding," etc.). In *Discipline and*

Punish Foucault has suggested how, at the same time as that about which Kierkegaard is writing, the detailed inculcation of mechanical processes for extending power throughout society led to both the formation of the self and the "human sciences" as well as various apparatuses internalizing the need for social uniformity in "individuals." Kierkegaard's concern with the hegemonic extension of power throughout the culture, resulting in the leveling of individuals, is analogous to Foucault's discussion.[12] In fact, Kierkegaard's remarks on "training" and "education" as well as on the homogenizing effects of "the press" and schools gain considerably in resonance when considered in light of Foucault's discussion of disciplinary machinery. This is an idea to which I will return a bit further on.

Kierkegaard goes on to offer a utopian image, again in musical terms, for the ideal order he envisions:

> When individuals (each one individually) are essentially and passionately related to an idea and together are essentially related to the same idea the relation is optimal and normative. Individually the relation separates them (each one has himself for himself), and ideally it unites them. Where there is essential inwardness, there is a decent modesty between man and man that prevents crude aggressiveness. . . . Thus the individuals never come too close to each other in the herd sense, simply because they are united on the basis of ideal distance. The unanimity of separation is indeed fully orchestrated music. . . . The harmony of the spheres is the unity of each planet relating to itself and to the whole. Take away the relations, and there will be chaos. (TA, 62–63)

Of course, this is the fullest representation of Kierkegaard's vision of a society united "indirectly," seemingly the only mode of association available to the antagonists of the disciplinary unanimity. Kierkegaard's description of the alternative world resulting from a failure to sustain this harmony is meant to be a representation of the "present age":

> Remove the relation to oneself, and we have the tumultuous self-relating of the mass to an idea; but remove this as well, and we have crudeness. Then people shove and press and rub against each other in pointless externality, for there is no deep inward decency that decorously distances the one from the other; thus there is turmoil and commotion that ends in nothing. No one has any-

thing for himself, and united they possess nothing, either: so they become troublesome and wrangle. Then it is not even the gay and lively songs of conviviality that unite friends; then it is not the dithyrambic songs of revolt that collect the crowds; then it is not the sublime rhythms of religious fervor that under divine supervision muster the countless generations to review before the heavenly hosts. No, then gossip and rumor and specious importance and apathetic envy become a surrogate for each and all. Individuals do not in inwardness turn away from each other, do not turn outward in unanimity for an idea, but mutually turn to each other in a frustrating and suspicious, aggressive, leveling reciprocity. (TA, 63)

Kierkegaard's dialectic arrives at the conclusion that the age of reflection, of objectivity, of discipline and training produces individuals "united" as the "public" and leveled in competition and envy, but individuals who are absolutely alone and apart precisely because of this mode of social ordering that denies them any "conviviality" or "contemporaneity" (TA, 91). The "individuals" even among the bourgeois intellectual classes who think of their products as their own are only marking "the mechanical counting of the beat." Failure to examine their own relation to their society, to try to understand what makes possible their "success" and "individuality," indicates how the social order of the bourgeois has co-opted them, produced them, denied them a role in the process of challenging that society which they all, undoubtedly, sometimes call into question. They think they dance either to their own tune or to the tune of an "oppositional" group, whereas they are marionettes jerking to the rhythms of the metronome hidden from them in their modernity and power.

How has the individual lost the ability to act as part of a true association forming a counter-discourse to capitalism's hegemony? For Kierkegaard, the answer lies in the idea of "reflection." As he points out repeatedly, the "age of revolution" is a "passionate age," capable of action, of defining itself by movement and choice. It "has *not nullified the principle of contradiction*" (TA, 66). This is another way of saying that it has not yet entered the period of bourgeois domination which marks the end of history and finds in Hegel's insistence upon speculation the perfect emblem of its endurance. History is formed by action and its consequences are inescapable. The age of reflection makes no choices because its will has been suspended to maintain the status quo. Its "actions" are calculated to extend itself. Kierkegaard remarks repeatedly upon the expansionary powers of "reflection." (See, e.g., TA, 97.) The intellectual cannot understand his life because it cannot be a life or take on shape if he cannot act; his "life" degenerates into "gossip": "the coherence of his life became a garrulous continuation or a continued garrulity, a participial or infinitive phrase in which the subject must be understood or, more correctly, cannot be located at all because, as the grammarians say, the meaning does not make it clear for the simple reason that it lacks meaning" (TA, 67).

The loss of the subject which Kierkegaard identifies here in the intellectual discourse of the bourgeois produces precisely the effect of *anonymity*. Rather than speech, the intellectual chatters, that is to say,

> The comments become so objective, their range so all-encompassing, that eventually it makes no difference at all who says them. . . . And eventually human speech will become just like the public: pure abstraction—there will no longer be someone who speaks, but an objective reflection will gradually deposit a kind of atmosphere, an abstract noise that will render human speech superfluous, just as machines make workers superfluous. (TA, 104)

The final term of this figure is not accidental, but part of an entire network of images drawn from the mechanical and financial world of capitalism. Kierkegaard has perhaps not been given enough credit for his recognition of the economic causes of the cultural alienation he describes. While his analysis is hardly systematic or prolonged, it is recurrent and intertwined with his exposure of the leveling of its products of society to commodity status through the disciplinary practices of capitalism. For example, he immediately juxtaposes the following figure of the disciplinary apparatus to the previous quotation:

> In Germany [had he known he could have added "and England"] there are even handbooks for lovers; so it probably will end with lovers being able to sit and speak anonymously to each other. There are handbooks on everything, and generally speaking education soon will consist of knowing letter-perfect a larger or smaller compendium of observations from such handbooks, and one will excel in proportion to his skill in pulling out the particular one, just as the typesetter picks out letters. (TA, 104)

This is not merely an objection to false learning of codes which stifles individual "authentic" expression. Kierkegaard is pointing, rather, to the proliferation in his culture of the various "conduct books" and other "media" which created ideologically "acceptable" representations of social behavior. The final part of this figure, with its allusion to mass circulation of ideas and images, its echo of the previous image of empty but decorated books, its suggestion of the automatic, self-perpetuating, "neutral" commodification of "culture," is only one of many figures aligned with the metaphor of writing in the text. Consistently, allusions to typesetting, to written grammar, and to sentence structure point to the absence of the subject from any adequate means of social symbolization; they point, in other words, to anonymity. The direct writing of "commodities" upon the basis of which "authors" become successful in their "anonymity" is only a form of chatter and garrulity, of self-interest and self-deception. *Chatter* is not just what we know in everyday life as "gossip" but it is the commodification of discourse, the means of usurping what Kierkegaard obviously sees as the most important element in the formation of a counterculture: language in history as a means of association.

The power of the systems of representation of capitalism leads, for Kierkegaard, to the fetishization of money. Everything is sacrificed to its gain. "The present age" is an age without passion; "but an age without passion possesses no assets; everything becomes . . . transactions in *paper money*. Certain phrases and observations circulate among the people . . . but there is no person to vouch for their validity by having primitively experienced them." But it must be clear that Kierkegaard is not, like some antiquarian historian, calling nostalgically for a return to species, hard currencies: "Just as in our business transaction we long to hear the ring of real coins after the whisper of paper money, so we today long for a little primitivity." But so awesome is the expansionary power of the network of systems of representation which have alienated men in a capitalistic society that even "wit," which Kierkegaard claims is more "primitive" than spring itself is transformed into a commodity. Kierkegaard's satire ironically sums up his vision of this expansion: "suppose that wit were changed to its most trite and hackneyed opposite, a trifling necessity of life, so that it would become a profitable industry to fabricate and make up and renovate and buy up in bulk old and new witticisms: what a frightful epigram on the witty age!" (TA, 74–75). The nostalgist's prose is a production of a "need" created by the alienation of the present. But the nostalgic grasping for "origins," the "primitive" species is incapable of escaping from the context that gives rise to it. Such antiquarian turning backward to better times is a diversion of the intellectual's life away from the confrontation with the present. And how disturbingly like the modern critical academy Kierkegaard's "wit" industry seems to be!

Kierkegaard is remarkably alert to the ways in which the "age of reflection" deludes its intellectuals into believing that they are, in fact, establishing a willful opposition to the general hegemony of industry and finance. It is not necessary here to point out how important action is for Kierkegaard in the formation of self and society. What is important, though, are his perceptions into the mechanisms the hegemonic culture applies to divert its "opponents" away from passionate action against it. These mechanisms exist on the level of discursive representation and on the level of social structure. All of these are represented by Kierkegaard under the category of "reflection." The effects of "reflection" on both these levels are described by Kierkegaard in this comparison:

> A passionate, tumultuous age wants to *overthrow everything, set aside everything*. An age that is revolutionary but also reflecting and devoid of passion changes the expression of power into a *dialectical tour de force: it lets everything remain but subtly drains the meaning out of it; rather than culminating in an uprising, it exhausts the inner actuality of relations in a tension of reflection that lets everything remain and yet has transformed the whole of existence into an equivocation that in its facticity is—while entirely privately a dialectical fraud interpolates a secret way of reading—that it is not.*
> (TA, 77)

The success of Kierkegaard's use of the figure of "reflection" as the sign of "the present age" stems from its adequacy as a representation of both the states of "inwardness" he is analyzing and the "outward" or social reality he is describing. Inwardly, "reflection" indicates the age's fascination with the endless play of the dialectic which Kierkegaard credits to Hegel and especially his Danish followers. Outwardly, or socially, "reflection" represents the mechanisms for ensuring the hegemony of its own cultural reproduction.

The single individual cannot act because "reflection" neutralizes the will. It valorizes cunning, shrewdness, and "understanding," that is, the calculating intelligence, at the expense of the will and thus makes decision, self-definition, resistance, and change impossible. Change becomes simple "flux, a blend of a little resolution and a little situation, a little prudence and a little courage, a little probability and a little faith, a little action and a little incident" (TA, 67). Indolence results from reflection's enervation of passion.

How can this "enervation" be enforced? How is the habit of mind created and maintained? The individual cannot "tear himself out of the web of reflection and seductive ambiguity of reflection" (TA, 69). Reflection displaces one from historical reality into an erotic relation with the infinite ambiguities of endless beginnings. Consequences apparently never exist for the reflective individual; there is always the possibility of creating another, sometimes purely personal myth for escape. Energy is exhausted in the act of loving one's own self-projection. But this death-dealing enervation is internalized because of the external, social modes of organization which in the name of "common sense"—that is, ideologically approved patterns of behavior in which the public is well-disciplined—transform "actuality into a theater" (TA, 72). Everywhere in society the effects of "reflection" are legitimatized in signs which mirror its authority and obscure other perceptions.

The machinery for establishing and maintaining the hegemony of capital in culture can be described by Foucault's phrase in *Discipline and Punish* as the "micro-physics" of power.[13] As Kierkegaard says, reflection turns power into a "dialectical tour de force." The paradigm of the disciplinary apparatus for Foucault is Bentham's panopticon, the ultimate penitentiary; since the observing authority in the panopticon is himself never observed, the responsibility for regulation is internalized by the inhabitants of the prison and they guard themselves, so to speak. The disciplining of the body extends to the training of the mind to guard against rebellion. Kierkegaard identifies the social equivalent of the panopticon's internalization of regulation and authority as the means by which his reflective age extends itself.

This fact is evident not only from Kierkegaard's adoption of the penitentiary as a metaphor to describe the entrapment of even the individual who hopes to rebel against the forces of alienation and oppression, but by his recourse to visual metaphors in his discussion of how society can regulate itself and homogenize its misfits. When analyzed on the social level, "reflection" is discussed as "envy," the metaphor for the leveling process which acts as a barrier against escape from "reflection." "Envy becomes the *negatively unifying principle* in a passionless and very reflective age" (TA, 81). "Envy" is part of the central process for deluding the intellectuals in their "rebellions": "The environment, the contemporary age, has neither events nor integrated passion but in a negative unity creates a reflective opposition that toys for the moment with the unreal prospect. . . ." (TA, 69). "Envy," the "negative unity" has the power of "tyrants and secret police," to level all distinctions and to maintain itself by thwarting all perception of its actions, a thwarting made possible by the universality, the ubiquity of its insinuating powers. "Negative unity" is the parodic inversion of association in which subjects, history, and their products can be united: leveling takes the form of the illusion of "equality": "the negative unity of the negative mutual reciprocity of individuals" (TA, 84). Under the ideologically acceptable guise of "equality," the disciplining machinery takes effect: "The *participants* [in a world-historical event] would shrewdly transform themselves into a crowd of *spectators*. . . ." (TA, 73). Kierkegaard's statement suggests not only how the *visual* becomes in the age of the panopticon the all-absorbing sign and practice of discipline and hegemony, but also subtly points out that the power of this disciplining process is so dialectical and reflective that the people who are exploited, dehumanized, and oppressed are made to *transform themselves* into distanced, alienated abstractions furthering the expansion of the power of capital.

"Equality" produces *peers* who live only in the *form* of relationships learned "piecemeal"; the forms of these relationships have been kept; in fact, they are only recently being abandoned by capitalistic society. But when they were maintained they were only parts of the disciplining of the culture: "No, the relation as such is impeccable . . . but the relation itself has become a problem in which the parties like rivals *watch* each other instead of relating to each other, and count, as it is said, each other's verbal avowals of relation as a substitute for resolute mutual giving in the relation" (TA, 79; my emphasis).

The Kierkegaardian analysis of the age returns to the principle of indirection to revalidate the will within culture. For the nature of this culture is such that no direct representation of an alternative can escape cooptation. "Leveling is not the action of one individual but a reflection-game in the hand of an abstract power" (TA, 86). Kierkegaard here is prefiguring Foucault's suggestion that in modern society the property metaphor may not be an adequate way to understand the operations of power. But the conclusion that Kierkegaard draws from the abstract, or what we might say, "micro-physical" nature of power is that it is self-reproducing and when challenged directly *always* victorious: "the individual who levels others is himself carried along, and so on." "No assemblage will be able to halt the abstraction of leveling, for in the context of reflection the assemblage itself is in the service of leveling" (TA, 86, 87). Of course, Kierkegaard will opt for a religious answer to this dilemma. That is, he will insist that the only idea capable of motivating the relation of one's self to an idea and through that idea a relationship to other selves is the belief in God. Nonetheless, despite the particular theocentric dimension of his argument, Kierkegaard's insight remains substantively useful. Capitalist, disciplinary society has appeared until now to be voracious: "it has cunningly bought-up every possible outlook on life" (TA, 89). But from Kierkegaard's point of view, this is because all of its antagonists have acted "willfully" to gain recognition as alternative, representative figures. And in doing so they have merely succumbed to the process of commodification.

Kierkegaard is suggesting here, in other words, a strategy of indirection, of pseudonomy, of "unrecognizability" that attempts to redeem history and the will from the abstraction of leveling by renouncing the direct pursuit of power, by refusing to offer oneself as representative, as hero or leader. Kierkegaard presents an analysis of the will to power which suggests that it is the defining quality, the sustaining core of the disciplining society. Finally Kierkegaard offers not a social revolution as a response to alienation, but an association of those who have renounced the appeal to and pursuit of authority; an association of those who value their suffering as "witness" to the possibility of maintaining a consciousness of full human association. In a passage near the end of *Two Ages*, Kierkegaard returns us to the problem of his quietism raised by Mark Taylor, a problem placed now in a social context which allows us to understand what he is suggesting and why he is doing it:

> The unrecognizables recognize the servants of leveling but dare not use power or authority against them, for then there would be a regression, because it would instantly be obvious to a third party that the unrecognizable one was an authority. . . . Only through a *suffering* act will the unrecognizable one dare to contribute to leveling and by the same suffering act will pass judgment on the instrument. He does not dare to defeat leveling outright—he would be dismissed for that, since it would be acting with authority—but in suffering he will defeat it and thereby experience in turn the law of

his existence, which is not to rule, to guide, to lead, but in suffering to serve, to help indirectly. (TA, 109)

(It is, of course, obvious that three figures lie behind this conception: Christ, Socrates, and Kierkegaard, himself.) The ubiquity of power drives the witness to a nonalienated life underground. It causes him to despair of the possibility of this life ever existing within the social world; in that sense it succeeds in alienating even such a sensitive analyst of alienation as Kierkegaard from the idea of a social order not spontaneously and inevitably oppressive in its use of power. Faith is indeed seen as the only possibility remaining for the renewal of human possibilities when one believes that society inevitably alienates man from those same possibilities. Kierkegaard's analysis of "the present age" seems to have fallen short. By not wondering himself what role the oppressive forces he presents so brilliantly might have played in helping to lead him to his conclusion in favor of unrecognizability, he lets us wonder if he has not been marking—on a very sophisticated level indeed—only "the mechanical counting of the beat correlative with the lacklustre of the dance." He seems not to have realized that the final hegemonic effect of social alienation is the alienation of the individual from the idea of the positive possibilities of society.

But, yet, as we have seen, Kierkegaard often does attend to and his works do emerge out of social phenomena. However, he does not conclude from the possibility for hermeneutic association between Gyllembourg, himself, and their understanding readers—those who are attentive to the indirection—that a reformation of society could put an end to the need for this association to be underground. Rather, he calls victim to one version of the myth of the end of history. He decides that the disciplinary society of the bourgeois is not only expansive, but permanent; one must tend one's garden.

The bourgeois intellectual's pessimism over the nature of the social order seems linked, even in Kierkegaard's case, to a position which reenforces the entrenched social order it so dislikes. This pessimism contributes to the mythology of capital's invincibility and permanence, to its mystique of inevitability. Critical activity designed to account for the effects of capital in society and to understand its cultural products is needed to offset this pessimism. Most importantly, critical practice must self-reflexively look to its own assumptions and conclusions to understand its relation to the conditions of its own social being, that is,

the extent of its own inevitable participation in maintaining and changing society's institutions—particularly, in our case, the university. As
Kierkegaard's theory and practice both suggest, this can only begin to
happen when the critic no longer sees himself or herself as merely an
academic transmitter of knowledge or as author of formalist or abstract
studies which disregard their own origins and effects in lived-history
and experience. If criticism is to be more than a "wit industry" it must
risk its own (minimal) stability to enter into the mainstream of cultural
understanding. It must abandon its fascination with the belletristic,
with bourgeois conceptions of textuality which neglect the subject—
but do produce sophisticated "readings"—and confront instead the
crisis of its own history, role, and future.[14]

3

......

Variations

on Authority:

Some Deconstructive

Transformations

of the New

Criticism

Recently there have been many attempts to describe, rebut, "go beyond," and account for deconstructive criticism. They have come from Marxist, phenomenological, humanistic, and political quarters. Occasionally, there have been sympathetic accounts, sometimes bordering on the apologetic, from a younger generation of scholars nurtured in the excitement of the Derridean era.[1]

Jonn Brenkmann and Michael Sprinker, for example, both remark on the power of deconstructive discourse within the academy and account for this fact by seeing deconstruction as the mirror image of contemporary society. Sprinker specifically identifies the source of deconstruction's power in the "technicality of [its] procedure." For this reason, Sprinker concludes, "Deconstruction . . . mirrors the effacement of ideology under the mantle of technical rationality which is the principal feature of ideology under late capitalism. . . . Deconstruction is the specular image of the society of the spectacle."[2]

Far from the rigor of such a critique, Gerald Graff, in *Literature Against Itself*, asserts that deconstruction is the heir of earlier modernist formalisms which deny reason, common sense, and referentiality.[3] Unfortunately, Graff's characterization is too broad and fails to account for its own position, thereby devaluing his genealogical insight. His polemic attempts too naive a recuperation of conservative humanism to fulfill the scholarly demands for historical precision required by this topic.[4]

In a closer focus, Jonathan Arac identifies the New Critical and deconstructive fascination with Coleridge, rather than Shelley, as a mark of their common genealogy. For as Arac suggests, "Even the rhetorical subtlety of Paul de Man . . . may remain as partial a tool . . . as Northrop Frye, or . . . the New Critics, in its restriction to discourse, in its attempt to deny the possibility of any other realm than that of the text."[5] In thus suggesting the continuity of deconstruction and New Criticism— indicated by the conservative reappearance of Coleridge and the persistence of textual priority—Arac identifies a persistent trend in modern American criticism. For the similarities in technique between New Criticism and deconstruction produce a critical impasse not easily broken. Since neither New Criticism nor deconstruction bothers to account for its own function and position historically in society— precisely because they are both radically anti-historicist—even the most sophisticated employment of the latest reading techniques merely repeats and extends a power formation already in place. I will return to this idea in the body of this essay.

In a remarkable series of essays, Daniel O'Hara has recently outlined a history of the romance structure of interpretation in modern criticism. Taking the case of Walter Pater as paradigmatic, O'Hara has specified that in Eliot, Valéry, Bloom, Frye, Ricoeur, Said, Graff, Lentricchia, Hartman, and Derrida a certain ironic repetition encircles all these and others in a pattern of (self-) parody. O'Hara finds: "The oppositional critics of our culture would simultaneously critique the last vestiges of the ascetic ideal [which Arac identifies with Coleridge, O'Hara with Kant] as it makes its appearance in the work of art of our culture and the latest models of the revisionary ideal by mating with their own self-created phantasmagoria in the voids of past texts. Their aim is to reproduce themselves as the divine child of yet another potentially liberating vision that deserves to be parodical."[6] O'Hara's devastatingly all-inclusive critique denies the critical intelligence any easy hope to make a new beginning or to avoid the ancestor's romance pattern. For his reading is not led by the witty inventiveness of deconstructive play to forget its place in an ironic tradition or to accept deconstruction's goal of hearing "unheard of thoughts."

Invoking Heidegger's phenomenological destruction, W. V. Spanos finds terms to analyze not only humanistic and New Critical procedures but also deconstruction, discovering the persistence in our recent criticism of the critical impulse to spatialize time. Spanos has produced a cumulative indictment of the New Critical-structuralist-poststructuralist hegemony which cannot be ignored. Focusing his attention relentlessly on the areas of nondifferential identity between humanism, formalism, and deconstruction—Babbitt, the New Critics, Derrida—while bracketing their reducible differences, Spanos has now named the deconstructors the true heirs of the modernist critical aesthetes. Spanos's opinion on this matter is seminal and needs quotation:

> In thus reducing the signifiers emerging from and addressing *different* historical/cultural situations to a timeless intertextual (ironic) text, deconstructive criticism ironically betrays its affiliation with the disinterested—and indifferent "inclusive" formalism of the New Criticism . . . which it is one of its avowed purposes to repudiate. The deconstructive reader, like the New Critic . . . , becomes a distanced observer of the "scene of textuality" or, in Kierkegaard's term, an aesthete who perceives the text from the infinitely negative distance of the ironic mode. With his levelling gaze, he, too, like his adversaries, refines all writing, in Derrida's own phrase, into "free-floating" texts. All texts thus become the *same* text.[7]

One cannot allow the deconstructive response to such charges too much authority. Such a response might, for example, fasten on terms like "time" and "aesthetic" and on "oppositions" like "interested" and "disinterested" to mark their metaphysical entrapment and perhaps "totalitarian" implications. Of course, conceding authority and persuasion to such a response is, in advance, to concede the argument. The temptation to do so testifies to the power of deconstruction. But it also testifies obliquely to the truth of Spanos's claim; for the ubiquity of the dissent to his position from critics of all camps reveals the very relationship he is trying to name.

Perhaps the argument needs to be developed in a complementary direction. The authority and dissemination of deconstruction can be accounted for by seeing it as a transformation of the critical variation called "New Criticism." But one must not insist upon the repetitive or recuperative nature of deconstruction too exclusively. One must not attempt to "reduce" it to a preexistent "tradition" or "institution" which, for various reasons, it cannot escape. Yet one can recognize that deconstruction is a redeployment of the forces which sustained academic literary study in its univocal, pluralistic, and New Critical modes, that is to say in critics as seemingly different as W. K. Wimsatt, E. D. Hirsch, and Wayne Booth.

Literary study is an institution with certain persistent as well as vary-ing characteristics. Like all institutions, academic criticism repeatedly "reforms" itself, transforming its appearance while elaborating and conserving its institutional power and thus ensuring its survival—or delaying its demise. Persistent "right-wing" critics of deconstruction argue that it is a threat to the civilization, a threat to the profession, and furthers the separation of academia from the public.[8] But is it not possible that the decade of deconstruction encompassed by Paul de Man's brilliant performances in *Blindness and Insight* and *Allegories of Reading* has helped preserve the academy during economic and methodologi-cal changes, and epistemological and evaluative doubts, so grave as to mark a "crisis"? Is deconstruction not the perfect institutional response to this crisis (rather than its cause)? Is it not a strategy for taking up the crisis into the academy in a self-preserving act which, as Donald Pease has suggested, fuels the institution with its own impotence?

For there can be no denying that the representation of "crisis" in criticism in the late 1960s is the work of deconstruction and those it influenced. Nor can it be denied that the polemical conflicts which resulted both from this declaration of crisis—to which deconstruction is the rigorously appropriate response—and the rising prominence of deconstructive techniques sustained the seeming vitality of the institu-tion through the 1970s and into the 1980s. Careers have been made, books published, journals begun, programs, schools, and institutes founded, courses offered, reviews written, and conferences held. The point is simple: no matter which "side" one takes in the battle, the fact is that deconstruction effectively displaced other intellectual programs in the minds and much of the work of the literary avant-garde—a group of which M. H. Abrams is as much a member as J. Hillis Miller.

In fact, if one concedes that repetition is a sign of institutional per-sistence and identity, then two parallel gatherings at Columbia Univer-sity must be remarked. On February 23, 1978, in a Lionel Trilling Semi-nar, before several hundred people including Stanley Fish, Abrams delivered "How to Do Things With Texts," a critique of Derrida, Harold Bloom, and Fish. Edward Said and A. Walton Litz responded. On Febru-ary 19, 1981, Frank Kermode presented, again to a Trilling Seminar, "To Keep the Road Open: Reflection on a Theme of Lionel Trilling." His respondents were Abrams and de Man. Kermode, too, chose to address the issue of the burgeoning of theory, of the threat this poses, "from above," to the identity and survival of the institution—illiteracy is the threat "from below"—and of the difficulty for critic/teachers to carry out their "pastoral" role of producing what Kermode calls, borrowing rather ironically, I think, from Fish, an "interpretive community." One is, of course, tempted to open an ideological critique of Kermode and Fish, to remark that the old and new criticisms are linked by this common traditionalist goal to reproduce, so to speak, the means of production. This is especially true when Kermode—in a passage the sentiments and figures of which are traceable back, at least, to Irving Babbitt and I. A. Richards—points out the dangers to the institution and the society it serves in the tendency to authorize various and competing canons.[9] "Yet it must be obvious," says Kermode, "that the formation of rival canons, however transient, is very dangerous; that in allowing it to happen we risk the death of the institution. Its continuance depends wholly upon our ability to maintain the canon and replace ourselves, to induce sufficient numbers of young people to think as we do."

One must suspend the tendency to demystify, or to defend, this position long enough both to mark its genealogy throughout the history of critical study and to understand that this position is a necessary and repeated element in a debate so central to the "pastoral" mission of literary study that it may be said to be a constituent element of its discourse and its institutional survival. Indeed, the tendency to demystify this position is one of the relays of power sustaining and implementing the institution by pressuring the dominant discourse— here represented by Kermode—to reshape and defend itself. The institution is not then simply represented by Kermode's variation on Richards. But this variation is itself supported and identified by the various antagonists attacking, "defeating," and sustaining it. The institution is the terms of the debate. It is historical variation without rupture, crisis, or new beginning.

We may conclude that deconstructive criticism and its interpretive, humanistic opposition function as specular images within an institutional and discursive system akin to Lacan's idea of the Imaginary. This specularity is clearest in charges which, on the one hand, accuse deconstructors of chaotically threatening civilization and, on the other hand, denounce humanists as totalitarians. Even J. Hillis Miller's outrageously inventive play on the host-guest paradigm points to this "unity" of antagonists on the practical, semantic level of critical performance (DC, 217–53).

To accept Spanos's perhaps too unqualified certification of the identity of New Critic and deconstructor is impossible for the academy so long as it sustains its own power structure by waging these endless battles between civilization and chaos, or, in the latest version, between man and language. It must be stressed that the critiques of Arac, O'Hara, and Spanos which I have mentioned do not simply cry, "a curse on both your houses." On the contrary, these analyses draw detailed attention to the ways in which the institution of academic letters sustains itself in service to our society.[10] They point out how the institution has managed, within variable limits, continually to redeploy itself around a central, functional structure whose rules for producing "knowledge" about literature, texts, reading, and writing we are only now beginning to understand.

A description of some of the various deconstructive transformations of the New Criticism would be useful in understanding the nature of academic institutions. For it would provide an opportunity to test methods for evaluating the various tactics and strategies adopted by such institutions in relation to and as a reflection of their larger socioeconomic contexts. A preliminary sketching of these transformations would reveal how deconstruction has redeployed the discursive power of the New Criticism's representations of irony, author, the ideogram, propositional language, etc. A complete list will have to await the production of a full institutional history of criticism.

What is beyond doubt, however, is deconstruction's attempt to represent itself as "different" enough from its American predecessor as to be "distinct." The *locus classicus* of this representation is de Man's "Form and Intent in the American New Criticism." In this essay, de Man argues that the New Criticism is essentially contradictory. For the poem, as Wimsatt and the others saw it, must be "hypostatized" to be an object of critical concern. Yet, as such, the fundamental structures of the poem appear to be irony and ambiguity. De Man charges that the New Criticism does not fully understand the nature of the hermeneutic circle as an ongoing, open process of interpretation occurring in time. Since Wimsatt's and Beardsley's "intentional fallacy" demarcated the limits of critical activity and investigation, it prevented the formation of "a truly coherent theory of literary form." The New Critics rested their readings on an incorrect boundary of poetic closure even while correctly affirming "the necessary presence of a totalizing principle" to any critical project (BI, 32). The New Critics conceived and treated of the poem as a natural or an organic object rather than as an act or intentionally produced "object." For de Man, this ontological error results in the New Critic's belief that complete understanding of the organic form of a poem is, in fact, *possible*. Upon this idea, de Man's essay brings to bear Heidegger's notion of the hermeneutic circle to point out that the "dialogue between work and interpreter is endless. . . . Understanding can be called complete only when it becomes aware of its own temporal predicament and realizes that the horizon within which the totalization can take place is time itself. The act of understanding is a temporal act that has its own history, but this history forever eludes totalization. Whenever the circle seems to close, one has merely ascended or descended one more step on Mallarmé's *spirale vertigineuse conséquent"* (BI, 32).

De Man effectively subverts the New Criticism's already declining authority by this epistemological assault. He has indicted the Americans for theoretical naiveté while acquiring for himself the authority of their practice. They had, after all, in their reading succeeded in correctly revealing the unstable and indeterminate nature of ironic texts, but had been woefully blind to the insight of their own practice. So de Man is successful in his struggle with a dying enemy and carries off as spoils the riches of their accomplishment: "It is true that American textual interpretation and 'close reading' have perfected techniques that allow for considerable refinement in catching the details and nuances of literary expression. . . . The ambivalence of American formalism is such that it was bound to lead to a state of paralysis. The problem remains how to formulate the model of totalization that applies to literary language and that allows for a description of its distinctive aspects" (BI, 27, 32). De Man's deconstructive project can be described as the attempt to solve this problem, but certainly his rigorous mode of disciplined and self-reflexive ironic reading acquires power in the very scene of communion with and cremation of the dying fathers of American formalism. In a way which we have long since come to think of as de Manian, his precise, studied ambivalence in this scene effectively disarms his subject by remarking the inevitable and previously unnoticed *aporia* while equally effectively conserving those elements constituent of his own procedure and project.

Despite the erudition, intelligence, and persuasion of "Form and Intent in the American New Criticism," its most remarkable feature is its intentional forgetting of New Critical moments of de Manian insight. It is precisely such forgetting in such a formidable scholar and critic as de Man which indicates that a transformational struggle for authority is going on.

In "The Heresy of Paraphrase," Cleanth Brooks, the most redoubtable of critical totalizers, at a strategically important moment hesitantly acknowledges the impossibility of producing critical closure. Brooks is arguing the impossibility and yet the simultaneous necessity of paraphrasing a poem in propositional language. Suddenly he suggests that the allegory of closure cannot be sustained, for the critical text is itself metaphorized and destabilized as it tries to be more "adequate" to the poem, that is, as it tries to close off its metaphorical play:

> As [the critic's] proposition approaches adequacy, he will find, not only that it has increased greatly in length, but that it has begun to fill itself up with reservations and qualifications—and most significant of all—the formulator will find that he has himself begun to fall back upon metaphors of his own in his attempt to indicate what the poem "says." In sum, his proposition, as it approaches adequacy, ceases to be a proposition.[11]

In other words, the critic's language becomes more similar in kind to the language of the poet the closer he comes to "adequately" representing the "meaning" of the poem. This may mean that the New Critical text aspires to be a stable simulacrum of the poetic text, an imagistic or ironic totalization of the infinite possibilities of the poem; but it might better be seen differently. For this passage testifies above all to Brooks's sense that the attempt to close the poem in the discursive language of heretical but inescapable critical paraphrase throws the critic into the dialogue of understanding de Man describes. Paradoxically, the attempt to find "adequacy" in a critical reading merely destabilizes critical discourse to the point—not of silence or reduplicating the poem—but of producing a text itself the record and process of the discovery of critical discursive inadequacy. Put simply: the ubiquitous ironic structure the New Critics, like de Man, attribute to all poetry, reflexively destabilizes the attempt to duplicate it in closure. Closure gives way to *aporia*, if you will, as the critical text indecisively oscillates between its own tendency to allegorical closure and its own ever-increasing awareness of its metaphorical status.

The most amazing thing about this passage is that it self-consciously announces the instability of the New Critical project in one of the most dogmatic essays of that school. Moreover it is a climax of sorts in the essay, marking the final turn in Brooks's argument on the alienation of poetry from proposition. And while the essay sadly marks the inescapability of propositional contamination of poetic discourse in the critical attempt at closing the text, it extravagantly remarks the equally inevitable "transcendence" of that contamination into metaphor as the result, and, therefore, as the root, of the New Critical project.

De Man's essay is not "in error." It joins the analysis of the limits of the New Criticism in the work of Northrop Frye, Murray Krieger, and R. S. Crane.[12] De Man's particular contribution is to accuse the New Critics of failing to transfer the practico-semantic knowledge produced by their techniques and readings to the theoretical or syntactic level. Without this oscillating self-reflexivity, the New Criticism, de Man charges, is paralyzed and doomed. It is typical of de Man's ahistoricism not to describe the beginning, survival, and persistence of this paralytic. For the very possibility of New Criticism is defined by its separation of syntactic and semantic, or theoretical and practical levels. The supreme and ubiquitous reflexivity de Man finds missing is an ecological mode of safe (nonparalyzing) relations between levels of discourse which are not epistemologically or syntactically homogeneous. Brooks's essay indicates that the New Critics are not ignorant of the "arrangements" they have made in their practice to ensure the continuation of their project and its authority. Transporting the practico-semantic discovery of irony to the technico-theoretical realm of stylistic reflexivity would, in fact, have paralyzed the New Critical project of presenting, in poetry, a form of nonlinear cognition and signification as an alternative to "positivism," "journalism," and the social sciences. De Man's critique displaces the goals of this project while preserving both the theoretical and practical insights—totalization and irony—of the New Critics. The effects of this acquisition, the preservation of irony as the trope of tropes, the production of an authentic "totalization," mark deconstruction's remaking of its predecessor's program.

The continuities of this remaking appear both in the deconstructive revision of New Critical touchstones and in the way the practice of certain deconstructive essays echoes the formalist paradigm. The Derridean critique of the "author" in *Of Grammatology* is an example of the poststructuralist extension of that very New Critical assault on "intentionality" which de Man studies. So, too, influential pieces like J. Hillis

Miller's reading of Shakespeare's *Troilus and Cressida*, "Ariachne's Broken Woof," illustrate the reformation of the New Critics' practice and the form and shape of their essays.

Miller's essay is important not for its speculative contributions to deconstruction, but for its success in putting deconstruction into play as a literary critical practice which can be schematized, abstracted, copied, and disseminated. While Miller argues for the radical and destabilizing effects of deconstruction on the critical establishment authorized by and sustaining metaphysics, the uniqueness of his achievement consists in his simultaneously providing brilliant examples of how deconstructive reading "is done." Miller's antagonists frequently concede him his destabilizing goals and accuse him, too, of being a threat to civilization. Others suggest that like de Man and Derrida, the other "boa-deconstructors," as Geoffrey Hartman calls them, Miller is a "negative theologian," an ironic metaphysician. While the first charge must be acknowledged by those who feel threatened by Miller's antihumanistic project to destabilize the univocal or privileged "reading," it is obviously unfairly leveled against a critic of such erudition, sophistication, and wit. As to the second charge that deconstruction is itself metaphysics—this is something the deconstructors have themselves first made us aware of. For as Miller tells us himself, the irony of deconstruction is that its texts "contain both logocentric metaphysics and its subversion" (ABW, 59). It is this "double-bind" which marks all deconstructive projects and which seems to escape many of its critics. "Deconstruction," Miller concludes, "attempts . . . a consequent vibratory displacement of the whole system of Western metaphysics. That this attempt always fails, so that it has to be performed again and again, interminably, is indicated by the way my terms . . . imperturbably reaffirm the system that I am using them to challenge" (ABW, 60). Deconstruction is not naive, and the power of its self-reflexivity which redeploys the power relayed by the figures of failure always already preempts those criticisms which impotently name it metaphysics.

Yet the interest of Miller's concession of failure and the need for repetition of the deconstructive move is not so easily exhausted. Abrams charges that deconstruction is parasitical upon "the obvious or univocal reading." Miller's response in "The Critic as Host" subverts the set of oppositions that lie unquestioned in Abrams's discourse.[13] Miller effectively demonstrates that such notions as "priority" and "secondarity" are metaphorical, unstable, and constantly oscillating in crosscurrents of figural exchange. So Miller disarms Abrams et al. and further extends the deconstructive weaponry in the academy by demonstrating and enacting the repetitive nature of his critical project and its extensive subversive implications for critical shibboleths.

But would Abrams's charge have more force if it included Miller with himself, Wimsatt, Trilling, Bloom, etc. as paragons of the profession empowered by the conservative transformation of the system he believes he is challenging? I take it that Miller's text confesses to this complicity when he remarks that "my terms . . . imperturbably reaffirm the system that I am using them to challenge." Quite rightly, in the context of Derrida and de Man and of Miller's own questioning of logocentrism in this essay, the passage must be read as a sign of the closure of metaphysics, of the ongoing cover-up of the trace, and of the power of the system of presence. Yet, more specifically, the "system" Miller challenges is that of the critical machinery which produces univocal, obvious readings or determinate sense. In acknowledging the limits of deconstruction's ability to "go beyond" metaphysics, i.e., in marking the closure of metaphysics as the horizon of our reading, Miller defends the authority of his text against the charge that there is no distinction in being a deconstructor. But this self-justifying apology also confesses that it can do no more than continually transform the New Critical project or system in the very process of challenging it.

Yet Miller the etymologist must know that to challenge an opponent is not only to call an opponent into question by demanding its identity, but is also to attack an opponent with false accusations. A challenge is calumny. Having put "truth" out of the question, Miller's deconstruction aspires to power by means of a false accusation which ironically reaffirms the identity of the slandered opponent. Miller shows that the univocal or New Critical reading is mystified and more unstable than it suspects, so much so that it depends upon the self-reflexively destabilized deconstruction for its own determinate identity. So Miller reverses priority and secondarity. Yet none of this is true, since calumny is the "nature" of all challenge. So Miller's devastating critique of univocality, of the logocentric monology of narrative, not only reaffirms the authority of the system it accuses, but reduplicates its own oscillating status, its own crisscrossing claims to power and truth.

Simply and specifically, "Ariachne's Broken Woof" appears as the mirror image of such texts as Wimsatt's "Concrete Universal."[14] Miller's ability to represent *Troilus and Cressida* and, by implication, all narrative in the figure of anacoluthon simultaneously shifts and reaffirms Wimsatt's desire to represent the organic form of harmonious totalities by the metaphor figured in Hegelian terms. Miller has shown that editors and critics comically attempt to erase the absurd "i" in "Ariachne." He has also dismissed I. A. Richards's solution of the problem by demonstrating that "Ariachne" is not a portmanteau since the two stories— Arachne and Ariadne—are contradictory. So like Rousseau's *supplément* (as Derrida explicates it), Shakespeare's "i" is both too much and too little, differing and deferring the pursuit of presence in a transparent sign. Miller's figure for this recognizable deconstructive trope is "anacoluthon."

Most interesting is the way this term expands in its "reference" from the interpretive "i," to Troilus's mind, to Ulysses's speech on order, to the entire Western metaphysical tradition. Miller could not have done us a better service than so clearly to illustrate his deconstruction's conservation of New Criticism's universalizing tendencies. "Anacoluthon," Miller writes,

> describes a syntactical pattern in which there is a shift in tense, number, or person in the midst of a sentence so that the words do not hang together grammatically. An anacoluthon is not governed by a single *logos*, in the sense of a unified meaning.
>
> If the word "Ariachne" is an anacoluthon in miniature, a similar structure is repeated in the syntactical and figurative incoherence of Troilus' speech [which critics try] to reduce. . . . The grammatical anacoluthon parallels, in the other direction, the anacoluthon of Troilus' divided mind, the narrative discontinuity of the entire play, and so on up to the immense anacoluthon of Western literature, philosophy, and history as a "whole." (ABW, 56)

The point here is not that Miller has made a "negative metaphysical" category of anacoluthon nor that he has seen "ontology" as "rhetoric." More important, in his subversion of the Hegelian project of monology, Miller mirrors—albeit with some disfiguring intent—the New Critical play of extending rhetorical tropes like "paradox" and "metaphor" into versions of the Idea figured as verbal icons and well-wrought urns. Miller's transformation of the critical process is a substitutive, inverted mirroring of the New Criticism. More: it is a reversed replication of the New Critical structure de Man calls paralysis and I call survival. For with the partial exception of his etymological games, Miller's theoretical insight seems not always to transport itself onto the practico-semantic level of style or technique; for his prose preserves the same complex tension of clarity and irony as does Brooks's and his method the same contextual, global attention to detailed iconic read- ing as Wimsatt's. Miller's inversion of the New Critical project appears in his reiterated demonstration of a text's *instability* while offering *stable* representations of textuality in the figure of anacoluthon. Is this not analogous to Brooks's repeated claims for a text's *stability* while offering *stable* representations of closed form in the various versions of the well-wrought urn? And do not both Miller and Brooks inscribe in their texts tropes calling their projects into question and display these tropes at the center of their bids for authority?

While Miller may not so effectively transform his insight into the ironic play of style which marks Derrida and de Man at their best, it is also true that their stylistic play, crucial as it is to their success in unsettling academic criticism, must not obscure the variations in their works on New Critical tropes. Of course, these variations "define" themselves precisely in their play. Especially in the case of Derrida, "style" is the only space for his project. To reduce or minimize the nature and complexity of his prose is to neglect his achievement, to prejudice the case hopelessly beyond recall, and to announce one's own blindness to the entire deconstructive project. If deconstruction can legitimately claim any distinction in the academy, it is less on the level of technical reading power than on the level of style.[15] Even so, the frequency with which some readers and critics ignore the precision of Derrida's stylistic deployment of key nonconcepts, such as *supplément* or *différance*, suggests that the utility of these "terms" for the institution should be momentarily considered apart from the style of their repre- sentation.

The point is not just that, as Edward Said suggests,[16] certain of Der- rida's neologisms taken together form a deployed system of reading— despite his intentions; but that, in some cases at least, this happens because Derrida *appears to be offering* only more vigorous and severe forms of common critical tropes. This is perhaps more true of the early Derrida, especially in *Of Grammatology.* It is certainly more obviously true of some "nonconcepts" like "supplément" or "trace" than of others like "hinge" or "différance." Perhaps the clearest example of how Derri- dean deconstruction is, as it were, already written into American academic criticism involves not a neologism at all, but Derrida's critique of "author," "intentionality," and "proper name."

Wimsatt and Beardsley had, in "The Intentional Fallacy," effectively made the "author" a function of the text: "It is only because an artifact works that we infer the intention of an artificer" (The Verbal Icon, 4). Explaining the paradox that "internal evidence" of a poem's working is also "public," they go on to write of it: "It is discovered through the semantics and syntax of a poem, through our habitual knowledge of the language, through grammars, dictionaries, and all the literature which is the source of dictionaries, in general through all that makes a language and culture" (10). While this rhetoric can be easily deconstructed by examining the figural priority of "literature" to "dictionaries" and the sense of causal opposition which masks the "leakage" of each figure into the other, it is worth seeing how this presages Derrida's demonstration of the textuality of the author, even of the autobiographical "je." In fact, Wimsatt and Beardsley, like Derrida, point out how the text is a record of the struggle to master tropes rather than be mastered by them. For them, this insight is couched in the psychologistic language of contextualism and in the aesthetic rhetoric of the pure art object. But there can be no ignoring how for them the battle to control or efface "context" and "life" to produce a text is a conflict between self and language waged for control of tropes: "There is a gross body of life, of sensory and mental experience, which lies behind and in some sense causes every poem, but can never be and need not be known in the verbal and hence intellectual composition which is the poem. For all the objects of our manifold experience, for every unity, there is an action of the mind which cuts off the roots, melts away context—or indeed we should never have objects or ideas or anything to talk about" (12).

In the "Introduction to the 'Age of Rousseau'," Derrida, with pointilliste precision, thematizes exactly what is going on in Wimsatt and Beardsley. This should not be surprising since at the "center" of Derrida's project is the recognition that this epoch announces itself as the "end of metaphysics" precisely in the way in which it seemingly everywhere calls into question the fundamental tropes and functions of logocentrism only to reestablish them. Derrida's writing on the "author" brings out and supersedes Wimsatt's and Beardsley's assault on authorial intention as a designation of writing's once again remarking on itself and its previous obscurity.

Derrida, of course, unlike Wimsatt and Beardsley, realizes that the mere substitution of terms—"internal" for "external," "public" for "private"—does not allow one to think the problem of poetic or any other discourse outside the realm of metaphysics. So Derrida can write: "The names of authors . . . have here no substantial value. . . . The indicative value that I attribute to them is first the name of a problem" (G, 99). Derrida moves *to open* the text by reinscribing the "author," whereas the New Critics try *to close, to totalize* the text in the same movement. The New Critical move, we can see with Derrida's help, exemplifies the inevitable entrapments of a restricted economy. Derrida refuses to consider discourse in terms of the "author" since it is one of the primary signs of metaphysical closure; but, unlike the New Critics, he also refuses to attempt such a consideration by a mere substitution of "poem" for "author": "I think that *all concepts hitherto proposed in order to think the articulation of a discourse and of an historical totality are caught within the metaphysical closure that I question*" (G, 96). The "autotelic text" becomes, in Derrida, a metaphor for exploring the theory of writing. Derrida examines texts, free of the traditional authorial illusion, to discover and question their internal structures, not for formal closure and meaning, but as symptoms of the problematic of the closure of metaphysics. Inscribing texts into this problematic further extends the "dehumanization" of writing which is itself enabled by the detachment of text from consciousness. This leads Derrida to a statement remarkably similar to that of Wimsatt and Beardsley on the way the mind de-contextualizes itself to produce a poem. Since for Derrida the "proper name has never been . . . anything but the original myth of a transparent legibility present under the obliteration" (G, 109), the "author" cannot function as cause, origin, or source of texts. In a passage which recalls Wimsatt and Beardsley, Derrida articulates the deconstructive desire to speak an unheard-of thought on the matter of a text's production:

If in a rather conventional way I call by the name of *discourse* the present, living, conscious *representation of a text* within the experience of the person who writes or reads it, and if the text constantly goes beyond this representation by the entire system of its resources and its own laws, then the question of genealogy exceeds by far the possibilities that are at present given for its elaboration. We know that the metaphor that would describe the genealogy of a text correctly is still *forbidden*. In its syntax and its lexicon, in its spacing, by its punctuation, its lacunae, its margins, the historical appurtenance of a text is never a straight line. (G, 101)

Although most often the New Critic allegorizes these lacunae in a myth of totalization, the deconstructor duplicates the traces of the genealogy in the text with a rigor exceeding that of the "writer." If anything defines in common the best work of Derrida and de Man, it is this duplication. "We should begin," Derrida writes, "by taking rigorous account of this *being held within* [prise] or this surprise: the writer writes in a language and in a logic whose proper system, laws, and life his discourse by definition cannot dominate absolutely. . . . And the reading must always aim at a certain relationship, unperceived by the writer, between what he commands and what he does not command of the patterns of language that he uses. This relationship is . . . a signifying structure that critical reading should *produce*" (G, 158). This statement, of course, summarizes the deconstructive reversal of the New Critical project. It authorizes the redeployment of critical energies into a new alignment of forces which preserves the integrity of the institution while providing original and praeter-naturally subtle insight into both the operations of textuality and the primordiality of writing "as the disappearance of natural presence" (G, 159). Ironically, the very critical movement which *produces* the abysmal (*en abyme*) relationship between authorial control and linguistic excess in fact sustains the institution of literary study. While Kermode and others might see deconstruction and literary theorizing in general as a threat to literature and criticism, precisely because of its abysmal concerns, because of its subtle perceptions into the theory of writing, it seems that deconstruction is, despite its "radical" impulses and procedures, truly conservative. "Contrary to received opinion," de Man remarks, "deconstructive discourses are suspiciously text-productive" (AR, 200).

Deconstructive reading is a writing. It is a necessary doubling commentary which must be transgressed *to open* a text and a reading. For de Man, the perpetuity of text-production is a function of error: "There can be no writing without reading, but all readings are in error because they assume their own readability" (AR, 202). Deconstruction appears to name and seemingly dispel this error. But such error is ubiquitous, a function of the sign itself: "The problem is . . . that a totally enlightened language, regardless of whether it conceives of itself as a consciousness or not, is unable to control the recurrence, in its readers as well as in itself, of the errors it exposes" (AR, 219, n. 36). De Man's "reading" of *Julie* leads him to offer an emblem of all error in a textual image of demystification: "The paradigm for all texts consists of a figure (or a system of figures) and its deconstruction. But since this model cannot be closed off by a final reading, it engenders, in its turn, a supplementary figural superposition which narrates the unreadability of the prior narration" (AR, 205). So reading/writing produces allegory. One cannot say of these remarks with Gerald Graff that they are referentially self-contradictory. Such a comment is unappreciative of de Man's ironic play with the levels of discourse in such a statement. Nor can one argue that this is *merely* pessimism or impotence. The difficulty consists in realizing how these seemingly despairing remarks *produce* texts and representations of writing/reading and criticism which have power.[17] It is the quintessence of deconstruction that it responds to the decline of academic literary criticism by inscribing within the academy a project for preservation. The repetitiveness of deconstruction is an institutional necessity fortunately fulfilled by the vigorous texts of subtle critics.

In a sense, Edward Said's objection that deconstruction becomes by repetition merely a "new" system, a "new" method of reading is unutterably true and moot. Deconstruction can be nothing else. It is always already the case that the ubiquity of error in the sign determines deconstruction as an institutional practice, as a succession of more or less interesting misreadings. "Deconstructions of figural texts" (and what other kind are there?), de Man writes, "engender lucid narratives which produce, in their turn and as it were within their own texture, a darkness more redoubtable than the error they dispel" (AR, 217). One could speculate upon or play with the figure of darkness de Man so trenchantly probes. One might even offer a "counter" idea of darkness or condemn de Man for moral or political reasons for making darkness such a key element in his representation of literature and criticism. But doing so would, of course, testify to the ecological success of the figure as it emerges in de Man, with a complex genealogy—a success in sustaining the institution ironically marked by its power to provoke so many *challenges*.

No legitimate argument can be made denying the importance of ethical, political, epistemological, or pedagogical critiques of de Man, Derrida, and the other deconstructors. But political critiques of deconstruction must take into account the subversive effects it has had on an academy still largely unwilling either to accept the rigor of its analyses and the intelligence of its speculations or to employ its students. Similarly, a complete genealogical analysis, of which I have presented here only the barest outline, would have to describe deconstruction's specific turns upon the shape of the academy in order to avoid merging deconstruction back into the relief of institutional criticism out of which it has raised itself. A criticism which sees no differences between deconstruction and its predecessors is naive and does a disservice to our self-understanding. Yet such an understanding requires an awareness that deconstruction, in a seemingly paradigmatic way, redeployed critical power and sustained much of the institution. The curious can only ask if the increasing number of intelligent and distorting attacks on deconstruction, from both right and left, as well as a sense in some quarters that it is "finished," mark the beginning of another local variation in the forms of the institution. Has the energy of deconstruction begun to flag, and is all the current critical dance around it a ritual feast of renewal? Has it been co-opted or will it persist and flourish? Is a new transformation of the New Critical-deconstructionist "line" to appear? If so, then we might ask, what dark shape marches forward threatening to be born?

4

......

The Metaphysics of
Textuality: Marx's
Eighteenth Brumaire of
Louis Bonaparte
and Nietzsche's
Use and Abuse of History

Just as little must one imagine that the democratic representatives are indeed all shopkeepers or enthusiastic champions of shopkeepers. According to their education and their individual position they may be as far apart as heaven from earth. What makes them representatives of the petty bourgeoisie is the fact that in their minds they do not get beyond the limits which the latter do not get beyond in life, that they are consequently driven, theoretically, to the same problems and solutions to which material interest and social position drive the latter practically. This is, in general, the relationship between the political and literary representatives of a class and the class they represent.—Karl Marx

Like the artist, theoretical man takes infinite pleasure in all that exists and is thus saved from the practical ethics of pessimism, with its lynx eyes that shine only in the dark. But while the artist, having unveiled the truth garment by garment, remains with his gaze fixed on what is still hidden, theoretical man takes delight in the case garments and finds his highest satisfaction in the unveiling process itself, which proved to him his own power.—Friedrich Nietzsche

The question of style—it is always the question of a pointed object. . . . Style will jut out, then, like the spur on an old sailing vessel. . . . With its spur, style can also protect against whatever terrifying, blinding, or mortal threat might present itself or be obstinately encountered: i.e., the presence, and, hence, the content of things themselves, of meaning, of truth. . . .—Jacques Derrida

Throughout the late 1960s and early 1970s both Paul de Man[1] and Jacques Derrida unveiled the pervasive presence of Hegelian metaphysics within the history of philosophy and modern critical practice.

For both theorists, this metaphysics was a closed economy of significa-tion.[2] Derrida, as he himself points out in *Positions*,[3] is attempting simul-taneously to carry out a general economy and a general strategy of deconstruction which would always and everywhere be directed against the Hegelian dialectic.

Derrida's and de Man's anti-Hegelianism has had a profound and apparently lasting influence on an entire generation of literary critical intellectuals. I would like, in this paper, to consider some of the effects of this influence and to suggest some of what is lost to criticism as a result of following in the footsteps of these great masters. Let me say at the beginning that I will make no effort to "refute" the basic claims which others derive from these critics and which they make authorita-tive: such claims as those about the relationship between textuality and allegory or the so-called deconstructive inversion of hierarchies. My point is that I have found no convincing demonstration that these terms or "non-concepts" are, indeed, as unavailable to *all* critical discus-sion as the ephebes of Derrida and de Man often claim. On the con-trary, I want to make a small case for what is ruled out of the proper domain of critical thinking by those who give their strongly committed allegiances to the most extreme forms of deconstructive skepticism. Another way to put this would be to say that I will make no attempt to contest with Paul de Man's preternaturally sensitive readings of the characteristics of textuality in those texts by Rousseau, Nietzsche, and Proust which he could make so interesting for us. Rather than enter those lists and fail or be marked by the paralysis of discipleship, I want to engage in a somewhat different critical discourse secure in the irrelevance of the deconstructive critique to its value—despite its own traditional and, indeed, apparently "metaphysical" nature.

The shape of this essay is somewhat convoluted. I intend to derive and outline what I take to be a more powerful and attractive mode of oppositional practice from two central works of the radical intellectual tradition: *On the Uses and Disadvantages of History for Life* and *The Eighteenth Brumaire of Louis Bonaparte*.[4] Yet before going on to Marx and Nietzsche, I would like to outline part of Derrida's anti-Hegelian stance, particularly as this emerged in the late sixties and the early seventies, that is, at the moment when Derrida became attractive and influential among a num-ber of soon-to-be-powerful literary critics. But even before opening that parenthesis on Derrida—which is necessary to my general argument—I must take a somewhat different look at another aspect of Derrida and de Man's work and influence.

Both de Man and Derrida repeatedly announced, from the late sixties onward, that critical thinking about language had, for far too long, been secondary to other intellectual projects and concerns: phenomenology, structuralism, and humanistic literary history are cogent examples. In fact, we can see now as many did even then, that they were absolutely correct. The late sixties and the early seventies give abundant evidence of the failure of both New Criticism and liberal bourgeois humanism to ground the intellectual and social importance of the critical academy.[5] One can find the evidence of this failure not only in the heap of unimportant scribble conjured by those pursuing the seductive spectre of academic success, but much more importantly in the despair of the young in literary study, a despair which turned them away from critical studies to sociology, law, social work, and other then fashionably "relevant" or rewarding disciplines and careers. This same despair is found among the "me generation" of the seventies and the insecure youth of the Reagan revolution in the eighties as they turn to journalism, business school, advertising, and engineering: caught in the illusion they can securely ground their future's happiness and freedom in the sacrifice of their present to a practice they see as at most second best.

A certain set of questions come easily to mind: could it be said that American literary education was felt by the majority of students, and often by the "best and brightest," to be unimportant, culturally irrelevant, and not just a dead-end kind of professional training? Could this mean that literature itself is closed finally in a casket locked beyond all exhumation?[6] Might it not even mean that the nature of the intellectual study of literature in the American academy is at fault? It seems obvious, one might assert, that too many, perhaps even a great majority of American teacher/scholars dance to tunes piped on horns blown in previous ages. Might we not ask, though, if literary study has lost its value, and importance to the social order because it has stopped being critical, it has stopped practicing negation and opposition to what is given and so has failed to provide the only thing critical practice can offer which can be found no where else: the ability to see, to study, and to call into question all the inadequate institutions, discourses, and practices of our culture and political order? Might one not also argue that Americanized deconstruction did not in any way revise this circumstance, but rather became merely the institutionalized response to the loss of social power, of cultural relevance, a response which, in effect, sustained the given order of the literary institution when it was in crisis?[7]

De Man and Derrida were and, to some extent, still are phenomena. Not only did what they say effectively alter the way many of us who listened, thought about, and studied literature, but they were also (and perhaps this is even more important) sources of excitement and energy for an academic literary establishment seen as haggish, passive, repetitious, and historically very inappropriate. De Man and Derrida were seducers; whether they were sirens or Socrates is a question that should perhaps be answered. Edward Said, for example, seems to be himself unsure: in his discussions of Derrida he takes him far more seriously than those who either follow him professionally or repudiate him blindly. Said would seem to take Derrida and other "systematic" critics[8] with about the same degree of seriousness as an Athenian court might take Socrates. It would be inappropriate to picture Said as Odysseus tied to a mast listening to the sirens. Yet, it seems to me, an important question whether the criticism of textuality is sirenic or Socratic. No doubt both de Man and Derrida in their consummate displays of irony, in their propulsion of mind along previously blocked paths of thought are like Socrates. But they are also like Nietzsche's image of woman—the figure of distant promise whose dangerous powers of seduction exist both at a distance and in close proximity.[9] Admiring from afar or closing to grapple with truth—both bring exhaustion and death—can I say then I won't enter the lists with de Man, and can that mean anything in our profession but succumbing from a distance? In *Positions* Derrida analyzes this same problem in this way:

> If we have to keep our distance from the feminine operations of *actio in distans*—which doesn't amount to simply not approaching it, except at the risk of death *itself*—it is because "woman" is *not* just an identifiably determinate appearance that is imported at a distance from somewhere else, an appearance to draw back from or to approach. Perhaps, as non-identity, non-appearance, simulacrum, she is the *abyss* of distance, the distancing of distance, the thrust of spacing, distance itself—distance *as such*, if one could say that, which is no longer possible.... There is no essence of woman because woman separates and separates herself off from

herself. From the endless, bottomless depths, she submerges all essentiality, identity, all propriety, and every property. Blinded in such a way, philosophical [one can say critical, as well] discourse founders, and is left to dash headlong to its ruin. There is no truth about woman, just because this abysmal separation from the truth, this nontruth, is the truth. Woman is one name for this nontruth of truth. (P, 179)

The proof of de Man's and Derrida's seduction of the youth of academe is that they are themselves names for the truth of nontruth, and, of course, for the nontruth of truth—if one could any longer speak even in that way.

Beginning in 1967, de Man insists that there is a crisis in criticism:

Well established rules and conventions that governed the discipline of criticism and made it a cornerstone of the intellectual establishment have been so badly tampered with that the entire edifice threatens to collapse.[10]

As de Man repeated this claim throughout the early 1970s, after 1968, after Tet, after Nixon, to many of us it seemed as if the entire edifice of Western life were about to collapse—and some of us wished to hurry it along. De Man's nearly apocalyptic statement sat well with those who were living through a horrible imperialist war and painful civil war in the streets and on the campuses. Paradoxically, de Man's call attracted those who hoped to turn the university away from its associations with a racist and imperialist state. But de Man's work is nothing if not reasoned and mocking; even in 1967 and 1970 he was prepared to admit that to many academic critics there appeared to be no crisis at all. Of course, as all those concerned with contemporary criticism now know, de Man argues that all criticism is generically "crisis"; it is always insightful only because blind; always undergoing hermeneutic and methodological upheaval. Yet he daringly intimates that speaking of crisis in American literary criticism might be "out of tone." Americans are eclectic, less concerned with polemics, and satisfied that all previous "crises," so-called, have only been stages along the progressing and progressive way.[11] But de Man quickly adopts a rather harsher tone toward this characteristic American cultural optimism:

This kind of pragmatic common sense is admirable, up to the point where it lures the mind into self-satisfied complacency and puts it irrevocably to sleep. It can always be shown, on all levels of experience, that what other people experience as a crisis is perhaps not even a change; such observations depend to a very large extent on the standpoint of the observer. . . . No set of arguments, no enumeration of symptoms will ever prove that the present effervescence surrounding literary criticism is in fact a crisis that, for better or worse, is reshaping the critical consciousness of a generation. (BI, 5–6)

The crisis of which de Man speaks seems to be safely located in the past for most academicians. Perhaps we can see this in the appearance and reappearance of such essays as Walter Benn Michaels and Robert Knapp's "Against Theory."

There are, of course, many reasons why the crisis in criticism seems to have faded from the consciousness of the profession—especially its upper reaches—even as the financial crunch and the Reagan-initiated assault on educational funding grows worse. I want to restrict my comments here to matters largely internal to the profession. Of course, I realize that the literary institutions are not independent of the larger world, but I want to isolate some specific institutional realities to understand the profession's own role in neutralizing this critical consciousness.[12]

The American literary institution has had two powerful ways to overcome this crisis in criticism. The first is the increasingly seductive voice of the past represented best in the late sixties and early seventies by M. H. Abrams and more recently and more publicly by Denis Donoghue, Susan Sontag, Robert M. Adams and the like. The second is the institutional machinery of cooptation and dispersal which simply incorporated the rhetoric of crisis into academic publications, curricula, and prizes thereby disarming its critical implications. *Diacritics*, *Glyph*, *boundary* 2, *Critical Inquiry*, *The Georgia Review*, and others—all these journals to differing degrees and at various times in different ways became sites for the initiation of many into *la nouvelle critique*—which was good—and into the hierarchical reward structure of the university—which is unavoidable. Yale responded institutionally to the intense awareness of change in New Haven with the Literature Program, an undergraduate curriculum for literary theoretical, comparative, interdisciplinary study (a program now moving in somewhat different political directions) and with several issues of the *Yale French Studies* on French Freud and the pedagogical implications of contemporary criticism.[13] The University of California and the NEH combined to form the School of Criticism and Theory at Irvine under the direction of Murray Krieger, himself no friend of poststructuralist criticism.[14] For a time, even the generally moribund *PMLA* found it acceptable to publish poststructuralist articles and to note the frequency with which the name of Derrida appeared in its pages.

Rather than see these events as openings in the essentially closed economy of American criticism, I take them as movements of domination which make overt exactly how dependent upon the central institutions of state, bureaucracy, hierarchy, and capital so-called "advanced" criticism really is. Deconstruction is, as Derrida himself might put it, always already coopted; it is always and everywhere hard to differentiate from its avowed academic antagonist.[15] One can see how difficult it is for the American academy to take seriously, that is, to take in any critical and reflexive spirit, the crisis of criticism when one considers the celebrity and authority of Jonathan Culler who professes throughout his work to be providing "guides" which essentially commodify serious critical work and deny that work all of the power of negation.[16]

The effects of the critical crisis have not been as irreversible as de Man supposed because the liberal humanistic tradition is still ideologically quite powerful and has, in a generally conservative historical moment, regained much of its former strength. When Abrams debated J. Hillis Miller, for example,[17] Abrams's role or function was to place the massive authority of his reputation as a literary humanist in opposition to "deconstruction's" "threatened barbarism." In effect, Abrams granted many academicians a dispensation from studying the newer critical texts and those of their forebears: Hegel, Nietzsche, Marx, Saussure, Lacan, and Heidegger. Abrams intends his work to further civilization by enhancing knowledge and communication; but during the seventies his most important function within the academy was as a force for closure, a full-stop authoritatively representing both the unwillingness of too many to study a new point of view and the stake which the humanistic institutions of literary study have in closing out (except for the tokens) serious consideration of the work of recent critics.

II

I would like to move from the margin of my proposed topic and return to the parenthesis of de Man and Derrida on Hegel which I opened so long ago. The reason for having moved to the margin is quite simple: my topic itself always exists on the margin of the American literary critical establishment and I have been confronting it all along. My primary concern is with Marx and Nietzsche's interest in criticism's relations to institutions and education.

But before I can move directly to that topic, the issue of deconstruction's relation to Hegel must be taken up very briefly.[18] In "Genesis and Genealogy" in Nietzsche's *Birth of Tragedy*, de Man claims that literary criticism is largely carried out within a Hegelianism. Modern literary criticism attempts, like Hegel, to totalize different elements of textuality and literary history—which de Man finds incommensurate in themselves—within one circular figure where the beginning and the end of interpretation are similar because the beginning is the end. De Man argues that *The Birth of Tragedy* is a double text, a deconstruction of the very genetic and genealogical metaphors which structure its own narrative model. He also says that, despite the claims of the high modernists and their explicators, linear and circular models of history are analogous. De Man claims to have found in Nietzsche's text a rigorous demonstration that the apparent differences between the teleological structure of linear consciousness associated traditionally with the hierarchical model of Christianity[19] and the dialectical or "evolutionary" forms of history represented in Hegel's *Erinnerung* both emerge from one important interest: the desire to develop continuous, teleological models for the interpretation of the history of the West which culminate in the highest possible parousiacal synthesis of temporal events in a transcendent whole. This abstract, unitary, historical model, de Man concludes, obscures the consistent interruptions into narrative continuity which plague all texts—novels, critical books, and histories. Nietzsche's text has, he tells us, enacted the universal situation of all writing, that is, the duplicity of writing in a multiplicity of ironic voices which inevitably subverts its own movements of cohesion. In writing, "truths" cannot be brought to rest; if they appear to be stabilized conceptually "within" texts, especially within narratives, as in Fichte's narrative of subjectivity, that is only because the improvisatory, buffoon-like generative power of irony as the trope of tropes, as the "permanent parabasis of allegory," has been obscured by a technologically based culture, the stable forms of which cannot seriously open themselves to the freer circulation of signifiers in a non-narrative, non-teleological writing. In fact, for de Man, the primary location of the suppression of language's ironic duplicity is historical narration.

History-writing's adaptation of the genetic model of continuity is a transference from a level of scientific reference in biological sciences to a metaphoric level in narration—a transference which, according to de Man, cannot be made with epistemological rigor. Therefore, he concludes, since there is no reason for this transference, an explanation for its pervasive occurrence, particularly in literary history, can be found only in the power of its effects. Hence de Man's preoccupation at that time with analyzing major literary figures, such as Rousseau, Shelley, and Nietzsche, to show that they are already demystified, that their texts are already aware of their own status as double-writing, and time and again demonstrate how the disfigured, fragmentary nature of writing prohibits its historical hermeneutic recuperation and always anticipates its best (Hegelian) interpreters.

Derrida in a similar movement—Derrida's differences from de Man are not crucial here—repeatedly figures the Hegelian dialectic as a recuperative machine which totalizes and synthesizes by taking up all binaries into a third term moving irrevocably toward totalization. This is an all-powerful machine of interpretation: it first dissolves complex differences into antitheses and then sublimates them "in an anamnestic interiority (*Erinnerung*), while *interning* difference in a presence to itself" (P, 36). Derrida represents the Hegelian hydra as a perpetual reconstitution of the "dual opposition." And the object of this Hegelian assault is always the

> undecidables, that is, simulative units, 'false' verbal, nominal or semantic properties, which escape from inclusion in the philosophical (binary) opposition and which nonetheless inhabit it, resist it, and disorganize it, but *without ever* constituting a third term, without ever occasioning a solution in the form of speculative dialectics. . . . In Fact, it is against the incessant reappropriation of this simulative activity in a Hegelian type of dialectics . . . that I am attempting to channel the critical enterprise. . . . (P, 36)

De Man and Derrida feel the Hegelian model must be displaced since it is the most powerful and closed economy epitomizing Western metaphysics and its critical substratum. Derrida always sets himself "against thought" precisely because, as he learns from Bataille, whenever Hegelianism appears to be displaced, there it is most effectively controlling language and *producing* thought: "It is the emptiness given the substance of a highly derivative ideality: the effect of a difference of forces, the illusive autonomy of a discourse or a consciousness whose hypostasis must be deconstructed. . . ." This general deconstruction, we learn, is an attack on history and hermeneutic understanding:

> Must I recall that, from my first published texts, I have attempted to systematize deconstructive criticism precisely in opposition to the authority of meaning (*sens*) as a *transcendental signifier* or as a *telos*, in other words against history ultimately understood to be a history of meaning (*sens*), history in its logocentric, metaphysical, idealistic representation . . . going so far as to include the complex imprints it was able to leave on Heideggerean discourse? (P, 39)

Yet, Derrida uses the word "history" himself, but not in either its linear or circular sense; by his definition, both of these are inside the closure of metaphysics: a set of "faults always different from one another, of divisions whose mark or scar is born by all philosophic texts." What Derrida offers as history is repetition and trace; it is, in other words, textuality. The central movement of deconstruction, then, is the displacement of history as a sense of reference and content by a "general text" (P, 43). Derrida's struggle against unitary history means there are, indeed, many different histories to tell, but all these different histories are marked by the same: they are "different as to their kind, their rhythm, their mode of inscription, unbalanced, differentiated histories. . . ." Always and everywhere, only textuality is an alternative to the closure of metaphysics; history is recording, retrieval, and transposition of meaning: "What I call text," says Derrida, "inscribes and extends beyond the limit of such discourses. . . ." (P, 42).

That Derrida's speculations have been productive for critical writing is beyond doubt.[20] Yet—and now I wish to move out of my parenthesis into the main text of my argument—this concept (or non-concept) of a pervasive textuality which alone struggles against metaphysics—this too is an idea or movement caught up in metaphysics, but not simply in the same ironic Derridean sense that deconstructors such as J. Hillis Miller all too readily admit.[21] Nor do I mean this in quite the same sense that Derrida anticipates in *L'Ecriture et la différence*.[22] That is to say, I do not mean merely that deconstruction's troping of "history" with "textuality" is a metaphysical figure because, like Lévi-Strauss's use of the sign, it is an unavoidable bricolage of the rhetoric of presence. I mean rather that in its totalizing preoccupation with textuality—despite the ironies this allows—deconstruction is the highest form of metaphysics.

While the deconstructors hope to reveal the possibility of a general economy in various writers, and thus the closure of metaphysics in the trace, irony, or the uncanny (one can, of course, with Derrida and some of his followers proliferate "non-concepts" here), they reproduce the essential movements of Hegelianism—its idealistic abstraction from concrete history and matters of power and institutions.[23] One must concede, as Said has done,[24] that deconstruction is intended as an oppositional practice; but for that very reason one must repeatedly point out that, in its failure to understand the materiality of the very discourses it claims to deconstruct, it fails to understand the realities of power. Of course, this general claim has now been made many times, but perhaps its truth helps to explain many aspects of the contemporary critical scene in America:

(1) this valorization of textuality is itself one cause of the general failure of theory to sustain the crisis within criticism;

(2) the aesthetic dimensions of textuality and its refusal of historicity have allowed the American critical institution to ignore, disarm (by dissipation), and profit from deconstruction;

(3) focusing on only the rhetoricity of the dominant culture has played into the hands of the closed economy critical thinking hopes to negate;

(4) does this concern with "textuality" not too closely echo that of both the New Criticism and liberal humanism in their fascinations with rhetoric, romance, and separation of text and history?

III

I would like to illustrate some aspects of this deconstructive misunderstanding of the institutional nature of empowered discourse by examining Jeffrey Mehlman's reading[25] of Marx's The Eighteenth Brumaire[26] and Paul de Man's influential reading of Nietzsche's On the Uses and Disadvantages of History for Life. I hope to show that in both cases the texts preempted and moved beyond the abstracting powers of their critics precisely because such abstraction is a tool or weapon of the dominant Hegelian model against which they are both partly in revolt.

In *Revolution and Repetition*, Mehlman attempts to show the universal presence of Freud's uncanny in writing. What is most uncanny about the uncanny, Mehlman claims, is precisely that it can occur in any guise, anywhere. Mehlman's desire is to show that *The Eighteenth Brumaire* is itself subverted from within as a historical recuperation of events by the uncontrollable and unaccountable presence of "Bonapartism." Mehlman's analysis convinces him that Marx intends to apply rigorously, to the events of 1848–51, a Marxist model of causality based on a direct reflective relationship between base and superstructure. In other words, Mehlman would have it that Marx is mechanically accounting for the history of this counterrevolutionary period in terms of a linear model of development which sees the necessity of proletarian revolutions following upon that of the bourgeoisie; in addition, he would also claim that Marx is equally mechanically asserting that the state is always and everywhere a simple mirror representation of the forces of oppression, in this case the dominant bourgeoisie. Into this recuperative model, which Mehlman rightly points out represents one line of thought in classical Marxism, comes the dictatorship of Louis Bonaparte as a trace, a farcical repetition of his uncle, to disrupt the Marxist dialectic of history: Bonaparte is a third term outside both specularity and representation. He is the return of the repressed in *The Eighteenth Brumaire* and the break or fold in Marx's text. He cannot be represented or inscribed within a specular system; he breaks the closed economy of Marx's representative interpretation of history. The state under Bonaparte is not the instrument of class oppression because Louis is not the representative of any class; he is, as a farcical character, completely *déclassé*. He destroys the Party of Order and thus oppresses the bourgeoisie; he allies himself with the *lumpen* and consequently is opposed to the workers; and while he may appear to represent the peasants, this is itself comical since he misrepresents himself as the son of his uncle, Napoleon Bonaparte, to gain their support and extend his authority. He hides the truth from the peasants: the reforms of the uncle are the exploitations of the nephew. Furthermore, as Mehlman's analysis goes on, he locates Marx's anxiety about Bonaparte on the level of economy as a sign of Marx's desire to repress what Bonaparte represents inside the general text of writing and history:

We have already linked the extravagent expenditure[s] of Bonapartism to a crisis of representation. But in that case, one is hard put
not to see in that frenetic circulation of money which exhausts the
fiscal policies of Bonaparte—Marx: "to steal the whole of France in
order to make a present of her to France"—a Marxian counterpart
to the extenuating circulation of meaning found in Freud. This
principle of absolute expenditure, in which we would see an
intuition of the utter mobility of terms within a fantasmatic structure, is even apt to play implicitly within Marx's theoretical formulations. (RR, 33)

One can, of course, hear echoes in Mehlman not just of Freud but of
Derrida and Laplanche as well. The move Mehlman makes here is that
typical of all deconstructive turns: the location of the repressed element
of textuality which resists efforts at its recuperation into a binary opposition and then a synthesis into a third term. Mehlman puts it this way:

If there is indeed a break in these texts, it is by no means between a
truth and an ideology which would have originally suppressed or
masked it. It is rather in the heterogeneous movement which
would endlessly emancipate an unheimlich dimension indifferent to
the distinctions: truth/error, suppressor/suppressed. (RR, 40–41)

It would seem difficult to fault Mehlman's reading to this point. One
feels he has shown that Marxist writing cannot escape from the problematic of the non-specular dimension of writing. Or put more positively, Mehlman seems to have advanced one aspect of the Derridean
project by going to the heart of the enemy—revolutionary historiography—only to find lurking there what, to quote Derrida again, are the
"undecidables," that is, simulative units, "false" verbal, nominal, or
semantic properties, which escape from inclusion in the philosophical
(binary) opposition and which nonetheless inhabit it" (P, 36). But
somehow, in his analysis, Mehlman seems to have forgotten that Marx's
text is also a political act and not only a segment, so to speak, of the
"general text." While one could easily extend Foucault's critique of
Derrida's valorization of l'ecriture as a negative transcendental to Mehlman's idea of the universal uncanny, this would itself remain merely a
philosophical distinction unless it were immediately shifted to the
material grounds of politics.

Critics must be cautious not to concede textual analysis in advanced scholarship to the deconstructors. On the contrary, an approach to texts as material events, such as those elaborated by Said or Foucault under the influence of Gramsci and Nietzsche, must be developed further. It might be useful to begin by examining the hypothesis that *The Eighteenth Brumaire* takes account of itself as a political text in a way which neither classical Marxist analysis, as represented by Maximilien Rubel,[27] nor Mehlman's deconstruction can recognize.

The essential flaw in Mehlman's understanding of *The Eighteenth Brumaire* is his insistence that Marx is trying to cover up the scandal of the detachment of the state from society in Bonapartism. But his error is based on the misconception that Marx always and everywhere systematically attempts to mediate the relationship between state and civil society. Rather than repetitively and universally carrying out such mediations. Marx often, especially in his more polemical pieces, uses his critical and historical tools to engage in a contest for power, in this case against Bonaparte immediately, in others, against capital in the long run. Hence Marx's famous statement about "the weapons of historical research, of criticism, of satire, and of wit" (EB, 8).

Critics of Marx have often noted that he positions himself to oppose Proudhon and Victor Hugo in describing the events of 1848–51. What they have noticed less frequently is that he also puts himself, as author, into direct competition with Bonaparte. For Bonaparte and Marx are engaged in a contest for the extension of authority into economic and social institutions. Louis originally has no tools other than those ambiguous ones granted him by the Party of Order's interpretations of the constitution; but through a careful analysis of the configuration of forces in France at that time, Bonaparte slowly gathers real power to himself. Whereas originally all of "his" power was derivative, he gradually assumes independent authority and detaches himself and the state from society as a whole. Within the narrative history which *The Eighteenth Brumaire* constructs, Bonaparte and Marx are parallels, or, if you will, protagonist and antagonist, in the same drama. As Marx represents the events of 1848–51 it becomes clear that only he and Bonaparte are able to see what in fact is happening in France—that is, only he and Bonaparte can construct an interpretation of the present events which will allow for a real grasp on the operations of power, politics, and culture. Only these two are able to appreciate the comic autonomy and self-conscious, parodic manipulation of both the Party of Order and the Napoleon legend. There are other parallels as well. Both Bonaparte and Marx exist outside the class structure, that is, they are the only actors on the stage of history whose perceptions are not obscured by the ideology of a class position. Consequently, their different political understandings of events are comprehensive and thorough in a way that no one else's can be. Also, they are both repetitions of previous figures and both are self-conscious of their belated position and employ that belatedness, paradoxically, to gain power resulting from the insight it allows:

> Hegel somewhere remarks that all facts and personages of great importance in world history occur, as it were, twice. He forgot to add: the first time as tragedy, the second as farce. Caussidier for Danton, Louis Blanc for Robbespierre, the *Montagne* of 1848–1851 for the *Montagne* of 1793 to 1795, the Nephew for the Uncle. And the same caricature occurs in the circumstances attending the second edition of the eighteenth brumaire. (EB, 15)

What is interesting in this passage is the way Marx's relationship to Hegel is a doubling of the nephew's relation to the uncle. While the nephew gains power as an "heir" to the "father," he is in fact comically a misrepresentation. But his authority is gained, Marx reminds us, not simply by an abstract manipulation of image or text, but by the real material reorganization of genealogical charts and the laws which regulate genealogical research. His swerve on the line of hereditary authority gains Bonaparte real power. Marx's swerve from Hegel is also materialist not just in its conception, but in his revision of Hegel for material effect in the world.

Marx appears to represent history as an evolutionary, dialectical event in the shade of Hegelian dialectics. But his writing diverges seriously from that set of figures. He not only "repeats Hegel with a difference" by insisting on the farcical nature of repetition, but he makes Hegel's into a materialistic dialectic and, thus, to gain his own authority, reproduces the product of his "father's" writing on a more powerful level of political competition.

While these comments on *The Eighteenth Brumaire* have not yet demonstrated the problem with Mehlman's reading, they do suggest that Marx is aware of the dangers of his relationship to Hegel. He intends to turn away from the ideal meaning of the spirit's history and toward the comic representation of concrete history—a move which assumes and enacts the existence of critical writing as an event within the material realities of the social world.

Marx's turn from Hegel does undermine Mehlman's reading. Marx self-consciously employs Hegelian forms of dialectic and recuperation neither to repeat them as such nor to undermine them deconstructively. Rather he employs them as tools useful to various degrees in grasping the situation as he sees it: this is the political use of bricolage. In this text, Marx does not valorize the dialectic. He merely employs it instrumentally in a contest with Bonaparte and capitalism so that his own analysis might gain authority from its exactitude. (I will return to the problem of the adequation of Marx's text to the historical situation.)

I want to stress that Marx is involved in at least a tripartite battle: first, with Hegel; second, with those others who have written about the events of the second *brumaire*—Hugo and Proudhon; and third, with Bonaparte and capitalism. The story of Marx's biographical and intellectual resistance to Hegel is too well-known and too nuanced to be treated here.[28] What has not often been noticed is that Marx is battling against Proudhon and Hugo's versions of these events because their texts, different as they are, *both* give authority and power to Bonaparte. So, consequently, Marx's attempt to displace their versions is only one stage in his own struggle with Louis. In fact, his text is a violent, polemical attempt to make room for an historical analysis which will not lend authority to the forces of reaction. There is, in other words, an identifiable strategy to Marx's satirical empiricism in this text: it is ideological and cannot be neglected in any attempt to get at the text's function. Marx is less interested in the so-called consistency of the "system" of history he represents than in both attacking Louis and also appropriating some of the forces of the economic, literary, and philosophical disciplines as weapons for the progressive forces of history.

Marx's own discourse acknowledges the complexity and contradiction of the events confronting his analysis and so as well, at least implicitly, the difficulty in constructing an adequate verbal model of the historical moment. He begins radically. In a completely un-Hegelian manner, he asserts that history itself as an orderly process, as it is usually understood in the contemplative German tradition, has been suspended. Disorder is not, as Mehlman would have it, the parasite in the body of Marx's repressive model of limited economy. Rather, it is the original scene of historical awareness. It calls upon Marx to produce a text which, while not systematic, is persuasive, powerful, demystifying, and irresistible: "This period that we have before us," says Marx, "comprises the most motley mixture of crying contradictions" (EB, 43). In fact, Marx ridicules any expectation of orderly, systematic, totalizing understanding of historical events as a naive belief in miracles. Ironically, his description of those naive Frenchmen who believe in such models sounds remarkably like the image of Marx the repressor which Mehlman conjures up: "As ever, weakness had taken refuge in a belief in miracles, fancied the enemy overcome when he was only conjured away in imagination, and it lost all understanding of the present in a passive glorification of the future that was in store for it" (EB, 20). It is precisely the temptation to repress the sudden and abrupt appearance of the unaccountable in the present which Marx is attacking here. He identifies such desires with poor historical understanding, a desire to replace actuality with language, and an abandoning of the present reality for possibilities contained in some hypothetically assumed-to-be future. Those who yield to this repression, or even further it by their service of the capitalist hegemony, close their analysis to such "undecidables," as Derrida would call them, and they are struck by unpredicted events as if by thunderbolts; their entire systems of representation collapse, leaving them at the mercy of those like Bonaparte whose understanding is not fixed and whose systems of representation are always modulating in response to changing circumstances. This ongoing modulation of understanding provides the linguistic basis for power because it copes with the continuing need to abandon or modify networks of representation as they become inadequate to the political task of the historical moment, that is, as they hinder an effective grasp on the social and political structure of the present.

I am not suggesting, as Mehlman does, that Bonaparte is the uncanny which must be repressed. Rather, in this view, Bonaparte is the principle of historical understanding and effective political action which must be illuminated. Marx and Bonaparte alone can develop complex, duplicitous, contradictory figures of representation which can empower language to function as an effective political weapon within a real struggle. As figures of declassification, they represent the possibility of escaping the mystification which comes from unconscious ideational formations. They can go further than all other Frenchmen in their understanding of the current events because they do not think in terms which are analogous to the way other members of society act—

that is, according to their class position. They are the process of historical action as representation freed from limits of delusion and, as such, they are alike and in competition. The struggle between Marx and Bonaparte is then an equal one—on the level of textual drama. But on the level of political power, it is a totally unequal one. Bonaparte governs and Marx is sent into exile. Marx has recourse to the weaponry of language precisely because recourse to other forms of action is largely denied to him.

Marx likens the effect of his writing to Bonaparte's act in staging the coup. The monster of Bonapartism was contained embryonically in the parliamentary republic which drafted the constitution, but could only be seen when the bayonet of the coup tore the womb to let the monster appear. Similarly, Marx's analysis of Louis's comic role as nephew effectively gives birth to the monster. In other words, Bonapartism has two births: one in political history and the other in Marx's representation of it as a monstrosity. Ironically this "second" birth is also its death; Marx removes the monster's power and authority by revealing the conditions of its existence. He employs the weaponry of criticism not only to clear a space inside his culture for a more effective representation of history, but also, and quite specifically, as a way to gain power for what he sees to be the forces of progress.

If Bonaparte and Marx are alike in their lonely understanding and representation of the contradictions of French society, then the only marked difference between them must exist on a nontextual level. Intention extends itself beyond textuality into other networks of power and determination and so requires that the critic deal with authors like Marx as historical actors and their "texts" as events. They are not merely textual counters available for academic analysis. The power of oppression and the restraints on revolutionary desire—this difference brings critics to the point of choice, where politics and morality dictate that the complex agency of authors not be reduced, by any one set of analytic tools, to a reality seemingly completely explicable by one academic discourse. Such reduction is always the danger of deconstruction. Because Marx's text confronts us with this choice and demands our involvement, we cannot as critics respond with scepticism regarding the value of Marx's project or with systems claiming to provide disinterested forms of verbal and psychological analysis which, interposing between us and the event of Marx's writing, keep us from recognizing our own need to assume a stance vis-à-vis the materials we read. If we allow this last interposition to continue, then we are no longer critics and we join forces with—in Marx's terms—Hugo, Proudhon, Bonaparte, and, we might add, Jeffrey Mehlman. In so doing, we deny to criticism the power of direct involvement with material realities of society and its institutions whose organizations are not, *a priori*, assumed to be textual in nature. Moreover, we would retreat to an idealist position which detaches language and action absolutely. We willfully forget the power associated with systems of representation and we try to continue to remove ourselves as critics from any position of responsibility.

IV

An analogous forgetting of the material and institutional position of writing has occurred in de Man's reading of Nietzsche. I cannot here do the detailed analysis needed to follow all the intricate movements of de Man's essay. His conclusion, however, is clear enough and is useful for the purposes of my argument: he claims one can account for the essential contradiction of all writings in rhetorical and performative terms.

One version of this contradiction can be found in the concept of the "modern": all writers try to be original, but the very attempt inscribes the writer into tradition and "he enters into a world that assumes the depths and complications of an articulated time, an interdependence between past and future that prevents any present from ever coming into being" (GGN, 161). De Man goes on to write that "The more radical the rejection of anything that came before, the greater the dependence on the past." He then draws a conclusion which seems to make a universal claim: "The distinctive character of literature thus becomes manifest as an inability to escape from a condition that is felt to be unbearable. . . . The continuous appeal of Modernity, the desire to break out of literature toward the reality of the moment, prevails and, in its turn, folding back upon itself, engenders the repetition and the continuation of literature" (GGN, 162). The problem which holds de Man's interest in this reading of Baudelaire and Nietzsche is whether or not literature allows escape into history, or, put differently, "whether a history of an entity as self-contradictory as literature is conceivable" (GGN, 162).

Nietzsche's text has a more specific, yet more general, concern. The interposition of the idealizing movements of deconstruction block access to it. Nietzsche directs his own deconstruction against the excessive incorporation of historical study in the German educational system which might prevent other types of thought:

> I have striven to depict a feeling by which I am constantly tormented; I revenge myself by handing it over to the public . . . most people, however, will tell me that this feeling is altogether perverse, unnatural, detestable and wholly impermissible, and that by feeling it I have shown myself unworthy of the mighty historical movement which, as is well known, has been in evidence among the Germans particularly for the past two generations. (UD, 59)

Even in his seemingly most anti-historical moments, Nietzsche addresses himself to the immediate institutional version of the problem that confronts him—not just the discursive formations which empower and control the circulation of the sign. He is aware of the ideological pressures in his society to close off the possibility of considering the ambiguous social purposes of historical and revisionist thinking—in a discourse of the historical. In fact, he suggests that the prohibition against his instrusive demystification of historical study has the force of law. Of course, one could, as Mehlman no doubt would, give priority in reading this trope to the Lacanian/Derridean uses of the figure. Such potentials should not be excluded. But one should also see that this reference to the law is part of an elaborate set of references to state, government, and educational institutions within the text and that these are, themselves, part of the struggle of the day over the forms institutions will take.

For example, in Nietzsche's discussion of antiquarian history, he specifically invokes the central organic figure of the tree from Hegel's preface to the *Phenomenology*. He juxtaposes this borrowing to other figures which suggest the reactionary and oppressive nature of the state of the Prussian monarchy at this time as well as the collapsing concord between state and intelligentsia. The allusion to Hegel not only reflects the crisis-like extremity of Prussian cultural oppression, but it is also a reference to the entire debate on the monarchy's relation to Hegel begun just a few years earlier in Berlin. In the 1830s, the conservative valorization of the state as the highest manifestation of reason in history was under some attack and the relation between the state and its legitimating intellectual servants was troubled. The state's response is typified by its asking Schelling to lecture in Berlin. He insisted that with the end of history, reflected by the flowering of the spirit in Hegel's system, there has also come an end to the evolution of the state. The tactic failed and the state, to ease the pressure on its cultural alliances, increased censorship.[29]

Nietzsche's allusion to the central Hegelian metaphor for totalization must be read in the context suggested by Schelling's reactionary claims. It is part of the struggle over the nature of the state and its relation to cultural institutions like universities and censorship.

Nietzsche's argument may briefly be summarized in this way. The excessive study of history in Germany and the absolute authority of historicism in aesthetic judgment are themselves aspects of social control and reproduction. He warns against the alliance between state and intellectuals precisely because the latter have not considered their utility to the state. Hence Nietzsche's own ironic self-figuration as a "nurseling of older ages." Hence also his ironically nostalgic advice at the end of the text to adopt the Greek classical model for each individual's rethinking of his own needs in a particular historical situation.

A fuller discussion of Nietzsche's text would have to go on to show Nietzsche's desire to negate Hegel's appropriation of all history for his own belated state as a latecomer. It would have to extend the homologies between the development of various closed cultural forms[30] in Germany and France in the second half of the nineteenth century. Nietzsche's text is, therefore, an example of how the intellectual disciplines of a culture can be used to disclose the ways in which systems of power and various nontextual configurations of forces make up a society and preempt the possibility of democratic self-determination on the part of individuals and groups. Nietzsche's attraction to the "folk"—in his discussion of antiquarian history—reflects his concern for the integrity and differences of local communities allowed to maintain themselves in evolving communal patterns of cultural relations. Furthermore, his discussion of this attractive communal image makes clear that the German state's disposition of cultural mandarins to valorize such antiquarian social values is in fact an appropriation of folk tradition meant to make them the province of the high cultural forces manipulated by the reactionaries of the Prussian monarchy. These newly produced objects of historical knowledge go on to become the "populist" base for an oppressive and absolutist state.

Two quotations from Nietzsche make clear the points I have just raised. In discussing antiquarian history, Nietzsche writes:

> The feeling antithetical to this [a restless, cosmopolitan hunting after new and ever newer things], the contentment of the tree in its roots, the happiness of knowing that one is not wholly accidental and arbitrary but grown out of a past as its heir, flower and fruit, and that one's existence is thus excused and, indeed, justified—it is this which is today usually designated as the real sense of history. (UD, 74)

This recuperative mentality leads to closed cultural forms which are essentially right-wing populism. Those, Nietzsche argues, who have no respect for every simple antique are "rejected and persecuted" (UD, 74). The result of this is that

> the historical sense no longer conserves life but mummifies it [and] then the tree dies unnaturally from the top downwards to the roots. . . . Its piety withers away, the habit of scholarliness continues without it and rotates in egoistic self-satisfaction around its own axis. (UD, 75)

This final image returns the argument full circle to the point of departure on the margins of this topic. We return to de Man's suggestion that too much literary criticism is simply habit, the institutional inertia of business-as-usual. Literary criticism rarely asks institutional and political questions about the nature of its own practice or its social function. But there is one ironic explanation which, in small part, accounts for the continuing inertia and the coming victory of reaction: deconstruction has failed to ask itself historical questions: why is it here now; why is it so readily adaptable to the conditions of American academia; indeed, how can it so easily coexist with its own apparent antagonist, that large body of literary humanists who think that deconstruction is mere careerism, or, at best, the obscurantist projection of addled brains?

What Nietzsche's and Marx's texts illustrate for us is the possibility of a critical act which takes on a full reflexive rhetorical role while at the same time confronting directly the material and institutional restraints and enabling conditions of its own existence. They show us once more that criticism which fails to do this is the worst sort of metaphysics; it hides in a web of textuality or "tradition," yielding power to the forces which limit and deploy it, precisely because such criticism is comfortable in the secure niche granted by the hegemony to which it is useful.

Like Abrams, most liberal educators and critics serve a function of which they are at best only partially aware. It is of the essence that humanism obscure such insights.[31] Until critics begin to use their training and tools to understand where they have come from and what purpose they serve they cannot hope to establish any cogent educational plan or purpose.

Ideology we know is inescapable; but quietism should not be the consequence of that insight. It is always the task of the teacher/scholar to help students to learn to use the tools of the critical disciplines in order to understand the origins of these tools, why they persist, how they are determinate, and to what ends they might be used. Demystification—escape from "false consciousness"—is not the answer. The critical act can at best allow for a partial understanding of the present, of one's political location. Even such limited knowledge is crucial because, as Marx and Nietzsche both suggest, metaphysics always takes the form of a preoccupation with the past and future, either recollection or teleology, and never with the present and its possibilities for human action to grasp and change the social order of discourse and power.[32]

Literary criticism which abdicates its responsibility to a historical analysis of its own institutional conditions of existence is both metaphysical and reactionary. Nietzsche and Marx both point the way toward a model of critical thinking and writing which insists on the scholar's newly acknowledged responsibility to help others determine their own lives. It is crucial that we literary intellectuals follow their lead; there are few if any other (respectable) locations within the intellectual world where critics can truly have a value and effect.

5

......

The Ineluctability
of Difference:
Scientific Pluralism
and the Critical
Intelligence

The idea that there is a postmodern literature different from and often
opposed to modernism gradually gained acceptance by scholars, critics, and teachers through the 1960s and 1970s with the result that the
term itself and the variety of often conflicting concepts it designates
have become awkwardly legitimate. A detailed genealogy of this process of legitimation which described the intersections of discourses
and practices from literature, art, and political philosophy would itself
tell a great deal about how the institutions for producing and circulating cultural representations work in our society and also how certain
parts of the intellectual elite understand our society and its recent past.
Of course, a genealogy of recent reconceptions of other representations such as "Romanticism" could tell us many of the same things, but
perhaps in not quite such an important or fruitful way; for theorists and
critics of the postmodern study and describe the present moment and
so enact the present while conceiving it. Examining the ways and
means by which representations of the postmodern proliferate may
well provide a privileged insight into the workings of our cultural
apparatus. It may suggest not only how we represent our culture to
ourselves, but also how we might develop alternative figures for this
task that could more closely approximate our developing perceptions
of the complexity of our social and historical existence.

There are, of course, many different senses to the term "postmodern," so that an initial "discrimination of postmodernisms" is in order.
But since space permits neither such a complete discrimination nor
such a genealogy, all I can hope to suggest are some of the defining and

limiting characteristics of theorizing about the postmodern in literary criticism as well as some additional directions for further study.

Attempts to constitute the postmodern have provided the academy with some of the most excitingly inventive speculative analysis and critical writing of recent years. They have added a new dimension to the critical lexicon, employed and expanded innovative methods, and helped redefine our conceptions of the modern canon. One need only invoke William Spanos's "phenomenological destructions," Joseph Riddel's "deconstructions," Ihab Hassan's "paracriticisms," and Alan Wilde's studies of irony to perceive the richness and power of critical speculation on the postmodern and the way it has affected the landscape of literary study.[1] There are as many differences as similarities among these critics and their works so it would be foolish to suggest any underlying harmony of assumptions or intent. Yet, on the very broadest level, they all conceive the postmodern and their own critical practices as alternatives both to the established values and beliefs of our mass culture and to the habitual linguistic forms of critical practice which legitimate those values. In other words, put simply, in their highly various ways, these theoreticians and practitioners of the postmodern stand in opposition to the institution in which they labor and the culture which that institution, even in its current reduced state, continues to support. The postmodern appears in the work of these critics as something suppressed by modernity or as a new mode of "value-production" more suited to our world than the strategies and tactics of previous literary forms or conceptions of language. Spanos argues, for example, that postmodernism counters the aesthetic disinterest of modernism's spatialized forms by returning to the temporality of Being. Alan Wilde suggests in The Horizons of Assent that the postmodern, especially in American fiction, is a generative, mythmaking response to the shallow egotism of late modernism and its anomie. And Riddel's insight into the metaphoricity of language allows him to dissolve hardened critical patterns and to open textuality to the play of difference.

At times, critics of the postmodern reach beyond the traditional limits of "literary criticism" and enter directly into the intellectual debates on the social order and cultural life. For example, Spanos and Wilde both attempt to relegitimate a realm of social value in literature and criticism by developing phenomenological models of consciousness and language that "reflect" the nature and achievement of postmodern writing. Such models also require from critics and audiences an ideological commitment to the "worldliness" of art and criticism as well as to the priority of time and becoming.

These few comments on postmodern criticism suggest, even if they do not demonstrate, that constituting the postmodern as in opposition, or, at least, as an alternative to the "modern" or "metaphysical" is itself an oppositional act intended to be counterhegemonic. That is to say, it desires to break up and displace the modernist legacy, for that failed ensemble of social and linguistic relations acts hegemonically to mask social difference and the possibility of achieving even tentative but stable human values in postmodern consumer culture. That the original impulse of theorizing the postmodern is oppositional is a fact perhaps not fully explored even by its strongest representatives. Spanos has developed most keenly the antipathetic stance of his criticism, attempting explicitly to make over literary history and the purpose of criticism. His antagonistic, often violently counteractive position suggests further questions about theorizing the postmodern as an oppositional practice.

The most important of these questions is quite simple: can theorizing the postmodern be a successful oppositional practice if it remains within the limits of "lit. crit."—even as they have been broadened by these critics to include philosophy, art, and linguistics? Or to put the same question differently: is the "literary critic" the appropriate intellectual figure for carrying out such a project? Recent changes in the relation of the literary profession to society as well as the results of various nonliterary investigations into society, language, and power suggest that these questions can only be answered negatively as long as "lit. crit." refuses to take seriously the effects of the social world on the aesthetic and visionary figuration which it values, defends, and studies. Furthermore, the critic must recall that the critical act is a social act and attempt to understand and theorize the role the critic plays in culture in relation to matters of power, interest, and knowledge in our increasingly information-based media-culture. Of course many critics have attempted to develop theories and analyses that keep in sight the social-historical nature of literary production.[2] But for the most part, critics of the postmodern have not treated literature as one element in a historical culture. Rather, instead of analyzing the postmodern as a cultural configuration of social practices and discourses, they have tended to treat literature abstractly, as an "object," in its own right, of *literary* critical investigation. At times, at its best, as in the works of those critics previously mentioned, this analysis points beyond literature as a "discrete" phenomenon and exceeds the limits of "lit. crit." to touch on ontology, painting, and language theory. But these extensions suggest the need for others. Why not attempt, for example, to constitute the postmodern in the context of feminism, ecology, "interest-group politics," or cybernetics? Should not "literary critics" recognize that the therapeutic discourses of an interventionist social order may be as "postmodern" as the forms of John Barth's fiction or Robert Creeley's poetry? Indeed, that the latter cannot be satisfactorily analyzed outside the historical social order constituted by the discourses of the former?

Of course these objections to literary criticism are old ones. They can be countered on at least two levels: no critic can realistically hope to "master" the range of material needed for such contextualized cultural studies; and, literature is a social institution, but a "semi-autonomous" one with its own internal system of rules and traditions that can be studied and understood largely independently of other socially powerful discourses. To the second of these objections one might answer that it is incumbent on anyone holding such a belief to demonstrate that these rules and traditions are generated internally, independently of any other actions in the social world. It would be necessary to show that the reconstruction of these rules on something like a competence model is not ideology but the critical science about which scholars from Northrop Frye to Jonathan Culler have fantasized. They would have to show, in other words, that there is an "inside" to literary history that is independent of the "outside" history of other material practices. Or, alternatively, they would have to admit that what they produced was a static ideological model representing present interests. As to the first objection, it is simply not true that one cannot work in more than one discourse. In fact such a restrictive belief is the result of the specialized education that fragments knowledge and the intellectual labor process. Although Antonio Gramsci may be right to say that writing the history of a party is a way of writing the history of a nation, the first cannot be written as the second in the abstract, without a precise sense of how a party intervenes in society, how social needs impinge on the party, and how the party directs action and thought in response to the real needs of the people.[3]

Both objections to the necessary recognition of the social dimensions and intersections of literature merely echo the traditional division of labor that is a hallmark of the hegemony that postmodern critics hope to counter. Until and unless critics alter that division of labor by associating literary with sociohistorical studies or by carrying out group research projects to minimize the individualistic ethos of critical production, they cannot provide successful opposition to the ruling hegemony; they will too often simply replicate it. The advanced practice of critics like Wilde, Riddel, and Spanos in defining the postmodern has begun to break down this division of labor; their researches, although different, are also complementary. Moreover, their work has serious political implications primarily in its "deconstructions" of texts and false assumptions about language: thus not only do they reveal the "roots" of our representations in inescapable yet hidden linguistic processes, but they also undermine them and attempt to present alternatives. Unfriendly critics who argue that these works are abstract/ nihilist games produced by a dying bourgeois institution fail to understand adequately the very material effect that changing discourses can have on the ruling representations of even our media-centric mass culture. A more serious question is: what can be done to extend the oppositional intentions of this critical work?

It seems that a turn away from the individualistic focus on "authors" is in order along with a turn toward a more group-based research and criticism. Daniel O'Hara has elaborately demonstrated the maddening failures of individualistic strategies for visionary projection and revision throughout modern and postmodern literature and criticism.[4] Other communally based projects must be developed. Scholars must treat "authors" not only as inscribed within a great tradition—in whose techniques a writer becomes competent—but also as within a set of discourses that constitute the social world to which a writer comes. No matter how interesting, immanental studies of the internal achievements or failures of an oeuvre place a mistaken emphasis on "genius" or some "universal human nature" and do not take the opportunity to move from the oeuvre into the historical world of social discourse of which it is a (dependent) part.

Postmodern criticism cannot be oppositional if it remains within the disciplinary division of intellectual labor, no matter how hard it tries to broaden or undermine its own discipline. To theorize the oppositional effectively, a self-conscious attempt to be individually counterhegemonic is not enough. Postmodern critics must develop a detailed, scholarly comprehension of their own location within the field of discourse and cultural practice. A counterhegemonic or oppositional criticism has certain minimal requirements: a historically specific research project oriented by autonomous developments elsewhere in culture and guided by a political program that avoids, as far as possible, the suppression of memory and the division of labor that are the hallmarks of the academy's general subservience to the hegemony. In other words, radical critical intellectuals must understand the historical specificity of the cultural practices of their own period with an eye to bringing their own practice and discourse in line with other oppositional forces in a society struggling against hegemonic manipulation and state violence. Postmodern critical intelligence can complete the legitimation of its oppositional ideology only if it becomes part of the public sphere by placing itself within the context of other oppositional forces and theorizes the counterhegemonic in light of their local struggles. Such a repositioning of critical intelligence would allow it to do what it alone can best do: change the relationship of the power-knowledge apparatus to the hegemonic culture that exploits and deploys it. Only by moving in some similar direction can critics of the postmodern complete their transformation into postmodern critics.

But how can this transformation be completed? And what might a postmodern critic look like? These are questions the answers to which cannot be predetermined. The work of Jean-François Lyotard is intimately connected with the general question of postmodernism, yet in *The Postmodern Condition* his writing is hard to differentiate from that of any historian of ideas. It seems clear that "high" intellectuals are reluctant or unwilling to abandon the recognizable forms of their cultural traditions, even when theorizing what they agree is a new form of culture. Of course in studying the postmodern—as we have known to be true of the modern at least since C. S. Peirce and Walter Benjamin—critics must be concerned with popular and mass culture, and they must bring to bear on this increasingly wide range of cultural production and consumption entirely new forms of critical power. But until and unless these critics consciously position themselves within the structures they hope to identify and work upon, they cannot respond adequately to the pressures that the cultural and political present imposes on them. Critics are not "navel gazing" when they study their own history as part of their intellectual and political function.

There is still much resistance, especially among so-called humanistic literary critics, to the demand that critical intellectuals do an inventory, as Gramsci would have it, of the forces that form and determine them and their institutions. Resistance from figures like W. Jackson Bate can only misdirect the critical project of determining the role criticism and its related institutions should be playing in this postmodern Western world—especially as it impinges, and often violently, upon non-Western peoples and traditions.

Stanley Aronowitz can help us understand the nature of the task facing the postmodern critic. He has outlined in detail the changing social forces of our society and has studied the challenges they pose to the continuing intellectual usefulness of some of the major assumptions underlying important oppositional discourses. Examining Aronowitz's recent work provides not only a sharp outline of the problems and opportunities facing the radical critic, but also a strong theory of how best to deal with them to achieve counterhegemonic effects.

II

Stanley Aronowitz is not a literary critic. After years of union organizing and political activism, he is now a professor of sociology and editor of *Social Text*. His major book, *The Crisis in Historical Materialism*, is divided into two parts: the first, the long title essay, and the second, an assemblage of previously published shorter essays on a variety of topics such as political economy, narcissism, film, and historiography.[5] More than impressive, the range of Aronowitz's research is an essential aspect of radical intellectual oppositional practice.

The Crisis in Historical Materialism begins as a self-critique that outlines how the paradigms of historical materialism no longer describe our social order. Aronowitz is one of many radical intellectuals for whom orthodox historical materialism is in a crisis. Anthony Giddens perhaps puts the dissatisfaction with Marxist political economy most succinctly: "Human social life neither begins nor ends in production."[6] For Aronowitz this means essentially that Marxism has denied its own historicity and no longer can show that its basic principles—structured around the priority of production—"remain adequate to both past and present" (CHM, 7). Paradoxically, this crisis arose at the moment when "Marxism became the leading theoretical premise" of history writing, economics, and sociology. Since the late sixties, Marxism has become a central university-based paradigm for intellectual investigation. "The academic recuperation of historical materialism," Aronowitz writes, "attested to the heuristic importance of material conceptions of social and historical structures. Yet," Aronowitz goes on, "Marxism had claimed to be a theory of revolution—a discourse of social transformation and emancipation—as much as an alternative to bourgeois social theory" (CHM, 7). In *The Crisis in Historical Materialism*, Aronowitz describes the theoretical and historical events that have cumulatively escaped Marxism's paradigms and concludes that Marxism can no longer satisfy radical needs and desires for cultural change and social harmony. These needs have taken new and different forms of expression and, as Aronowitz sees it, their heterogeneity provides radical intellectuals the opportunity to reconceptualize their role in a fragmented society. Perhaps more important, he suggests that radical intellectuals should call into question the previously ruling idea that there is or should be a master discourse of liberation and social change. Indeed, Aronowitz's book is most importantly a theoretically and historically specific defense of the idea that, in our postmodern world, no single ruling discourse of social life or autonomy is possible or desirable. It is a book about the relation of radical intellectuals to theory and it asks the question: "how do radical intellectuals theorize?"

The Crisis in Historical Materialism argues that critical theory too often models itself on a false perception of science; it refuses to recognize that our knowledge is constituted by basically discontinuous discourses and that there are multicausal explanations for social structures. It is also a critique of all theories that postulate a transhistorical subject—such as the "proletariat"—as a privileged term in a scientistic, totalizing, and centered description of history. Aronowitz recommends a theorizing that never loses its critical purpose, that pursues an alliance with practice, that is always historically specific, and that, because it rejects the vanguard party and a role for what Foucault would call "representative intellectuals,"[7] accepts and advocates a self-managed society formed from an alliance of autonomous, sometimes competing, groups. In other words, rejecting the Leninist model of the vanguard party and following one aspect of Gramsci's thought, Aronowitz advocates a "theory of the historic bloc [as] a more adequate formulation of the politics of the present period" (CHM, 127).

Blocs replace class-based parties for both historical and theoretical reasons. Aronowitz finds in Adam Przeworski's structuralist analysis a historically specific theory of class formation which calls into question the idea of a transhistorical subject and its class-based party politics.[8] Przeworski argues that as long as capital evolves, "classes are bound to form as the result of struggles (rather than the other way around)" (CHM, 73). The proletariat or any other class exists only insofar as it is constituted as the result of a struggle "about class" (CHM, 73). Struggles that form classes are struggles against domination and for autonomy; the politics appropriate to such struggles is a politics of association that, if necessary, alters its alliances as the forms of capitalism evolve.

Just as it is central to his revisionist thinking about class, his attack on scientism is crucial to Aronowitz's revisions of intellectual practice. Following Paul Feyerabend and Thomas Kuhn,[9] Aronowitz argues that the cultural dominance of modern science must be explained in sociohistorical, not epistemological, terms. Foreshadowing the point he develops in "History as Disruption," Aronowitz writes that modern enlightenment science can no longer be "regarded as a continuous process of theory formation according to the dictates of reason" (CHM, 57). As Aronowitz sees it, Feyerabend analytically clarifies the ambiguous language of science itself to reveal that the philosophical and popular belief in an internally consistent developing "progress" in science is inescapably ideological. Aronowitz correctly points out that analytic philosophy cannot explain or change this and that society needs an ideology-critique of science. He finds the beginning of such a critique in Larry Laudan's recent work, which, although within analytic philosophy, suggests that the idea that science and knowledge "progress" is an ideological belief that does not reflect the way science works.[10]

Aronowitz's interest in these theories of science lies basically in his attempt to demonstrate the historical limits of Marxist discourse. His claims for the historical nature of scientific knowledge are not new or extreme among radical intellectuals. But the works of these theorists contribute to the crisis in historical materialism. Aronowitz writes that "the new philosophy of science, despite its reluctance to push further to a critique of society itself, has opened the way for the self-critique of Marxism as a kind of scientific ideology" (CHM, 57).

Aronowitz traces these scientistic errors in Marxist theory and practice from Lenin and Lukács to recent practitioners of "Lenin's theory of monopoly, capitalism, dependency theory, and capital-logic theory" (CHM, 144). Lukács, Aronowitz claims, develops his theory of mediation as an equivalent of Lenin's conception of the party as the voluntaristic location of "scientific politics" (CHM, 15). Mediation produces objective knowledge of social laws and structures. For both Lenin and Lukács, according to Aronowitz, "the reflection theory of knowledge" and "a correspondence theory of truth" (CHM, 15) guarantee the scientific status of the party's politics. Mastery over nature, Lenin felt, provides a closer and closer correspondence between reality and the laws of science. And since mastery over nature is a function of the productive forces of society, production, for Lenin as for Marx, is the central practical and theoretical source of knowledge and politics.

Although Lenin always adapted his position to changing historical conditions, his theory of monopoly capitalism and imperialism aspires to the condition of scientific consistency that Aronowitz also finds in dependency theorists such as Rosa Luxemburg. André Gunder Frank, and F. H. Cardoso as well as in capitalogic theoreticians such as Harry Braverman, Paul Sweezy, Paul Baran, and Paul Mattick. Aronowitz's arguments with these three theoretical models for explaining late capitalism are not systemic; he neither attempts simply to correct the models they develop nor to offer a competing model of his own. Rather, as in the case of his objections to Lukács's theory of mediation and to Lenin's theory of the vanguard party, Aronowitz argues against the scientistic impulse behind these theories by showing that they are not identical with the totality, as they claim, and that in their attempts to assert truths in identity theory they are as coercive as the hegemony they oppose. By accepting a scientific paradigm, not only do these theorists forget the degree to which their own "scientific" models are part of capitalist ideology insofar as they share formal structures of argument and evidence with technology and modern science, but they also uncritically accept science's most powerful and insidious proposition; the development of a paradigm that will function as a field-theory of explanation.

In his critique, Aronowitz tries to displace this central tendency of Marxist analysis to form "field-theories." His objections to Lukács and to the more recent theorists of late capitalism focus on their various attempts to generate master discourses that either claim to take all culture and economy within their descriptive, explanatory, and predictive range or else reduce those phenomena they cannot subsume to marginal areas of art and emotion. Aronowitz contrasts these theoreticians to those like Althusser and Gramsci who place greater emphasis "on the centrality of ideological structures as elements of capitalist hegemony" (CHM, 170).

Hubristic intellectuals generate master discourses and they are, in turn, betrayed by the complexity of the very history they fail to encompass.[11] Lukács's theory of mediation, for example, develops Marx's previously ignored remarks on the fetish into an explanation of the proletariat's refusal to accept its own historical role. Reification and commodification of social relations in capitalist societies make it impossible for the proletariat to recognize the underlying forms by which capital rules. As Aronowitz rightly points out, Lukács's analysis turns attention to culture as a location of capitalist domination and along with Gramsci's theory of hegemony revives "considerations of ideology and culture within Marxist theory" (CHM, 19). Lukács remains an optimist: with the aid of the party, workers will acquire revolutionary consciousness, see the real relations of capital, and rise up in revolt. Although Lukács's theory is more satisfactory than Lenin's conception of a "labor aristocracy" bought off with the spoils of imperialist warfare, it is, for Aronowitz, nonetheless a "total field theory" that, in its implicit commitment to models of single causality and progress, fails to comprehend historically specific conditions that call for alternative discourses to describe multiple causations.

The Frankfurt school attempts to provide one such alternative; it points out the socially *regressive* nature of fascism and concludes that there is no necessity or inevitability to the constitution of the proletariat as a revolutionary class or subject. There are, of course, problems with the Frankfurt school's methodology. For example, it undermines the legitimacy of its analysis with its despairing conclusion that there is no possible opposition to the authoritarian state. As Aronowitz helps to show, in its important reversal of Lukács, the Frankfurt school ignores the oppositional impact of certain everyday modes of resistance to the state as well as certain contradictions within mass society. But, despite its own tendency to project an absolute hegemony as the fate of capitalist society, Aronowitz takes hope from the Frankfurt school's work that we may find acceptable alternatives to thinkers like Lukács who, in their attempts to build unified field theories, reproduce scientistic ideologies of causality, progress, and prediction. Such ideologies are not adequate to postmodern society with the multiple foci of resistance to capital that have developed, for example, in feminism and no-growth movements, and they should be abandoned in favor of critical models of thought more like those of Max Horkheimer, Theodor Adorno, and Herbert Marcuse. I will return to Aronowitz's objections to the despairing conclusions of critique in its "pure" form.

For Aronowitz, capital-logic theory is a recent sign of the endurance of this scientistic model in historical materialism, and in finally dismissing this theory, he summarizes his attitude toward all unicausal, scientistic explanations:

> My argument may be expressed in one final principle: the counterlogic of the erotic, play, and the constituting subject may not be reduced either to the mode of production of material life or the mode of social reproduction (family, school, or religion in their capacity as ideological apparatuses of the state). Political economy ends when theory seeks to specify the conditions of transformation. Marxism as critique consists in showing that the science of political economy is descriptive of the commodity fetish. The apogee of critical science resides in specifying the non-subsumable. (CHM, 196)

For Aronowitz, all unified field theories are reductive because either they ignore those elements of cultural life that they cannot subsume or they marginalize them as "anomalies" to be incorporated at some future time into the paradigm. The political effect of such theories is either the coercive inclusion of the anomalous in a total order or a discriminatory exclusion that denies their reality as agents in society. "Critical science" attends to those anomalous people and movements; it confronts "theory" with them as proof of its untruth, of the nonidentity of a theory with the totality. Moreover, critical science tries to find in those "marginalized" figures traces of a reality that has escaped capital's hegemony and evidence of the theoretical and political possibility of noncapitalist social organization. In "specifying the non-subsumable," critical science locates those forms of life, action, and thought that are the necessary condition for the future transformation of society. It does not involve predicting the unknowable, that is, "the conditions of transformation." Such prophetic, prescriptive attempts are coercive and require, by definition, the deployment of a unified theory that functions, at least instrumentally, as "true." Yet theory can "specify" those nonsubsumable elements of society by describing them and theorizing their forms of resistance and association. Such specification may indeed aid in bringing about the "conditions of transformation" because it shows the untruth of all field theories and undermines their legitimacy as prescriptive, but coercive, worldviews.

Aronowitz's commitment of "critical science" to specifying the non-subsumable elements of the counterlogic of oppositional groups and practices will not eventuate in mere empiricism. Rejecting the urge to totalize allows the intellectual to see the "*partially* realized elements of an oppositional culture within the framework of mass culture." Ernst Bloch has shown how capital conflates need and desire.[12] "The counterlogic," Aronowitz writes, "is to maintain their separation, to define desire as that which goes beyond need and is unrecuperable by the prevailing structures" (CHM, 196). Aronowitz and Bloch are both developing Marx's insight that capital will produce its own gravediggers, but not on a class-based productionist model. Aronowitz suggests that critics and scholars should study the marginal elements of society and culture; but since capital can subvert the margins by making them fashionable, marginality should not be valorized per se as a form of subversion. Intellectuals should study the margins to describe and theorize the counterlogic of opposition to hegemony as it appears in the crevices of capital's dominance. Aronowitz clarifies how the very conditions that capital generates limit its development and so create crises: "What I am saying is that the dialectic of accumulation consists in its reliance on the conditions that produce its own limits. The study of the counterlogics to capital is long overdue. For it is here that the crisis will be discovered, not in the operation of 'objective' laws" (CHM, 197).

In his discussion of "scientistic" elements from Lenin and Lukács to the capital-logicians, Aronowitz integrates three crucial themes: first, the changed role of the radical intellectual from descriptive scientist to critical scientist; second, the need to rethink the relationship between nature and society in light of feminism and psychoanalysis; and third, following Adorno's thesis, the need to develop a new dialectics which will not suppress difference or negation in the name of a formal logic of identity or an a priori concept of a transhistorical subject.[13] Since master discourses subject nature, humanity, and history to distorting models and plans for action, radical intellectuals can no longer legitimately adopt the role of the traditional intellectual who produces totalizing and representative theories if they intend their work to be part of the struggle for social self-management and cultural autonomy. This changed role for the intellectual has both a theoretical and a political consequence, although the two cannot be in any serious way divided. Theoretically, radical individuals must follow Adorno's critique of Hegelian identity theories and accept negation, not the "negation of negation," as the determining moment in developing a dialectics of difference. Important political consequences follow from accepting negation's role in a liberating project. To accept this role requires an antihegemonic politics of association between different, sometimes even contradictory and competing, autonomous groups—in other words, the politics of the bloc.

Aronowitz's discussion of theory shows the importance of historical specificity and difference in developing a radical theory. Adorno's "negative dialectics" provides a philosophical explanation of the compelling need to adjust scientistic models to the demands of changing social formations. In discussing the failure of historical materialism to live up to its "vision," "Adorno attempted to show that the very *categories*, the presuppositions from which Marxism springs, were misdirected" (CHM, 25). The "necessity of philosophy" that Aronowitz tries to reestablish consists in critically clarifying the appropriateness of theoretical categories to the specific historical formations of the period to which they are applied.

Adorno's critique of Leninism not only explains the importance of critical negation and the errors of totalization but leads as well to the recognition of the importance of nature as itself a nonsubsumable category of theory. By analyzing Lenin's refusal to consider epistemological problems in *Materialism and Empirio-Criticism*, Adorno shows that this Marxist dialectic culminates in a formal logic of identity like Aristotle's. The power of negation for Adorno consists in its ability to discredit all theories of totality, which are, he holds, always theories of identity and merely based on formal logic: " 'totality,' " Aronowitz quotes Adorno as saying, " 'is to be opposed by convicting it of nonidentity with itself' " (CHM, 27). In a way that prefigures Habermas's work[14]—although with different results—Adorno insists on a return to the kind of questions raised by Kant and not answered by Hegelian and Marxist dialectics, which suppress difference in the negation of the negation. "The recuperation of difference," Aronowitz writes, quoting Adorno, "by a higher identical synthesis is 'a primal form of ideology' " (CHM, 27). Adorno denies that any subject exists a priori and transhistorically; insofar as any subject exists it is formed by and in history. Adorno accepts Freud's demonstration of the insurmountable divisions in the self and, in a way that prefigures Derrida,[15] Adorno writes that " 'the most enduring result of the Hegelian logic is that the individual is not flatly for himself, he is his otherness and linked with others.' " Aronowitz's comment suggests the link with poststructuralism: "nonidentity is not difference *between* two things (subject/object) but exists within each" (CHM, 27). The "difference" within the subject is, thus, never negated, suspended, or overcome. Subsumption of difference is not legitimate. Difference can only be repressed through social and discursive power. A subject fully present to itself will never emerge in history.[16]

Politically, Adorno offers a critique both of Western liberalism and of Stalinism. Both attempt to suppress and contain difference; both think it can be overcome. The present situation in Poland reveals how actually existing socialism cannot concede the nonidentity of the party and the workers's desires and needs.[17] Liberal Western society tolerates pluralism only as long as it creates no authentic opposition that cannot be contained by a system of hegemony and bureaucracy.

Aronowitz finds in Adorno's critique of Enlightenment reason and politics a critique of science that allows for a reconceptualization of nature. Science is capitalism's attempt to deny the difference of nature. Aronowitz claims that the very institution of probability theory and the introduction of the complementarity principle into physics "all show the will to totality in modern science," by incorporating uncertainty and instability into a unified, predictive system. On this model, for Aronowitz, the "rationalization of difference is reproduced in social science" in its quantifying techniques for prediction and control (CHM, 28). Demonstrating the illegitimacy and inadequacies of totality theories and of identity logics means that both science and Marxism must change to accept nature's difference and to theorize its relationships with history in such a way that the counterlogic to capital can be described and extended.

Throughout *The Crisis in Historical Materialism*, Aronowitz complains that Marxism's enormous stress on the development of the forces of production as mastery over inner and outer nature does not allow Marxist materialism to theorize nature's resistance to mastery and its "priority" to history. Marxism's sense that human labor can produce an identity between nature and society obscures the point of departure for theorizing that very relationship: " 'The objectivity of historic life,' " Aronowitz quotes Adorno as saying, " 'is that of natural history' " (CHM, 28). Adorno recalls that Marx himself recognizes the equally determining role of natural history on human affairs, something that Aronowitz feels Marxism has forgotten. Adorno thinks that Marx's "critical" use of a "socially Darwinian" theme is important because it testifies to Marx's acceptance of an independent natural limit upon social consciousness and historical practice: " 'Even if a society has found its natural law of motion,' " Adorno argues, " 'natural evolutionary processes can be neither skipped nor decreed out of existence' " (CHM, 28). Adorno criticizes not only Marxism's failure to acknowledge the independence of "external" nature, but also its failure to acknowledge the autonomy of "internal" nature, of desire, which expresses itself, even if distortedly, throughout capitalism. Adorno's position "recognizes the disjunction between human desire and its object, but at the same time understands that nature gives rise to the social process and becomes part of the process as its 'unconscious' " (CHM, 28).

Aronowitz returns to Marx to legitimate his departure from Marxism on the issue of nature's relation to the social process. "The principle of historical materialism suggests that Marx be read in order to be forgotten." The dead should bury the dead, for the job of radical intellectuals is to change, not repeat history: "to find those changes in theory needed to comprehend changes in the development of human societies and the evidence that contravenes our expectations" (CHM, 46). On this matter, radical theorizing means rejecting basic Marxist notions such as "nature is congealed in the products of labor" or "that nature is a 'tool house' and a 'laboratory,' an object to be worked up into use-values" (CHM, 47). Aronowitz, of course, also rejects idealistic alternatives to these figures of speech; describing nature as a pure, abstract "Other" to the social is an ahistorical idea that ontologizes nature.

But above all, Aronowitz stresses that a radically historicized sense of nature has disastrous social as well as ecological consequences. Aronowitz argues that none of Marx's "technological metaphors" can be a philosophical basis for rethinking nature's relation to society because like Lukács's historicist rejection of the immanence of nature "as part of the social problematic" (CHM, 49), these metaphors are part of an Enlightenment ideology. Sounding his theme of the historical difference between the postmodern era and those in which the orthodoxies of Marxism developed, Aronowitz argues that "the historical conditions that necessarily prompted both Marx and Lukács to insist upon the centrality of the social dialectic have been surpassed" (CHM, 49). Epistemological questions that challenge realist views of nature and knowledge are just part of a series of events and critiques that no longer tolerate the reduction of historical materialism to economic categories. Aronowitz suggests that Engels's "view of nature as a constant process of coming into being and passing away" is a more acceptable starting point for a historical materialist conception of nature (CHM, 48). Among other reasons for accepting Engels's position, not least is its compatibility with some recent structuralist and poststructuralist attempts to rethink materiality itself. Noneconomic determinations of social process are material in nature. Sexual and linguistic relations contribute, for example, to the repression of women by preventing the symbolic representation of woman as anything but the "Other," as the absent "Other" of the Western imaginary. In effect, language, discourse, and desire represent noneconomic but material forces.

Louis Althusser writes that "an ideology always exists in an apparatus, and its practice or practices. This existence is material."[18] Aronowitz argues that a recognition of this broadened sense of materiality, combined with Freud's demonstration that self-knowledge is not possible, will compel a revision of Marxism that leads to acceptance of the idea of "*the substantiality* of human nature" and "of the constitution of the subject at the conjuncture of nature and history" (CHM, 51). Following Adorno's critique of Marxism's logic of identity, Aronowitz writes that:

> Marxism's will to uniformity constitutes its very weakness. . . . It is no longer acceptable in the light of the discovery that the "mastery" of nature is not unproblematic. Therefore, production itself becomes problematic, and history can only be made consciously by recognizing nature's "needs." The rational management of society would entail recognition of what Leiss has termed "limits of satisfaction."[19] (CHM, 60)

The "needs" of "internal" nature, made clear by psychoanalysis, have serious repercussions for social theory. In *Civilization and Its Discontents*, Freud shows that sex and desire constitute a counterlogic to socially productive labor: the interchange between work and the erotic is one location of the subject's constitution in and of civilization.[20] Sublimation provides certain forms of socially useful gratification, but by no means settles the struggle between nature and history; these are incommensurable realities, but they are dialectically related. This difference between nature and history is the transhistorical mark of negation that Adorno regards as the necessary basis for a critical dialectic, and it is what Aronowitz makes the basis of his "scientific criticism." Aronowitz urgently attempts to form this new criticism because he believes it will help prevent the revolt of nature against a coercive society. Capital no longer only oppresses society, but by its attempted domination of nature and the psyche threatens to end it as well.

Radical theory can join other forces in preventing this apocalypse by recognizing the independence of nature and by theorizing desire as part of the counterlogic of postmodern society. The possibility and efficacy of such theorizing is strengthened by feminism and ecology and by the counterhegemonic speculations of writers such as Gilles Deleuze and Félix Guattari and by Jacques Lacan's subversion of the determining power of the Oedipal structure. The shift of capital from production to consumption along with the development of advertising and other aspects of the "production of signs" has released desire from some of the more familiar and repressive forms of bourgeois reproduction. In other words, capital catches itself in a contradiction: the use of advertising to exploit desire to sustain consumer society has released desire itself as a "natural" force no longer contained by the repressions that directed all energy into production.

Marxism's commitment to production and the domination of nature sometimes prevents it from examining everyday life and the roles of language, sexuality, and women in constituting material life.[21] But such an examination requires going beyond historicist forms to a dialectic that will not subsume the ineluctable differences between nature and society into an exclusively social dialectic. Althusser's theory of ideology provides a beginning to such a theory although Aronowitz remains highly skeptical of Althusser's "humanistic" assertion of the radical disjunction of history and nature. Also, insofar as Althusser believes that the economic base, in the last instance, determines cultural life, he too is, from Aronowitz's perspective, part of orthodox Marxism. Nonetheless, in spite of these reservations, Althusser's theory of ideology— "as the lived experience of the relation to the real of that which is prior to symbolization"—is a significant advance because it severely limits the authority of rationalism and scientism—despite Althusser's own invocations of "science." Like the works of Walter Benjamin and Michel Foucault, Althusser's writings insist that "humans are constituted by non-commensurable rationalities that are in perpetual conflict" (CHM, 69).

The political equivalents of these conflicting and incommensurable rationalities in the postmodern period are the "new movements of liberation [which] insist that the multiplicity of voices of liberation must remain autonomous" (CHM, 131). The liberation of desire as a revolutionary force requires the renunciation of all institutional forms that might embody visions of centralized power or of new hegemonies. Like Foucault, perhaps even under his influence, Aronowitz concludes that the multiple, local, autonomous struggles for liberation occurring throughout the postmodern world make all incarnations of master discourses absolutely illegitimate.[22] The role of the intellectual must, therefore, change: "the liberation of desire requires a return to the notion of will, since it does not accept the claims of centrally-organized political parties to *represent* desire. The problem of representation is unsolvable by means of a master discourse" (CHM, 130). Like Foucault, Aronowitz rejects the traditional intellectual's role of producing representations of the desires of the oppressed. Such production is parallel to the forces of domination themselves, is always based on false identity theories, attempts to totalize social process, and denies radical difference. It is always a dream of a new hegemony. Despite its intentions, it represses difference. In the postmodern world, politics and social reality have so changed that struggling individuals and autonomous liberation movements will not accept the guiding role of often white, often male, middle-strata intellectuals.

One could argue that at this point Aronowitz's own argument leads to a typical and dangerous form of American pluralism. Aronowitz has considered the possibility that widely diffused oppositional groups can be subverted. As a tactic to prevent this outcome, he recommends a bloc politics, but with a stress, theoretically justified by Adorno and the theoreticians of desire, on the autonomy of groups within the bloc. Conceding that capital can recuperate almost any opposition—it has, itself, accepted the "logic" of decentralization ideologically and to some extent economically—Aronowitz insists that the demand for self-managed societies will force capital to take a stand: "The demand for a self-managed society on the basis of the formation of an historic bloc that is simultaneously anti-capitalist and anti-hierarchical remains beyond the recuperative power of the prevailing order" (CHM, 134). Although any specific reform can lose its subversive characteristics, the relentless drive for autonomy cannot. Capital cannot tolerate concessions neither it nor the state can control. "There can be no vision of homogeneity" (CHM, 135). This statement applies both to the existing hegemonic forces and to the antihegemonic, oppositional groups. There can be no unified strategy of revolution on the 1917 model because without a master discourse no image of a new hegemony can be projected and pursued. Alternatively, Aronowitz projects a utopian vision of sometimes conflicting heterogeneous desires coexisting without antagonism or hierarchy (CHM, 135).

Having refused all legitimacy to master discourses, Aronowitz cannot produce a theoretical model to clarify his vision or to explain how to bring it about. But without such a discourse, he seems unable to explain how the society he envisions will escape the pessimistic conclusions of Freud and Nietzsche. But the essence of Aronowitz's vision, the optimism of his will, depends precisely on leaving the answer to these problems to the social struggles of everyday life waged by liberation groups and individuals.

III

The role that radical intellectuals can play in developing the moral and intellectual leadership of this utopian society depends on fulfilling the ideological potential of what Aronowitz calls "critical science" or "scientific pluralism." Initially, this critical practice must be separated from other phenomena. It is not a version of bourgeois pluralism,[23] nor does it share scientistic commitments to unified field theories, unicausal models, and the commensurability of discourses. Finally, it must be separated from "pure critique," which often results in either determinism or voluntarism.

"Critical science" places limits on the voluntaristic aspirations of radical intellectuals to produce master discourses and turns theory toward the specificity of historical trends. Although critical theory does reestablish the authority of resistance to the "immutable" laws and forces of development and oppression and so politically restores the individual subject to a role in social formation, this does not simply abrogate the operation of laws in social development. Rather, it mediates them, "rendering them no more than tendencies" (CHM, 198). Critical practice that associates itself with struggles for liberation cannot naively assume success based on desire or will or the inevitable coming of a socialist society. If such criticism is to be efficacious, it requires detailed research into the concrete and specific constitution of the historical moment in which it is placed. The "romance of interpretation," as Daniel O'Hara calls the foolish aspirations of critical thought to sublimity, is a hindrance to liberation.[24] As long as it refuses to abandon a belief in what Jonathan Arac calls the "heterocosmic autonomy of literature," it will remain acceptable to liberal pluralism.[25] Capitalist, patriarchal society has no trouble tolerating or ignoring it.

Aronowitz points out a useful alternative direction for criticism in a postmodern world, especially for a criticism that attempts both to theorize and to embody the postmodern:

> The problem is to construct a critical science whose "last instance" is the concrete, the historical specificity of social praxis while, at the same time, making the rigorous distinction between praxis as the constituting moment of history and the way in which history as already constituted takes on the appearance of the social formation's impenetrable facticity. Thus, there is a *positive* moment in all critical theory, a descriptive moment when the unfolding of capital's forms of appearance appear to possess the weight of natural law. The critical moment consists in the activity of showing how these forms are produced by classes and masses. The task is to integrate the descriptive into the critical, making the return to the concrete the dominant moment of social theory. (CHM, 198)

Critical description denaturalizes the appearances of capitalist society and reveals the origins of these appearances and their underlying forms in struggles for dominance and hegemony. This is a genealogical moment in the line of Nietzsche.

But if the radical intellectual adopts this critical science of tendencies in place of the attempt to develop and transmit a master discourse, the question still remains: how does this provide social leadership? For whom does the intellectual work? To whom does the intellectual *show* "how these forms are produced"? What are the social consequences of this educational gesture? How will it help bring about the nonantagonistic forms of autonomy that constitute Aronowitz's utopia?

On these matters, *The Crisis in Historical Materialism* is not completely clear. The refusal of the representative role of the intellectual could result in the dispersion and co-optation of intellectual practice. One possibility is that intellectuals might become "specific intellectuals," as Foucault suggests, engaged in the struggle of autonomous groups in their local situation. But Aronowitz is clearly concerned that such dispersed actions can be co-opted. Fragmented groups and discourses "are, by themselves, not adequate to global structures whose mode is to subvert the autonomy of the margins and the underclasses" (CHM, 196–97). Scientific criticism can form the ideology of the autonomous groups, "leading" them into an association that will not subsume their specifiable differences. Criticism becomes the ideology of bloc politics.

The crucial role of ideological criticism has come about because social changes in advanced societies will be determined by cultural questions. Economic struggles among elements of an ever more proletarianized population will expand, but their potential for liberation can only be fully cultivated insofar as they become battles for cultural autonomy as well. A utopian vision of nondomination will guide this scientific criticism. Theoretically and ideologically, it will show to all those counterhegemonic groups that no alternative hegemony is consistent with human aspirations for liberation and equality. Politically, critical science will theorize how "building from a micropolitics of autonomous oppositional movements, whether derived from production relations or not, a new historical bloc may emerge" (CHM, 127). Scientific criticism would theorize a bloc that is, by definition, *antihegemonic* in its politics and culture, in its ideology and the forms of everyday life. Theory must refuse doctrine if it is to assume the perspective of self-management.[26] It must describe and defend the "*permanence of difference*" against the common sense of identity in both socialism and liberalism.

Of course, Aronowitz's position faces severe criticism. Questions will be posed by both economistic and critical Marxists. Also, he will be questioned about the efficacy of his defense of the power of historical "tendencies" as opposed to "laws." Is this an adequate way around scientism and extreme voluntarism? Is it an adequate description of the strength of certain existing historical social configurations? Can this be reconciled with his acceptance of Althusser's theory of ideology? Does not his preservation of critique's positive moment—showing the real structures behind reified appearances—preserve some elements of Lukács's theory of mediation? Does the incommensurability of discourse allow for a sort of eclectic borrowing from other theories to form an ideology of the "bloc"? Does Aronowitz avoid structuralist rhetorics in order not to circumscribe the desire of autonomous groups and individuals? Indeed, it seems Aronowitz has not fully come to terms with the implications of Lacan and Althusser on the transhistorical persistence of ideology. How will this affect the utopia he envisions? Can critical science become the ideology of that society and of all its autonomous groups? Without leading the way and representing that utopia to these groups as the best of all possible worlds, how will it become their ideology? How will education avoid *leading* groups to their goals? How will criticism avoid the advocate's role of convincing others that the utopia of ineluctable difference is exactly what we all desire?

These are not caviling questions, nor do they undermine the significance of this book. Aronowitz himself writes in his "Prospectus" that he will "open up more questions than [he] can as yet hope to answer" (CHM, 8). I certainly cannot offer a full answer to any or all of these questions. It would be useful for critics to carry on the historical research required for understanding how these questions have come to be so important to intellectuals now. We might better see what needs they express and what we might hope to gain from answering them. In other words, we could learn their political origins and consequences and so might better judge what our own actions and institutions should be.

As I have argued elsewhere,[27] there is good reason to be suspicious of all institutions that establish or depend on structures of "representative" or "leading" intellectuals and parties. The long-growing historical and theoretical dissatisfactions with the Leninist party and its Lukácsian justifications have led intellectuals to pose questions such as those Aronowitz treats and those others that arise in any reading of his work. Such questions try to find for critical intellectual work a political role that is not part of some antidemocratic ideology or apparatus.

We might sketch our problem in this way: on the one hand, critical intellectuals concerned for the values of participatory democracy and sensitive to the hope that people can control their own representations cannot accept the many self-justifying professional and pragmatic models for critical practice so common today;[28] on the other hand, Lukácsian and Althusserian models of englobement and totalization sustain Leninist practices and visions that often blunt decentralized drives of particular groups toward democratic forms of self-determination. Aronowitz's work greatly aids efforts to get beyond the double obstruction posed by professionalism and by leftist totalization. He has demonstrated how critiques of science, the analyses of various feminisms, and the development of local forms of political struggle must all be taken into account in any effort to theorize the political position of a critical intellectual.

The critical mind must address the politics of the moment, but must also avoid being bound merely to the rhetoric and concepts of the narrowly defined present. One might, for example, use the skills of literary criticism to study the discursive structures at work in the representations by American media of current struggles to eliminate apartheid in South Africa. Such a critical project might have a doubly beneficial critical and political result. It might not only elucidate the dominant structures of race, economics, and ideology involved in such representations and their effects on United States policy, but might also help to develop new ways for the Western intellectual to defend what is valuable in his or her own tradition, despite the endless need to revise most and discard much of it. That is, such a political critical move—based on a refusal of totalization and the representative intellectual—could be liberating in two ways: it might help to weaken the support of a reactionary American government for a tyranny it claims to dislike, and it might strengthen the critical, self-examining tendencies that are what is worth preserving in our tradition.

This small example does not in any way answer the many far-ranging theoretical questions provoked by Aronowitz's work. My sense is that the answers are needed but that they can only be found in the process of trying to adapt critical motives to the values and projects of participatory democracy. I see no other conclusion to be drawn from Aronowitz's analysis of the politics of the bloc and of the new and important decentralizing movements of feminism and ecology. For literary critics to join in this movement of forces opposed to tyrannical totalization and representation, they must begin by offering a thorough critique of the new ethics of professionalism that some leading figures and their followers now propel into the market of critical celebrity. Critical intellectuals will have to investigate the origins and contemporary functions of those ethics in order to negate them; then perhaps the work of building more positive institutions and progressive critical practices can begin to go forward.

IV

One of the most marked changes in the elite culture of postmodern society is the decline from the late 1950s in the importance of so-called advanced literary study. There are many economic, cultural, and ideological explanations for this decline. Any literary criticism that does not take this decline and other related changes into account is simply refusing to recognize a discomforting reality. Furthermore, this situation in English studies should no longer be described in terms of a crisis-rhetoric for it is a permanent feature of our society and critics have no right or reason to assume it will pass away. Residual formations persist when societies change and "literary" criticism as an academic profession is largely a residual formation. With the exception of certain aspects of minority and women's studies and some advanced literary theory, the profession seems to have little "liberating" role to play in our society. Some debate could be staged about composition theory and teaching; perhaps it is finally beginning. But the *normal* criticism produced and published by dozens of academic journals and presses seems more and more indifferent to human desires and needs. Neither the program of "good citizenship" prescribed by Wayne Booth[29] nor Geoffrey Hartman's seductive arguments for criticism as art[30] seem very effective as antihegemonic tendencies.

What are the possibilities afforded by the specific cultural formations of postmodernism for human liberation and what role can the critical theorizing of the postmodern as antihegemonic hope to play? These are some of the questions that criticism and teaching can try to answer specifically by furthering the desire for autonomy and self-management among students and intellectuals inside the academy. If in so doing, support for other forms of struggle also emerges, then the critical project will have some concrete social effect. In any event, Aronowitz reinforces the sense that the future is uncertain. Despite the powerful, but flawed, vision of utopia he projects—which reminds us of our power to imagine alternative lives—he devastatingly exposes the residual myth of progress in our visions and strategies of liberation, and this leaves no easy place for assurance or optimism.[31]

6

......

Agriculture
and Academe:
America's Southern
Question

The relations of different nations among themselves depend upon the extent to which each has developed its productive forces, the division of labour and internal intercourse. —Karl Marx

In the period after 1870, with the colonial expansion of Europe . . . the internal and international organisational relations of the State become more complex and massive, and the Forty-Eightist formula of the "Permanent Revolution" is expanded and transcended in political science by the formula of "civil hegemony." —Antonio Gramsci

No student or historian of the Agrarian moment in American criticism has adequately analyzed either the political and cultural ideology of a handful of critics in Nashville and Baton Rouge or the national political function of their transformation into professional literary critics at the center of the American professoriat. Indeed, no analysis of the American New Criticism has told us as much as we need to know about its origins in nationalist struggles to integrate the U.S. culture and market as a condition and concomitant of its international or, we might say, imperial power.

None of the critics who represent movements meant to go beyond the New Criticism has explored historically its function within the larger political, cultural context I have just mentioned. Nor have the New Critics's still numerous admirers—those who accept its aesthetic canons for the most part and those who feel it progressively opened the study of literature and the university to the middle class—made a case for their founders based on this aspect of their history. Despite the

recent spate of institutional histories—conservative and liberal alike—
some of which are laboriously documented, these particular political
origins of the New Criticism in the Agrarian moment are left unex-
amined, indeed, they remain unthought-of.

Terry Eagleton's summary survey, "The Idealism of American Criticism," exemplifies the rush of critics on the left and right to repeat
what amount to received truths about its history and function:

> From the mid-1930's to the late 1940's, American literary theory fell
> under the sway of a curious hybrid of critical technocracy and
> Southern religious-aesthetic conservatism known as the "New
> Criticism." [Eagleton at this point refers us to John Fekete's *Critical
> Twilight* (1977) for "an excellent study of the movement."] Offspring
> of the failed agrarian politics of the 1930's, and aided by the col-
> lapse of a Stalinized Marxist criticism, New Criticism yoked the
> "practical critical" techniques of I. A. Richards and F. R. Leavis to
> the re-invention of the "aesthetic life" of the old South in the
> delicate textures of the poem.[1]

Eagleton must be congratulated for noticing what most U.S. commentators on our literary history ignore altogether: the connection of our
dominant formational critical practice and discourse to a politics of
national importance. If Eagleton does not explore the texture of this
political history, no American scholar of the movement has deigned,
even in book-length studies, to treat the matter as a serious issue.

For example, in the standard work on this material, *The Burden of Time*,
John L. Stewart analyzes Agrarianism from within its own ideology,
reproducing the "line" which the Agrarians voiced themselves. In
other words, his is a work of "explication": the ground of the Agrarians's critique of "America" and of their own "aesthetic" commitments
is the alternative "image of man" they offer in their work:

> that image . . . is stoutly anti-progressive, anti-rationalist, and anti-
> humanist, for it insists on the irreducible mystery in life, the all-
> pervasiveness of evil in human affairs, and the limitations of man's
> capacity to understand and control his environment and his own
> nature.

In fact, when Stewart discusses the functional value of Agrarianism for
the group at Nashville and the possibility of materially situating this

ideology presents itself, he retreats to the idealist rhetoric he has inherited from and mistaken for the whole of the Agrarian legacy:

> Agrarianism furnished means for declaring and questioning what seemed most meaningful to them: it gave them problems of value and behaviour around which to organize their random thoughts and observations into beliefs.

Stewart misses the chance to probe the nature of this "organization" and its sources and effects, and he begs the question of how "random" and "disorganized" those "apparently disparate" thoughts and experiences really were. Stewart's book exemplifies (and helped create) the consensus in the profession about the Agrarians; we can see that even Eagleton, from a diametrically opposed position, operates within the same set of perceptions.

It is important that we understand how the difficulty in tracing the concrete history of the discourses and practices of our critical institutions is essential to their function within our society. In the case of the New Criticism, the transformation of Agrarianism's politics into the political quietism or conservatism of New Critical orthodoxy effectively blocks any investigation into the position of critical Agrarianism within the national and international arena of political contest. Precisely because the New Criticism succeeded in professionalizing the apolitical and disinterested study of canonized texts and facilitated the professionalized institution of academic literary study, for the most part literary historians have, until very recently, found it very difficult to orient themselves intellectually to the critically responsible task of writing politically directed history which is any more than mere polemic for one or another contemporary critical "school." A general phenomenon of the successfully bureaucratized intellectual institutions which form part of the imperial hegemony of the United States is that they are self-forgetting and encourage cultural and political amnesia. Furthermore, as exemplary elements in the strategy of "passive revolution," as Gramsci calls Western societies's change without substantial change, they sometimes incorporate bodily the random intellectual critic of their own legitimacy, the historian of their own complicities. Gramsci would have us see how, in so doing, they help tie even the "oppositional" intellectual to the state in its extended, late capitalist stage.

This blockage and its amnesic effects can be seen on both left and right, as I have tried to suggest. The result is twofold: on the one hand, left critics simply write off the New Criticism and its variations as understood and surpassed, at least in theory;[2] on the other hand, conservative critics repeat and defend its "values," "quarrel" with its ideas, and repeat the tale of its own history. The second of these results takes two troubling forms: one is the large number of professors with New Critical sympathies who teach and sometimes write, but with no rigorous or conscious sense of their indebtedness to or difference from the New Critics; the second is a subdivision of our professional bureaucracy: what I will call here the "Professional Southernist" (PS). (I will discuss the second briefly; I have treated the former at length elsewhere.)

The PS is both a monumental historian and an antiquarian. Too often, the PS is a hagiographer. The PS's reproduce, in the form of explanation and apology, the tragic image of the Agrarians and their allies as failed prophets, bearers of refused alternatives, preservers of a better way, and guides to spiritual, imaginative renewal. The endless number of symposia, collections, gatherings of memoirs, interviews, and re-editions—all having to do with the rather short-lived moment of The Southern Review or The Fugitive—all these show very clearly how ritualized the putative study of these writers has become among those professionally studying "Southern literature." The reissuing of The Southern Review and The Kenyon Review makes the point about the ritual desire for a return to mythicized origins among what must be seen, by any standard, as a leading conservative and still unyieldingly anti-Marxist element within not only the academic critical profession, but the Reaganized culture as a whole. The existence of "The Liberty of Southern Civilization," edited by Lewis P. Simpson (LSU Press) exemplifies the massive productive institutionalization of the PS. At least two things are to be said about it: first, that it preserves and organizes documents which embody essentially conservative ideologies, no matter if that conservatism is sometimes the ground for a critique of the extended American state; second, and more important, it contributes to the cultural bulwark of civil society essential to the hegemony of the extended state. It does this last, in part, by absorbing intellectuals into the state sphere and, more important again, by furthering the ahistorical, acritical practices upon which the U.S. (putative) national consensus rests.[3] In the guise of "critical histories," the PS often produces monumental studies of the Agrarian past which cast the events of that time in impressionistic, antiquarian literary critical terms. More specifically, it subsumes an entire set of issues and conflicts associated with the state's response to the critics of liberalism and the economy in the twenties and thirties, to the idealizing abstractions of the "history of criticism" or "literary history." In other words, in an act of self-preserving revision, the extended state institutionalized an entire set of discourses and practices that, in turn, submerged all of the political struggles enacted within literary and critical practices at the very time that the extended state set about raising itself out of the crises of liberalism and unregulated capital. Permanent revolution, the agrarian and populist ideal, a suspicion of power, a Jeffersonian tenet, gave way precisely to what Gramsci calls in my epigraph, "civil hegemony" through the techniques of "passive revolution." (I will return to this a bit further on.) And now we are trying to find our own recent political past through the defenses against just such political investigations and dissatisfactions that that hegemony has erected to maintain itself. The nature of Agrarianism as an event within the field of nationalizing struggles in an imperialist culture has been nearly obliterated.

The effects of such defenses, indeed their literal embodiment within the field of knowledge, that is, their embodiment as a positive set of practices defining the representations of our past—some of these effects can be seen in Thomas W. Cutrer's book, *Parnassus on the Mississippi*.[4] This text is part of the "Southern Literary Studies" series that interlocks with Simpson's "Library of Southern Civilization." It, too, is published by LSU Press and is edited by Louis D. Rubin, another leading PS. Cutrer dedicates his book to "Lewis P. Simpson in whose capable hands the *Southern Review* lives again." Cutrer's book is a mass of unhistoricized "facts," as if the accumulation of information itself produces critical history. He aims to tell us what Brooks and Warren thought and did, especially during those years before Warren left for Minnesota and Brooks for Yale. We should not be ungrateful to Cutrer. He has done the antiquarian work upon which critical analysis must rest. But the book essentially details already received opinion. It is not controversial in any way; it hardly modifies the image of Brooks and Warren or of Agrarianism that we see in Stewart or even in Louise Cowan's *The Fugitive Group* (1959).[5] The issues at stake are never explored on any level. For example, what does it mean that F. O. Matthiessen adopts Brooks and Warren's *Understanding Poetry* for his courses at Harvard in 1938, the year of its publication? In asking this question, we must remember that

Brooks and Warren, like the Agrarians, did not think too highly of Matthiessen, calling his work on Eliot introductory and not criticism; they saw in him a prime example of the historicizing criticism dominant in their universities.[6] It is remarkable that Cutrer can note this and think nothing of it just after he has allowed, following Brooks and Warren, themselves, that they produced their textbooks in part to counter Northern educational imperialism. The nationalizing of their supposedly regional and oppositional texts was of crucial importance to the integrity of cultural reproduction in the United States and a study of how this nationalizing came about and what about Brooks and Warren made it possible would throw considerable light on the complexity of the New Critics's position as Southern Americans. But such matters cannot be raised within the confines of PS discourse. Indeed, PS discourse exists as a comfortable part of the American academy just because it can attach a substantial and troubling part of U.S. history to the unifying institutions of national cultural circulation.

II

On August 10, 1931, Allen Tate writes a letter to John Peale Bishop in which he rehearses their common Agrarian grounds for thinking Edmund Wilson's call for a "planned economy" silly and fatuous:

> I've had some flaming controversy with Edmund. I reviewed his book in the current Hound and Horn, and simultaneously he wrote a piece (N.R. [New Republic], July 29th) about our symposium [I'll Take My Stand] entitled "Tennessee Agrarians," the tone of which was superior wisdom before our mere ancestor worship [Tate published The Fathers in 1938]. . . . In general, he accuses us of day-dreaming over the past, i.e., of non-realism; I answer that we are simply calling on the traditional Southern sense of politics, which was eminently realistic, while his Planned Economy, seen through the whiskers of Professor [John] Dewey, is the most fantastic piece of wish-thinking I've ever seen. As you say, they have no sense of actual economic structure, which invariably rests on the last, but think of economic organization as a matter of boards, commissions, controls, etc., which are purely arbitrary and unless backed by some powerful and interested motive, like practical communism, are merely a liberal's dream.[7]

This letter typifies the Agrarians's attitude toward the development of the extended state as a response to the crisis of capital in the twenties and thirties. The Agrarians are anti-statist on several levels. As classical liberals, they firmly hold the position that the state should operate only as a watchdog over the democratic operations of a society of small landholders. They are opposed to the development of state power to intervene and regulate the economy. But above all, they are aware of and bitterly opposed to the development of what we might call, following Gramsci, the "extended state." Gramsci's sense of the "extended state" is complex, but we can derive some sense of it from this explanation offered in a note on "political science":

> the State is the entire complex of practical and theoretical activities with which the ruling class not only justifies and maintains its dominance, but manages to win the active consent of those over whom it rules.

That the Agrarians oppose this extended state and not merely state intervention in the economy, not simply the imposition of Northern industrialism upon the agrarian South, appears in John Crowe Ransom's contributions to the second Agrarian symposium, *Who Owns America?* Ransom's essay, like Tate's in the same volume, is concerned with property rights and the status of corporate power. But Ransom's essay, "What Does the South Want?," does not stop at the abstract equation of controlling ownership of small landholdings with democracy that marks Tate's essay. Ransom is much more sensitive to the encroachments of the fully extended state, and particularly its noncoercive hegemonic apparatus for attaching the South to the core power of Eastern capital and empire.

For Ransom, the South has a tradition that makes it passionate about what sort of political economy it would like to have, that would best suit the South's "prejudices." "An orthodox capitalism for the South," he writes, "would be an economy with a wide distribution of the tangible capital properties."[8] This idea does not get beyond Tate's statement that: "The effective ownership of property entails personal responsibility for the use which is made of a given portion of the means of production."[9] Tate and Ransom agree that the threat to this Southern ideal is the large national and international corporation which dominates markets and supplies and so sets prices. Both worry that Americans have lost sight of the need, as Ransom puts it, "to guard the right to administer property."[10]

But when Ransom turns to the particular problems of the Southern farmer, we discover that he has an untheorized perception of the development of the extended state and the transformation of an entire civilization which goes along with it. His text reflects with remarkable clarity the most highly developed form of the contradictions at the heart of U.S. Agrarianism in the period of the twenties to the forties.

He begins by insisting that as late as 1936 Southern farming remains outside the sphere of corporate economics and intensive capital exploitation. (We need not argue the point that this claim is historically incorrect.)[11] As a result, the Jeffersonian ideal of independent landowners free of state and corporate intervention can still be found in large numbers. Of course, the ever-increasing accrual of power to the state and the corporate order threatens the final destruction of this population. Ransom does not desire, as some of the other Agrarians do, the elimination of capital-intensive, large-scale production. He rather desires that it be modified in the South and suggests two needed restrictions upon its growth and power. Interestingly, what he proposes sounds remarkably similar to policies followed in the post-war period by third world governments entering into a dependency relation to the imperialist core:

> the South . . . will make at least two major requirements toward the discovery of responsible business direction: a review of the easy bargain which the charter-granting power now makes with the absentee owners of capital properties; and every possible legal assurance to the small independents of their right to compete against the corporations without being exposed to conspiracies.

Ransom believed that a limited state apparatus would guarantee Southern property rights and so the South's unique civilization. He believed this because he was an agrarian, that is, because he believed in the necessity of farming as the very ground of all economic activity.

His thinking about farming is absolutely idealistic. So intent is he on establishing the inalienable superiority of agriculture that he closes his eyes to the worst abuses of tenant farming which involved, by far, the largest number of agriculturally dependent people in the South:

Farming has remained a private business; the joint-stock com-
panies engaged in agriculture in this country are as exceptional as
their economy is doubtful. Farmers are far ahead of the so-called
business men in the unanimity of their independence. Even the
tenant farmer takes his contract on broad terms which leave him
free to plant, tend, gather, and sometimes sell at his own discre-
tion; and even the day laborer submits to nothing like the bossing
of a factory foreman. Farmers are the most important bloc of free
spirits who have survived the modern economy.[12]

Ransom realizes that in a money economy these free spirits cannot last
long; farming, as a money-making project, will always leave the majority of farmers destitute. Of course, Ransom recommends subsistence
farming as preferable to factory labor and as the inevitable outcome of a
surplus of land in a basically industrial civilization. It is, Ransom writes,
the "individual economy of self-subsistence . . . by virtue of which
farmers are invincible."[13]

Why are the farmers and the agrarian way of life politically valuable?
In this essay, Ransom answers this question in terms which are specific
to the changing nature of agriculture and its relation to the state; he gets
away for a moment from the usual mythic explanations the Agrarians
give which personify the evils of machines and industry. In short, says
Ransom, the apparatus set up by the state for the transformation of
agricultural civilization is at fault. Ransom singles out the extension
services and the county agent system as well as the land-grant agricultural schools as the apparatus through which the farmers were influenced to join in the hegemonic money economy: "they were betrayed
into this decision [to rely on money farming] by unrealistic advisers,
including for the most part their instructors in the agricultural schools
and experiment stations."[14]

This is an interesting essay in the history of Agrarianism because it
shows both that the Agrarians understood something of the issues at
stake, particularly, here, the matter of the seemingly relentless extension of the state; but also it shows that despite all of the talk of regional
autonomy, of the South as an alternative to the North's industrial and
imperial drives, the Agrarians were really only trying to negotiate a new
relationship with what we can call the core of imperial power. Many
critics and historians suggest, for example, that the South offered itself

and its myths as alternatives to the national, unifying American myths; that it insisted upon its own difference and tried to maintain an alternative civilization.[15] There is a great deal of truth to this, but the matter must be stated more clearly: the Agrarians were trying to make a double move: first, as relatively traditional intellectuals they were trying to regain the leadership role usurped by county agents and agricultural schools; second, they were trying to negotiate the South's entry into the national hegemony on different terms than that hegemony was offering. The extended state operated through extension services, agricultural schools, and the Farm Bureau, for example, to expand its hegemony, to bring a large number of especially "advanced," that is, sizable and efficient, farmers into the "money economy" regulated, for the most part, by the economic core powers. The Agrarians wanted to be admitted to the hegemony on other terms and with other functions for themselves. They wanted, in other words, to occupy the place held by traditional intellectuals, that is, the role of intermediary between the state and the farming populace. But that desire rested upon a sense of the liberal state, one which did not so directly assume responsibility for the planning of economy and the formation of an entire civilization. In the extended state, which FDR simply developed, a newer type of technically trained bureaucratic intellectual incorporates the farmer to the hegemony. It is through the mixture of so-called "private" and "public" institutions that the state offers the compromise necessary to induce a large social class to join the hegemony directed by the imperial capitalists.

Ransom, for example, welcomes the Supreme Court's decision declaring unconstitutional the New Deal's Triple A. Farming, he admits, needs a subsidy, but it cannot come from a regulative government agency: "farming ceases to be farming when its direction becomes external and involuntary."[16] The matter is, of course, precisely one of direction; the extended state offers compromises to various social groups, offers to take them into the hegemony on the condition that they accept the direction of the leading groups in the bloc. Clearly, then, Ransom does not hope for a restoration of an agricultural civilization nor for a populist revolution which would break up the largest productive units into smaller regional concerns. Rather he wants the ruling powers to allow subsistence farming and at the same time subsidize the money-poor farmers so they can take part in yet be independent of the money economy. Ransom proposes the impossible, namely the arbitrary isolation of farming from the processes of capitalist society:

> But in view of the special liability of agriculture in this country, and the fact that farmers are a class whom the nation should delight to honor, there should be a special treatment for them.... The farmer should receive greater and not lesser services than he now receives.[17]

Ransom suggests that these services should include primarily good roads, rural electrification, and first-class education.

Ransom justly points out how the South's agriculture had been intensely exploited; as a colony much more wealth was withdrawn from it than was returned to it. (Progressive Democrats, we are told to this day, can carry the South if they promise enough internal improvements. Indeed, his list reminds us of Willie Stark's claim to have finally given the people some of the improvements they deserved.) But his recommendations, if carried out, as in part they have been, would only make the South that much more dependent upon the core to which it is the periphery. This is not just a conservative move but also a self-deluded one with unrealizable goals whose very pursuit extends the structures Ransom hopes to oppose; in fact, he is proposing that Southern farming and the state make a social contract wherein agriculture can be bought as a stable base for the state's otherwise imperial energies. This incredible proposal rests upon an enormous theoretical ignorance about the extended state and the crises to which it responds. Above all, it involves a betrayal of all those trying in any other way to resist or modify the practices of capital as they experience them in their locale. In effect, despite his concerns for noneconomic matters, Ransom is proposing a regional corporate model of organization. The result is to isolate the Southern farmer from all others struggling for their independence and align them in a dependency relation to the state. This is what we might also call "the treason of the intellectuals."

Fundamentally, Ransom cannot believe in the equality of men and women. He excoriates proletarian writers who "have liked the thrilling odors from the armpits of men who work with their hands, and ... have admired the ox-like strength of laborers, and still more the ox-like herding together in comradeship, and in the gregariousness of simple creatures they have seen the sublime consummation of human society. The generosity of this policy," Ransom continues, "is beyond praise.

But by an oversight they have forgotten to make room for the most distinguishing of the human qualities, which is—intelligence."[18] The aesthetic life is the agrarian life which needs those of "intelligence" to be perfected. This statement of condescending patriarchal class hatred registers the Agrarians's anxiety over their function as intellectuals within a civilization regulated by the extended state. How are they to become part of this hegemony? What compromises must be made to have a place in it? Ransom concedes that labor unions might improve the lot of the workers, but quickly dismisses any notion that he might concern himself with them. That is not to be his role.

In 1933–34, Gramsci, imprisoned in Turi, turned his mind to understanding the operations of the extended state in western societies and how to overturn it. He theorized the historical transformation of the state after about 1870 into a new entity which makes the putative classical distinction between the state and civil society merely methodological:

> Its [the extended state's] aim is always that of creating new and higher types of civilisation; of adapting the "civilisation" and the morality of the broadest popular masses to the necessities of the continuous development of the economic apparatus of production; hence of evolving even physically new types of humanity. But how will each single individual succeed in incorporating himself into the collective man, and how will educative pressure be applied to single individuals so as to obtain their consent and their collaboration, turning necessity and coercion into "freedom"?[19]

Clearly the Agrarians did not imagine themselves to be in the service of the extended state which hoped to educate farmers to collaborate with the hegemonic imperial bloc. But equally clearly they did not sufficiently theorize the state's adoption of a strategy of "passive revolution" as a way of dealing with the crises of capital in the United States from the 1890s until the 1930s. Ransom had some insight into the processes by which "agriculture" became a category of economic activity within the extended state. There had been farmers in the nineteenth century, but when they began to organize corporately rather than act politically in a populist struggle against concentrations of economic power within the state—at that point "agriculture" came into existence as a political weight within the state apparatus.

The state process of compromising with the populist masses began in the nineteenth century with the Hatch Act, extension services, and land-grant colleges. It was refined with the county agent system and fulfilled with the maturity of the Farm Bureau as the corporate representative of the most "advanced" and "successful" farmers. Although a "private" institution, the Farm Bureau acted as an extension of the state, incorporating a farming elite into the system of power which defined farmers's issues as problems of "price," "market," and "parity." Effectively, the Farm Bureau decapitated the already weakened populist movement that had been compromised by its Democratic alliances in the elections of the 1890s. The Farm Bureau is made up of member farmers who form local and state branches which pyramid into a national bureau and its executive leadership. The national organization represents "farmers's interests" in Washington and through local branches and in cooperation with extension services and land-grant colleges educates farmers in the leading technical innovations in intensive farming and orchestrates the farmers's relationship to markets in the United States and abroad. (The history of U.S. agricultural policy is too complex to deal with here, but it has always been a leading edge of American imperial policy in the third world, especially where it has often devastated local competition.) The history of the Farm Bureau is a microcosm of how the extended state establishes hegemony. Education makes for a scientific farmer, part of an international market, regulated necessarily by national governments; intensive farming involves credit, machinery, and chemicals. In return for entering this cycle of production and consumption, the elite among farmers—and this is increasingly a corporate elite—have their material and ideological interests satisfied. Above all, however, we should note that in this structure no form of consciousness or organization beyond the economic-corporate gets developed.

Above all we must see that this is not simply a mechanism of oppression. Farmers in large number are drawn to a bloc which satisfies many of their needs, in which, consequently, they have an interest, and to which, in turn, they owe a considerable loyalty. Of course, this is also a mechanism of exclusion. For example, the New Deal Triple A, which Ransom so happily saw struck down by the Supreme Court, was one of many welfare-state initiatives meant to tie the less well-off farmer to the hegemony. Sharecroppers and tenant farmers were to be given special education and subsidy. The Farm Bureau rightly felt this was unnecessary since, without leadership and direction, the poorer farmers were not a threat to social stability, profits, or state power. Their organizations were either the Masonic and politically ineffective Grange or the politically impotent Farmers Union.

The Farm Bureau came into its own precisely at the time when the Agrarians were writing their books. In some sense they were in direct conflict. Two different types of intellectuals—one traditional: clerical, humanistic, petite bourgeois; the other technical: bureaucratic, scientific, professional—belonging to two different social formations compete for leadership. The Agrarians could have no constituency since the leadership among farmers was already absorbed not by virtue of the industrialization of the South but by virtue of the state's expanded educative and civilizing role which resulted in the emergence of not only new types of "men,"—"scientific farmers"—but a new form of production—"agriculture"—and new kinds of social relations. This was surely not the kind of "social contract" Ransom envisaged in his own idealist speculations about the reality of farming or the reach of the state apparatus. Such immense ignorance of social and political forces assured the Agrarians's tactics to regain traditional leadership roles would fail—they had no organic relations to the groups they hoped to represent—and their failures prepared the ground for their own absorption into the corporate structures and consciousness of the bureaucratized academy and its bourgeois professionalization.

In other words, as we have seen in the discussion of Ransom, the Agrarians were unknowingly aligned with the practices and ideology of the Farm Bureau. Both finally developed into corporate elites; both at least aspired to replace the populist, radical farm leadership with more conservative ideologies; both even hoped to produce—although the Agrarians thought they were "reproducing"—new types of men: the Agrarians, new Cincinnatuses and the Farm Bureau's new "scientific farmers." Both tactics removed the traditionally populist masses from any political conflict with the core concentration of power. The key is that the Agrarians do so in a way less useful to the state. They, in fact, produce no new men in the social order, but only in imagination, which is to say that they generate ideology conservative and reactionary even from the point of view of the developing state's rationality; an ideology the state funds in academe where the increasingly apolitical mythmaking of aesthetic critics buttresses the hegemony not only by blocking the development of radical consciousness but also, and more important, by dulling aesthetics and critique within the normalizing, consensus making apparatus of the amnesic mass culture which most effectively regulates the political economy.

III

Gramsci's notion of "passive revolution" is immensely helpful in understanding Agrarianism's failure to alter U.S. society and culture in the way its adherents had hoped. In effect the Agrarians, like many other contemporary literary intellectuals, felt some fundamental change in the United States during the 1920s and the New Deal. Edmund Wilson, for example, no ally of the Agrarian cause although friend of many an Agrarian, writes to John Peale Bishop (May 12, 1931) apropos his forthcoming The American Jitters,[20] that he has "a strong conviction that this is a crucial time for the United States."[21] But no American critic of the period had a strong understanding of the reconfiguration of the state and society that followed the failures of liberalism.

Gramsci developed the concept of "passive revolution" in his analysis of the Italian revolution's failure and in opposition to the "Crocean construction" of history. In fact, Gramsci seems always to have intended "passive revolution" to represent the process in which the ancien regime comes to governing power through "reformist" action while at the very same time, and by virtue of a critique of Croce's History of Europe and History of Italy, to direct his analysis against the current fascist domination. In effect, Gramsci argues that Croce's failure to "make history" of the periods of struggle—the French Revolution, Napoleonic Wars, and the Risorgimento—follows upon fascism's early attempt to align itself with the traditional and "respectable" right and its tragi-comic efforts to reenact the "reformist" patterns of "the period of restoration-revolution." Gramsci's concept, then, functions as historical analysis and as critique directed not only at traditional intellectuals whose failure to understand history and power makes them allies of fascism, but also at those very political practices (and their histories) that these traditional intellectuals cannot understand.

In 1935, Gramsci figures "passive revolution" in this way:

> The ideological hypothesis could be presented in the following terms: that there is a passive revolution involved in the fact that— through the legislative intervention of the State, and by means of the corporative organisation—relatively far-reaching modifica-

tions are being introduced into the country's economic structure in order to accentuate the "plan of production" element; in other words, that socialisation and co-operation in the sphere of production are being increased, without however touching (or at least not going beyond the regulation and control of) individual and group appropriation of profit. (SPN, 119–20)

With Gramsci's concept in mind we can see not only that the Agrarians did not theorize the political economic changes in the United States between the wars; we can also see that the rapid development of state institutions in "agriculture" both displaced traditional intellectuals (and destroyed the social order in which they had a place) and developed new men, "scientific farmers," powerfully linked to the state. Furthermore, we can begin to understand how these conservative radicals were so easily incorporated into academic state apparatuses.

The Farm Bureau and its accoutrements gave the new technical men all they needed; and the New Deal Democrats, in particular, "offered the mass of the intellectuals all the satisfactions for their general needs which can be offered by a government (by a governing party) through the State services" (SPN, 104). Cleanth Brooks, Robert Penn Warren, John Crowe Ransom, and their heirs were firmly established in mostly elite universities—R. P. Blackmur was the only "New Critic" whose academic career was not secure until the 1950s; he had no "credentials" and was "difficult"—and able to influence academic publishing, program developments, career shapes, and teaching. The "traditional" intellectuals had been driven from the field of direct political conflict with the state into the academic arena of cultural, literary, and critical debate, but debate practiced within the state-supported institutions of the university. This is not to say simply that these intellectuals were "co-opted," or "bought-off"; such simple-minded rhetoric would be assuring if it were true. (I shall return to this point at the end.) On the contrary, the state we might say met some of the real needs of these intellectuals by allowing them to carry on their struggles in the international cultural arena of literary studies and production. They were, in fact, enabled to speak against the state's "planning" apparatuses and often to generate ideologically critical representations of the capitalist order in the United States. (Above all, they saw themselves as fighting a rear guard action to preserve a place for poetry in a scientific world.) In effect, the cumulative resistance of the literary intellectual caste to their progressive displacement by the "new men" of the extended state earned them, in turn, a new place to speak and new functions to provide: they taught the young, they produced new knowledge—now within the state's apparatuses—and they, thusly, became and produced other "new men," new "types": the academic critic and intellectual professionalized, specialized, and sometimes still politically oppositional.

Gramsci's concept would let us investigate several other phenomena: the continuing investment of the academy in the "Southern writer," testifying to the South's "human experience" caught within its own uniqueness: the experience of the South's intensive post-Civil War exploitation presented in thoroughly academicized aesthetic categories. Southern-literary-intellectuals-become-New-Critics "resist" the North by linking the South to England; they firmly establish, in other words, the good credentials, the international legitimacy of one main strand of U.S. culture. In opposition to "capitalism," they link themselves and U.S. modernism to the classical traditions of Western Europe, and so they join the legitimating work of F. O. Matthiessen[22] and the like in their studies of "American literature and culture." In other words, the academicization of the Agrarian resistance—and, indeed, of its various analogues—there are always partial exceptions like Edmund Wilson, Blackmur, and Van Wyck Brooks—creates a corporate set of relations among intellectuals that increases their ideological production. It serves both to create and disperse sets of representations about "America" to give the U.S. identity and legitimacy and it inscribes the U.S. within the cosmopolitan network of cultural relations appropriate for an expanding imperial power.

In many ways, the academicized Agrarians and their heirs are like the cosmopolitan Catholic intellectuals Gramsci describes in Italy, always conceiving themselves as part of "world-wide" discussions, transcending the narrow national interests of the local; yet, as we well know from critics like Wilson and writers like William Carlos Williams, U.S. critics never completely escaped into cosmopolitanism because the problem of the national identity has never been settled and, furthermore, because the very imperial prominence of the United States in the world order has made all things "American" peculiarly central. Of course, few of the New Critics ever attempted to think through the problem of the United States in the world system of things, although R. P. Blackmur's writings on the Middle East in the 1950s and Edmund Wilson's narrower concerns with Israel are partial and variable exceptions to the rule. It is as if colonialism never existed and wars of national liberation were trifling matters of no concern.

In short, then, "passive revolution" gets us at the sequence of structural events which invents the powerful academic critic—less entangled with extra academic institutions than the "man of letters" ever was—and creates the unique set of paradoxes that U.S. critics still live with: it is possible, even if not easy, to be politically "hypercritical" of the state, to reveal many of its effects and extensions, and even to modify, to some extent, state relations with academia, and yet belong squarely to the hegemony that one aims to critique, resist, or subvert. This anomalous position generates an all-too-common stoic sense that one does what one can—even if this means no more than "preserving one's own integrity," at the very point where such desires seem to become nonsense before the fact.

IV

The various structural and political complexities I have been discussing, largely derived from Gramsci, leave their traces in the narrative writings as well as criticism of the Agrarians. Their historical narratives are particularly interesting in this context because they both catch the Agrarians at the height of their struggle—when nonetheless the problems with their position are clear—and because they contain their most naive intellectual self-representations. The two most interesting texts in this regard belong to another time: Warren's *All the King's Men,* which is the pathetic elegy of Agrarian aspirations, and Donald Davidson's two volumes on the Tennessee River, which is the transformation of Agrarian politics into nostalgia and anecdotal folklore.

V

The Agrarians felt that their culture and history were the victims of Northern industrial imperialism. More precisely, and following the revisionist history written by Frank Owsley and his students, they felt that after reconstruction their history had been rewritten so as to affiliate it to the national myths of a victorious North which in turn disseminated its own regional, that is, Eastern myths, as myths of national origin. Having become dependent upon these nationalizing myths, the South had begun to lose all sense of its own history and had created no narratives of its own to compete with the established versions of the Southern past.

To reclaim the cultural identity lost in the years after reconstruction, the Agrarians set out to rewrite Southern history, focusing on the antebellum and Civil War periods. They hoped both to refocus the image of Southern society and to combat the political effects of Northern, that is, national representations of the previous century's competing ideologies and civilizations. To this end, the literary Agrarians set out to retell the lives of figures central to the Civil War. Allen Tate wrote *Stonewall Jackson* and *Jefferson Davis*[23] and Robert Penn Warren, *John Brown*.[24] In addition, Tate planned but could not complete a book on Robert E. Lee.

As a gesture of oppressed peoples, the will to narrate, as Edward W. Said calls it, is a form of cultural preservation, part of the struggle for identity, an act of resistance to the empowered other's definition of the self, and an element in the struggle to enter the archive of historical record. The Agrarians set out to resist the efforts of the victorious North to colonize their minds the way their economy had been enslaved. In *I'll Take My Stand*, Frank Owsley, the doyen of Southern revisionist historians put the issue clearly:

> After the South had been conquered by war and humiliated and impoverished by peace, there appeared still to remain something which made the South different—something intangible, incomprehensible, in the realm of the spirit. That too must be invaded and destroyed; so there commenced a second war of conquest, the conquest of the Southern mind, calculated to remake every Southern opinion, to impose the Northern way of life and thought upon the South, write "error" across the pages of Southern history which were out of keeping with the Northern legend, and set the rising and unborn generations upon stools of everlasting repentance. Francis Wayland, former president of Brown University, regarded the South as "the new missionary ground for the national schoolteacher," and President Hill of Harvard looked forward to the task for the North "of spreading knowledge and culture over the regions that sat in darkness." The older generations, the hardened campaigners under Lee and Jackson, were too tough-minded to reeducate. They must be ignored. The North "treat them as

Western farmers do the stumps in their clearings, work around them and let them rot out," but the rising and future generations were to receive the proper education in Northern tradition.[25]

Indeed, Owsley notes that this reeducation program had been accompanied by a similar campaign to represent the South as unjust and barbaric both nationally and internationally. He realized that, as a result, effective resistance involved more than "correcting" the scholarly record. After all the revisionist history has been written, he writes, "mass opinion, prejudice, and smugness have not been touched."[26]

For the Agrarians, then, Northern imperialism has successfully established a network of opinion and belief which dominates all discourse about the South. The Agrarian's resistance to the dominant discourse took many forms: Brooks's and Warren's textbook series which emphasized the quality of Southern writing of a nonlocal color variety; the *Southern Review*, itself, in its commitment to publishing Southern writing that could stand aesthetic comparison with the world's best literature; revisionist history; histories of locales and regions, best represented by Donald Davidson's monumental two volume, *The Tennessee*,[27] folk-type literature on regional themes, for example, Warren's "The Ballad of Big Billy"; and the narrative representation of the everyday texture of Southern life and ideology in the form of biographical histories of the South and its figures. In addition, Warren set out to set the record straight on the "heroism" of John Brown, and by contrast represented the structure of values which the South stood for at its best.

The three main narratives of this last group, the books on John Brown, Jefferson Davis, and Stonewall Jackson, exemplify the Agrarian tactic of getting on the record those aspects of Southern life and ideology which the dominant discourse excluded or wrongly interpreted. They share a basic tactic: they set out to "naturalize" the Southern agrarian slave system by aligning it with traditional European life forms. Their aim is to discredit the colonizing representation of the South as an unnaturally organized civilization associated with brutal repression, darkest evil, and cultural underdevelopment. Tate's first contribution to this project is to discover a specifically Southern hero, Stonewall Jackson, who cannot be made into an avatar of American, national virtue, as Lee has been made into the glorious representative of America at arms. His second effort is to find a nearly tragic figure, Jefferson Davis, whose weaknesses can be made to account for Southern defeat and can themselves be accounted for as traces of the already present infection of Northern civilization in the antebellum and Civil War South. Warren's representation of Brown demystifies the colonizers heroic myth and discredits the virtuous abolitionist movement at the heart of national discourse condemning the South to second-class status as an inferior "other."

There are profound contrasts between the work of Tate and Warren in this common project. Above all these center around matters of will and prophetic vision, of religion and the knowability of truth. Warren is profoundly suspicious of the willful truth-knower, of the Brown-like visionary whose imperious will enacts itself at the expense of all others claiming its privileged knowledge of providence as justification. Tate, by contrast, glories in the prophetic visionary possibilities of Jackson and Lee while he mulls the civic disasters that befall the South when less than iron will drives generals and statesmen toward what they would (correctly) know to be the truth. Warren can create Jack Burden to worry the possibility of knowing or discovering truth, especially at the cost of others; Tate can write to John Peale Bishop that "For some reason I never doubt that I know what the truth is; I doubt my capacity to state it."

These contrasts suggest some of the contradictions and conflicts at the heart of the Agrarian movement. Indeed, they reflect two different responses to the experience of colonization that motivate Owsley and the others to these projects. On the one hand, there is the struggle to employ the weapons of the colonizer against himself, to exercise will and vision to establish an alternative, a competing representation politically more amenable to the virtues and needs of the oppressed; on the other hand, there is the drawing of the moral that the oppressed must not become like the oppressor, that struggling with the same means furthers the dialectics of oppression rather than weakening them. We might speculate that the reason Tate never could complete the book on Lee was that Lee moved Tate too close to Warren's position—distrusting political action for limited goals based on private visions of what is correct and necessary.

All three of these narratives sound the typical Agrarian themes: they all insist on the determining influence of locale on personality, of the contrast between frontier and settlement, of the constitutional stability of a Southern civilization based on a personal morality of responsibility and practicality. They insist that the South represents the last bastion of resistance to industrialism, to what would be called after the Civil War, "Americanism," and what they often rightly called "imperialism." In many ways, Tate's book on Stonewall Jackson is the most interesting of these three narratives. In it we see not only the political program of the Agrarians, but some of the close ideological connections between the values they located in Southern civilization and its heroes and modern poetry and its tradition. It is also the text which most clearly shows the potential conflict within Agrarianism, what I am calling here Warren's distrust of the visionary will.

The story Tate tells about Jackson is a simple one: the highly intelligent orphan son of a frontier family whose fortunes fluctuate wildly, he manages despite all obstacles to attend West Point where his intelligent hard work earns him grudging respect despite his social awkwardness. He marries, develops his great religious sensitivity, fights in Mexico to some small glory, retires to run a military academy, and, following his own lights, rises to glory in the war, saving the South on occasion, and never earning his due: command of an entire army. He dies pathetically and the South, particularly Lee, never recovers from the loss.

Strung along this narrative are a series of powerful ideological representations of matters central to the Agrarian attempt to resist the colonization of their culture seemingly central to their acceptance within the national hegemony. For example, Tate insists that the South was always constitutionalist in its relationship with the North. The point of this argument is both to acquire the force of law for the South in the conflict over legitimacy—his irony is meant to make the victors into rebels so that foundational authority will remain with the South—and to discredit all but what we might call "strict constructionist" methods of interpretation:

> The Northern revolutionists chose to interpret the Constitution through some mystical sense that had no exact correspondence with the letter of that document. "The spirit" (because it is irresponsible) "killeth; the letter giveth life." They interpreted it by abstract right. The South interpreted it historically, literally. This interpretation guaranteed the South a continuation of its historical rights. . . . Secession was not revolution; it was constitutionalism. (SJ, 60)

Surprising as it may seem to find a New Critic insisting upon historical interpretations of texts which might seem to recover its literal intention, Tate commits himself throughout the text to a theory of interpretation and understanding that rests upon something like a correspondence theory of truth. Interpretations, whether literally those of texts or more complexly visionary understandings of qualities disposed in the world, are valid to the extent that they are homologous with their objects. As a result, there is a continuum between Jackson's superhuman visionary comprehension of war's complexity and the correct, Calhounian interpretation of the Constitution. The correct correspondence assures both military victory and moral and political legitimacy. The Southern constitutional tradition upheld a legally, morally, and politically legitimate society; Jackson's spontaneous apprehension of the order of battle made him all but invincible. Above all, both had the will to act upon their correct understandings, unlike, by contrast, General Lee who would neither destroy the Union armies nor become dictator to save his people; and Jefferson Davis, who neither saw the truth nor could act upon it when it was offered to him.

What accounts for the proper balance of vision and will in a figure like Jackson? What accounts for its absence from Davis and so assures the failure of the confederacy? Tate's stories are essentially genetic, recounting the relative strengths and weaknesses of frontier virtue and theoretical impracticality. Will dominates Jackson and Davis: for the former it is shaped by religion and a visionary imagination that provides it with an exact object upon which to act; for the latter it is distorted by an inflexible, doctrinaire intelligence neurotically committed to an abstract understanding of the state and politics and so without any fit object upon which to act. In a sense, and in terms more familiar to literary critics after Eliot, Tate tells us that Davis is a divided sensibility whose imagination cannot, therefore, have an objective correlative. As a result, and its consequences are political and military disaster, all that Davis's will can do is externalize his own subjectivity. Jackson by contrast is a true poet whose ambitions and imagination find an object their equivalent and result in the pure disinterestedness of his actions.

This reading of Tate's *Stonewall Jackson* suggests how these narratives were meant politically to compete for the South's consciousness. Tate would restore the aesthetic critical intellectual to a position of leadership within the South by assigning its strengths to virtues far from the technical, abstract civilization offered by an imperial Northern hegemony in the form of its technocratic intellectuals and colonizing education. As I have already suggested, key to understanding the Agrarians's struggles to revise history and reestablish the virtues of antebellum "aesthetic life" is the challenge posed by the extended state to the leading role of the traditional intellectual. The tragedy Warren has Jack Burden narrate about Adam Stanton's loss of place in the new order of Willie Stark represents the displacement of traditional classically educated Southern intellectuals from the positions occupied not just by the likes of Lee and Calhoun but by all the lesser figures—school teachers, ministers, lawyers, all educated men, as Tate has it—in the antebellum South. The tragedy of Southern defeat is the failure to replace Davis with a figure like Jackson or even Lee. In sum, this reading of *Stonewall Jackson* suggests that the Agrarians were competing ideologically to reacquire the leading role of traditional Southern intellectuals that had been eliminated by, above all, the pervasive extension of the state into Agrarian civilization.

As Tate represents Jackson, he was from youth a person marked by the will to knowledge: "Tom was religious in a way that probably kept people from seeing that he was. He certainly has no feeling for orthodoxy. . . . He must have been driven, from the time of his mother's death, to wonder, without knowing what he was doing, at the source of all power and influence" (SJ, 10). As Tate sees it, the peculiar social order of the South encouraged Jackson to develop this will to knowledge; left an orphan without property he had no identity; "Without possessions a man did not morally exist. . . . A man's property was his character." Tate develops the point by contrast with the New England or national ideology; in the South, a man had no "inner life." Without property, he had to find a substitute and education was one of the few acceptable ones, but, Tate writes, "not learning for itself but as a means. For learning has never been respectable in itself" (SJ, 12). Significantly, however, Tate casts Jackson's social obligation to define himself by education in terms once more of the will: "The will to property may require only a submissiveness to that symbol of order which is the local church. But the will to power sometimes becomes the will to God" (10).

The logic of Tate's position requires that the issue be developed in these terms. Discrediting the national or imperial myths requires that he yoke the will to power with New England, which metonymically represents the Eastern capitalist hegemony; while the more civilized will to knowledge or property be linked with the South. John Brown epitomizes the disastrous consequences of extending the will to power to godhead: "God had told him . . . it was a right to murder." New Englanders who had toured Europe and returned with the latest of fashionable ideas, "saw nothing irregular in the antics of a homicidal maniac" (57). Tate opens up the line taken by Warren in his text; the modernizing North having lost all morals in the process of adapting self to empire and adopting the private ideology of "the inner life" could justify all barbarisms for the sake of its expansion. It was a morally and politically bankrupt civilization.

Private property alone gave a man existence. This liberal tenet lies at the root of Agrarianism's distrust of the extended state. The will to property and its defense becomes the will to civilization; but, as I suggested in my reading of Ransom's "What Does the South Want?," it is a small-held property that exists outside a money economy, and not incorporated property, that alone provides this sense of self. Northerners and moderns cannot, according to Tate, understand the idea of non-money property; the vast extent of the old Virginia plantations, for example, "conceived as fixed productive property rather than as negotiable wealth, brings no image whatever to the modern urban mind which thinks, not in space but in time; for Time is Money" (17).

Jackson's will was then perfectly trained for the job at hand; his personal aspiration was this will to property sublimated, we might say, into the will to knowledge. His genius lay in the discipline he had acquired through long years of study habits adopted in the pursuit of his own knowledge; he could disinterestedly hold suspended in his mind enormously complex conjunctions and simply forget himself in the task of arranging and understanding the order of truth presented to him. This genius was perfectly suited to the military man needed to defend the very civilization which had made him in its own interest. In its defense, he was ruthlessly logical as well as brilliant. Unchecked by Lee he would have butchered the Union armies in the name of completing the order he perceived.

Until the war, Jackson resembles no one more than Hart Crane as that poet appears in Tate's criticism. In 1926, in the "Introduction to 'White Buildings' by Hart Crane," Tate had discovered "the leading contemporary problem" of poetry: the difficulty of finding a theme correlative to poetic vision. Crane's great achievement, for Tate, consists precisely in having realized "even partially, at the present time, the maximum of poetic energy." No great poetry will be possible, according to Tate, "Until vision and subject completely fuse. . . . The comprehensiveness and lucidity of any poetry are in direct proportion to the availability of a comprehensive and perfectly articulated given theme."[28] As a consequence of not having found his theme, Crane's poetry is "sometimes obscure . . . the vision often strains and overreaches the theme."[29] Crane has imaginative vision with no objective correlative able to sustain it; the victim of modernization, Crane, unlike Dante, must not only absorb the past, he must first discover and reorder it.

Jackson, by contrast, was not a modernized man: his will had had an appropriate because public task within an established civilization that did not yet question its appropriateness. Without property he set out to make a name for himself through education—and he did, in Mexico, and so earned the position in his academy. But his too was only a stop along the way to the disinterested self-fulfillment Tate tells us awaits the genius within traditional society. Tate develops a contrast between Jackson, Davis, and Lee in terms of the visionary qualities of their imaginations and the political consequences which followed upon them. Nothing less is at stake in this contrast, as they see it, but the fate of civilizations.

The first salient point about Jackson, as we shall see, sets up the crucial contrast between Tate and Warren. For Jackson, we are told, "the exercise of character for its own sake, becomes the unconscious aim. . . . It is the paradox of the great," Tate continues, "that the most ambitious are the most disinterested" (33). This last quality aligns Jackson, in Tate's view, with the great poets of traditional societies:

> I suppose the thin and sensational quality of much contemporary literature, European as well as American, is due to the general collapse of all bases of judgement, the disintegration of the old exclusive and self-contained societies. It is pretty obvious that the more intensely local literature was in that sense the more impersonal and universal it became.[30]

Above all, for Tate, disinterested impersonality assures the universality of action, thought, and vision. The Southern hero, like the traditional Southern intellectual who is to lead the region to its new existence within the American hegemony, earns his authority by virtue of his transcendent affiliation with other intellectual heroes who, throughout history, have created and sustained the best of traditional civilizations.

What we see enfigured in Tate's image of Jackson and the poet of "thick" literature is the conventional claim by the traditional intellectual to transcend class and other biases, to have access to "truth" embodied commonly within a heritage modern society is in danger of losing. In other words, for Tate, who claims to know the truth, the figure of Jackson functions not only as a Southern hero whose qualities testify to the superiority of Southern agrarian civilization, but also as an avatar of the kind of cultural and visionary leadership the traditional literary intellectual, free of any interested ambitions or desires, might provide to a South regenerate in its old life-style.[31] Jackson enacts Tate's image of himself: Tate knows the truth, but cannot say it; that is, no matter how successfully he expresses his knowledge, no matter how nearly complete his work as poet and critic, he, himself, as "character" would always be somewhere beyond the legacy he can create and leave behind. The poet-critic, in himself, as character, is the fulfillment of an ineffable truth that traditional societies can value and ritualize. Similarly, Jackson, Tate tells us, always "would be superior to the fullest achievement of his ambition" (63).

The poet-soldier is present as the hero of full truth whose existence defends and spiritualizes a civilization. He is marked by an awesome visionary power of synthetic understanding and by the successful deployment of visionary order upon the external world. From the full but disinterested self, will imposes vision upon the world. Jackson, Tate tells us repeatedly, turned into himself where he meditated with great concentration upon whatever order he could infer from the chaos of war about him: "He developed great power in the holding of complex, interrelated quantities before his mind" (52). Jackson saved the Southern armies by his "grasp of relations existing at every moment among the complicated forces of the battle" (91). This power, typical Tate tells us, of all great strategists develops throughout Jackson's career until it reaches nearly preternatural levels. His "visual imagination" was so developed that finally, Tate writes:

> The host of his enemies he held in the hollow of his hand. Every movement they made he visualized: the whole theatre of war stood immediately present, at every moment of concentration, in his mind. He played against his enemies as if they were pawns in a game of chess. But there was a difference: the pawns of war had will and feeling. From the conduct of a hostile cavalry regiment,

thirty miles from the main army, he could infer the Federal general's plans and state of mind." (281)

Jackson's talents had found an object absolutely correlative to their
nature. But the effect is grander even than the possibility of victory for it
involves the aesthetic fulfillment of vision, itself. Jackson, Tate tells us,
"had seized upon an idea that went beyond the marching of men to a
battlefield." His comprehensive vision imagined nothing less than the
destruction of the Union as a whole. And, we are told, readers of
Stonewall Jackson must turn their attention to "the unfolding of Jackson's
idea upon the hills and roads" of Virginia (113). Jackson, in other words,
possessed the directed will to enact and unfold his unique vision, one
shared we must recall by neither Lee nor Davis, upon the lives of
others. As a charismatic leader of awesome talent, he drove his armies
to the fulfillment of his projects.

Jackson possesses a talent not unlike that Tate finds in Faulkner. He is
capable of visionary projection. For Tate, Faulkner's greatness always
lay in large part in his mythical use of Southern history, indeed, in his
creation of the Southern myth. Significantly, Tate describes Faulkner in
terms which suggest how near in kind are his talents and Jackson's. For
what is the act of mythic creation? "By myth I mean," Tate writes
apropos of Faulkner, "a dramatic projection of heroic action, or the
tragic failure of a heroic action, upon the reality of the common life of a
society, so that the myth is reality."[32] Of course, we see readily that Tate
attempts just such a projection upon Southern civilization in his narratives of Jackson and Davis. But more important, we must see that it
follows from this that Jackson represents the desire and project of Tate
and much of Agrarianism: to project a myth, an order of action and
value upon a society so that it will be that society's reality. In other
words, as Jackson would deploy his forces upon the hills of Virginia to
lead his civilization to the fulfillment which his disinterested character
envisions, so Tate and the other Agrarians are aspiring for a leadership
role for the traditional literary intellectual, precisely in continuing conflict with the North. Tate's great general is the perfect military figure for
the battle the Agrarians wage against both the colonizer from the North
and the already colonized consciousness of the South which denies
these intellectuals the traditional leadership role which their caste
consciousness tells them should be theirs.

In other words, Tate's narrative of Stonewall Jackson represents the entire range of the Agrarians's understanding of the conflict between the colonized South and the imperial North. In Jackson's visionary will, Tate finds the perfect image of those virtues of an aesthetically based agrarian society which make it superior precisely to the materially and technically more powerful forces of empire. Moreover, Jackson's virtues, we can see by reference to some of Tate's other writings, are those of both the great poet and the traditional Southern intellectual—both of whom have lost their prophetic and directing role in a society effectively at ease with the compromises the imperial North offers through the operations of the national extended state. Not surprisingly, then, at first the traditional intellectuals organic to past social formations are alienated from the new state order; they resist it as an encroachment on the older civilization in which they and their values had a function. To criticize the Agrarians for being conservative or reactionary critics of late capital and its extended state is to fail to understand the historical significance of their struggle not just for the South but for all humanistic intellectuals in this country in this century. The extended state system has historically forced humanistic or literary intellectuals, perhaps even all "traditional" intellectuals into oppositional rhetorics and ideologies. Significantly, however, it never allows them to escape into true opposition, but manages almost always to affiliate them to state institutions wherein their oppositional practices can be carried out. I am not suggesting that leading intellectuals are merely coopted, as Gerald Graff, for instance seems to think I am saying. Such an idea misunderstands the notion of hegemony. Within the institutions which affiliate the intellectuals to the extended state, actual oppositional work can be carried out to a degree: the core powers do indeed compromise with the intellectuals allowing them certain resources and rewards in practical exchange for accepting the core's direction of the hegemony as a whole. Gramsci's notion of "passive revolution," as I suggested above, lets us see that this is precisely the way in which the imperial capitalist forces preserve themselves: by compromise which aligns, often in a relationship of tension, various social groups to the directing group.

In brief, one can trace how the Agrarian resistance to the terms offered by the core to the marginal South transformed itself into the literary critical institutions which largely replaced the historical and philological study of language. One must also remember, however, that although this compromise which affiliated the critics to the state revolutionized the literary academy, it resulted in an essentially conservative structure. Of course this had to be the case. Not only must that structure be fundamentally conservative to be affiliated to the state of which it is an integral part—integral to winning the consent of the governed— but it had to accommodate, at least ideologically, the interests of those with whom it was compromising. In effect, those who had adopted a reactionary position from which to launch their attack on the compromise being offered to the traditional aesthetic intellectuals and their institutions—literature, criticism, the "aesthetic life"—were provided with other institutions, mostly academic, within which their desires and values, born of a past social order, could be usefully satisfied. Critique of the extended state was thus inscribed within its institutions. Effectively, the state could legitimate itself by declaring its own tolerance and liberality and so fundamentally obscure the difference between the aesthetic "criticism" done in the academy and any real critique of the hegemony which might reveal its actual operations or challenge its totalizing legitimacy. Having created a "discourse of opposition" within its fundamental institutions, the state was relatively secure from attack by those intellectuals whom it had displaced into its own superstructures.

7

......

The Rationality
of Disciplines:
The Abstract
Understanding of
Stephen Toulmin

Stephen Toulmin's *Human Understanding*[1] is roughly contemporary with the beginning of Michel Foucault's explicit preoccupation with disciplines and power.[2] Yet the differences between Toulmin and Foucault are so great that a limited comparison of their approaches to examining the relationship of the past to the present, especially in terms of disciplinary institutions and discourses, points up the main distinction between the legitimating activity of Toulmin's evolutionary model of history and philosophy of science, and Foucault's genealogical critique of post-Enlightenment forms of reason.

As Toulmin sees it, his task is to account for the advances reason makes in solving the problems that human needs discover in our (often technologically) modified environment. He aims to redefine reason, to free disciplinary knowledge from the traditional need to be logically systematic, and to correct philosophy's repeated error of identifying reason with logic (understood as a system of internal self-consistency). (I will return to the problematics of error in a discussion of Georges Canguilhem.) Toulmin's disciplinary project is quite clear: to reconstruct history and the philosophy of science as a general model of collective understanding, as an account of disciplinary rationality which would make it immune to critique by either, as he puts it, the followers of Plato, such as Bertrand Russell and Gottlob Frege, or the "radical relativisers," such as R. G. Collingwood and Paul Feyerabend.

Toulmin insists that Philosophers[3] must find a way around the consequences of these two positions, because both threaten the truth-producing abilities of science and its legitimacy. In other words, for

Toulmin the problem is that science and the practical activity of scientists do not and cannot conform to the rationalist model of the Platonists; yet, science cannot be as anarchic as Feyerabend suggests and must be saved from charges of relativism to ensure the social efficacy and truth-value of disciplinary knowledge. The effect of Toulmin's project, however, extends beyond these two specific objectives and results in a general theory aimed at legitimizing and universalizing the social role of instrumental reason. Max Horkheimer, in the foreword to a late selection of his essays, *Critique of Instrumental Reason*, offers brief remarks on how this notion should be understood:

> Today . . . it is the . . . essential work of reason to find means for the goals one adopts at any given time. And it is considered superstitious to think that goals once achieved are not in turn to become means to some new goals. . . . When stripped of its theological garb, "Be reasonable" means: "Observe the rules, without which neither the individual nor society as a whole can survive; do not think only of the present moment."[4]

Horkheimer's critique bears on Toulmin's project. Although Toulmin claims a revolutionary potential for his conception of reason as practical,[5] ecological problem-solving (in contrast to the normal philosophical equation of reason with logical systematicity), the ideological effect of his scheme is to justify scientific and nonscientific discourses and disciplines without considering their position within the complex of affiliated social relations that make up and support the production of knowledge and value in postmodern societies. Toulmin seems to want to escape the dilemma he thinks follows from Locke's concept of reason; he hopes to show that disciplinary and professional structures ensure that the ends of reason are for human benefit, if not in every case, then in their institutionalized completion.

But Horkheimer, along with Theodor Adorno and many others, has struggled to drive home the historical implications of Locke's thought, that is, the concept of reason in a capitalist, instrumentalist society:

> The definition of reason in terms of individual self-preservation apparently contradicts Locke's prototypical definition, according to which reason designates the direction of intellectual activity regardless of its intellectual goal. But Locke's definition still holds true. It does not liberate reason from the atomic self-interest of the

individual. It rather defines procedures which more readily suit whatever goal self-interest may require.[6]

I submit that the ideological weight of Toulmin's project is to depoliticize thinking about reason and knowledge by detaching them from the sphere of self-interest, so that the entire cultural structure in which self-interest is inscribed can, in turn, be naturalized. In effect, Toulmin's writings exemplify how the Philosophy of Science is the high intellectual discourse of political obscurantism; it becomes, as Toulmin would put it, the only discourse that can speak unerringly of how complex matters are: it alone can address a "professionalized," state-funded audience of scientists and other professionals to explain how and why things must work as they do. As I shall try to show, Toulmin's populational and neo-evolutionary theories obscure the political functions of what he calls "irrational self-interest" in institutionalized, professional disciplines and their regulative discourses. In other words, it is the ineluctable and unavoidable linkage of error and truth in reason which *Human Understanding* tries to deny.

Although Toulmin's talk of knowledge as human activity recalls certain moments in Marxist theory and seems to correct more dominant modes of abstract or idealist History and the Philosophy of Science, his own sense of reason is very abstract, without content, formalist, and ahistorical. Moreover, despite the attention he gives to such professional institutions as journals, organizations, promotions, and grants, he provides little analysis of the specific place of particular professions and disciplines within the concrete and specifiable structures and functions of social material organization. In other words, he treats these professional social structures in a vacuum, as if they had internal rules and existed unaffected by any other aspects of the larger culture. His treatment of the various practices within the concept of self-interest is, as a result, undertheorized and undercontextualized; its lack of reflexiveness is common among high-powered technical academics in a society that is ideologically committed, as Toulmin himself argues, to technological or practical forms of rationalism.

Toulmin's adaptation of Darwin is ideologically and culturally bound by his own place within this technologized academic culture.[7] This is clear if we contrast *Human Understanding* with Canguilhem's *On the Normal and the Pathological*, which works out a powerful Darwinian model for the Philosophy of Science. This model influenced Foucault in his development of Nietzsche's genealogical method for investigating the cultural role of reason in modernity.[8]

The issues that Toulmin addresses are, in many ways, the essential ones for a study of intellectual disciplines: institutional authority, the transmission of authority within disciplines, the response of reason to social problems, the effects of professionalization upon intellectual disciplines, and so on. His fundamental response to these complex matters is the populational model of disciplinary reason evoked by a reading of Darwin.[9] As Toulmin sees it, the importance of this model lies not only in its revision of Platonic and Kantian models of logical systematicity, but also in its applicability to social as well as intellectual change. At points the populational model seems to converge with Foucault's interest in historical discontinuities. For example, Toulmin claims that "an entire science comprises an 'historical population' of logically independent concepts and theories, each with its own separate history, structure, and implications" (HU, 130). This recalls Foucault's notions of the episteme and discourse. But although this line of thinking corrects concepts of science which insist upon total logical systematicity and so total conceptual interdependence, in its insistence upon the discrete histories of various concepts and theories—unlike Foucault's notions—it effectively isolates these from each other, from other discourses, and from non-discursive social practices. Toulmin's correction results in atomistic, empirical history in which one can only study the evolution of particular concepts as individual responses to socially or naturally given contexts.

Foucault learned from Canguilhem that just this sort of history of science was neither necessary nor needed:

> If I have wanted to apply an identical method to discourses completely different from legendary and mythical narratives, it is undoubtedly because the idea came to me from the works of the historians of science that were open before me, especially those of M. Canguilhem. I owe him my understanding that the history of science is not tightly caught in this alternative: on the one hand, to chronicle discoveries or, on the other, to describe the ideas and opinions that border science either from the side of its indecisive origins or from the side of its external consequences [my translation; original is *retombées extérieures*]. But rather that one could—that one should—do the philosophy of science as an ensemble of

theoretical models and conceptual instruments that is at one and the same time coherent and transformable.[10]

The contrast with Foucault on this point lets us see some of the contradictions that reduce Toulmin's position to absurdity: although the very idea of a populational model implies a family resemblance that contradicts such isolated discussion of conceptual developments; and although Toulmin discusses how the ripeness of a problem often determines the direction of research (and not the money allocated for political and military purposes, such as "Star Wars"), his own analyses suggest that the proper mode of disciplinary study need not examine the way in which one concept or discourse comes to mean, to have authority. How problems come to be ripe and solvable in certain ways—these questions are not theorized. Toulmin gives no thought, for example, to how the inscription of a problem within an entire network of institutions and practices (many of them explicitly elements of the extended state which produce and sustain its knowledge and norms) might effect or modify practice within a discipline.

The populational model unduly restricts the politically motivated genealogist of the modern and postmodern "regime(s) of truth" in two ways. First, it prevents the critique of reason in its complicity with dehumanization, especially when enfigured as a commodity fetishism. (This complicity I call "error"—what Toulmin assumes shall be corrected and eliminated by rational practice.) Second, this model itself reifies the various disciplines and in the process blocks theorizing the estranged relationship between disciplines and their practitioners. A full critique of the limits of Toulmin's model, and hence of a great deal of neohumanist rhetoric that relies on post-Wittgensteinian models of Anglo-American ethics and the Philosophy of Science, would require at least two lines of thought: first, an application of the basic terms of the Frankfurt School to display the irrationality, reification, and authoritarianism implicit in these self-confident procedures; and second, a consideration of Toulmin's normalizing of values, practices, and discursive institutions within the context of the post-Nietzschean work carried out by Gaston Bachelard, Canguilhem, and Foucault. Furthermore, since intellectuals concerned with this entire set of issues have noticed the value of bringing Antonio Gramsci to bear, with Foucault, on a critique of intellectual practice, the full analysis I envision would also require a study of science in relation to the extended state within the terms of hegemony Gramsci has elaborated. But before this could be done, a theory of the relationship between Gramsci's fundamental analysis of the constitutive and oppositional roles played by intellectuals vis-à-vis hegemony and Foucault's analysis of the regime of truth would have to be formulated.

For Toulmin, the paradigm case of the rationally continuous development of a discipline is the displacement of the authority of mechanics by quantum physics. His discussion of this example is important because it illustrates the problems of his commitment to a common-law model as a means of understanding changes in the fundamental assumptions and practices of a discipline. Toulmin's summary of this example must be quoted at length:

> Our own task, here, is to make the implications of this switch from "codified" to "common-law" argument absolutely explicit. Before it, the argument over quantum mechanics had run into barren cross-purposes, just because both parties still assumed that some formal procedure or pattern of argument could be found, on whose authority they could jointly agree. (Given this, they could simply have agreed to "calculate" and accept the result.) After the switch, they no longer appealed to formal arguments since, as they now saw, there were no longer any formal arguments carrying conviction to both parties. Now, all the solid arguments were informal, consequential ones: designed, not to invoke or apply particular calculative procedures, but rather to come to terms with their strengths and weaknesses, their range and limitations. This meant appealing to considerations of an essentially historical kind: using the theoretical experiences of earlier physicists as a precedent, in estimating the most promising lines for future theoretical development. By this switch from formal (or codified) to historical (or common-law) arguments, the true character of the issues in debate was brought out into the open. The question now became at just what point it was legitimate to challenge claims to sovereign intellectual authority on behalf of existing standards of scientific judgment, and to begin looking for a Young Pretender to take over the throne. Such a question must certainly be resolved in a rational manner; but that could be done only by setting aside the formal demands of all theoretical principles, and treating the matter in broader, disciplinary terms. (HU, 238–39)

Although in this example we see both the strengths and weaknesses of Toulmin's method, his strengths are finally rather banal. He usefully reminds us that the history of disciplines is the history of changing guards and that guards change in accord with shifts in ruling paradigms. But despite this reminder, Toulmin tells us little more than Thomas Kuhn does. Toulmin would claim that by employing the populational and common-law models he is better able than Kuhn to account for changes within and from one paradigm to another. He feels he has discovered a model that describes the shift as a rational appeal to precedent and to the persistent ideals of a changing discipline. Common law, in other words, exemplifies the appeal to precedent and shared ideals which he feels not only regulates a discipline but ensures its legitimacy. Just as in common law, a judge "reanalyses the social functions of the law in its application to some novel historical situation" (HU, 239), so the physicist when confronted by novelty must reconsider the accepted authority of sovereign rules and procedures to determine the best direction in which physics should develop.

Toulmin's argument by analogy is just as unsatisfactory because it has the appeal of common sense. We need only recall Gramsci's warning that common sense is fragmented folklore, that is, ideology, to be wary of the attractions an English-speaking audience might find in Toulmin's work.[11]

The fetish character of intellectual disciplines in Toulmin is perhaps clearest in the way he asserts their self-regulating functions. At once this notion recalls Max Weber's theory of rationalization and Georg Lukács's counterpointed idea of reification. Toulmin's conception condenses the disciplines into merely formal regulations for producing knowledge which bracket the effects of other social relations on those regulations. Although Toulmin seems to propose a theory describing the practical interdependencies of persons and their discourses, his insistence on abstracting the ruling principles of organized attempts to produce knowledge into the rarefied model of common law and the instrumentality of practical reason results in a surpassing of human interactions by formalist procedures that, in turn, further displace considerations of the social into reified schemas that acquire independence and objective status. The common-law model has the opposite effect to what it seems meant to have: it closes off any consideration of the ideological component of these procedures.

At the strongest moments in the text, this model appears very attractive, offering a guarantee of commonsense practicality at the heart of an enlightened society able successfully to guard against incursions of the prophetic and irrational. The common-law model comforts Toulmin and his followers because they find in it instances of the success they desire: judges, for example, understand that they often come up against what Toulmin calls "rational frontiers" (HU, 241), that is, the points at which the established and up-to-that-moment efficacious rules generated and applied by tradition and the discipline of law are no longer applicable to the case at hand; judges must then decide on new directions for the law and their practice.

Toulmin concludes from this that when faced with novel situations, that is, when confronting possibilities for action in the present in light of their desires for the future, professionals steeped in the history of their discipline make the best informed and best intentioned judgments possible. Indeed, this is often just what does happen when individuals and their disciplines confront novel circumstances. Yet the problems with this attractive and humanistic commonsensical rationality appear on the surface of Toulmin's own rhetoric. In the following passage, Toulmin is speaking of the law but makes clear that the law is only the purest example of the process he has in mind, that is, it is the space in which the ideal comes to a certain amount of self-consciousness and so makes itself available for figuration and foregrounding:

> Pound and Holmes put their fingers, very precisely, on the point at which legal reasoning ceases to be a formal or tactical matter—of applying established rules and principles to new situations—and becomes concerned with strategic issues: the point (that is) at which the "just" way ahead can be determined, only by reappraising the fundamental purposes of the law in a new historical context. Over such strategic issues, they insisted, judicial decisions can no longer be treated clearly and definitively, as "right" or "correct"; yet such decisions are, in their own way, none the less rational for all that.[12]

Toulmin insists over and again that at these boundary lines, at these rational frontiers, when "strategic issues" arise in a discipline, the actions and decisions of humans are rational despite the failure or inapplicability of the established rules of the discipline to the problems created by the discipline's own crisis. In other words, for Toulmin, a discipline's efforts at revision and renewal are, in themselves, the highest examples of social rationality.

Toulmin, we should notice, has shifted rationality into the space of reappraisal and, with one stroke, legitimated all already established institutions intent on maintaining themselves and their social role through a process of reform and readjustment. Should a discipline continue? Should it alter entirely its organization? Can it do this from within, as it were? (It is worth noting that Toulmin pays no attention to the problematic of inside/outside in his discussion of the internal practices of disciplines.) Can it realign the complex relationships between disciplines and the largest of cultural and political organizations, for example, the state? Can it ever initiate relationships? Must it always only react to already given circumstances and changes? Can it even ask, let alone theorize answers to, these and other more fundamental questions?

Rather than approach any of these matters directly, that is, rather than offer a political analysis or justification for the expressly liberal ideology of his Philosophy, Toulmin falls back upon the populational model to ground his conclusions about the common-law model. But as if he implicitly understood the weakness of this form of argument, he often simply appeals to the essentiality of reason that is reflected in and guaranteed by the history of disciplines as rationally evolving practices. What this appeal to historical evidence amounts to, however, is nothing less than a confusion of categories as Toulmin transforms the rational into reason and vice versa.

It is not accidental that Toulmin wants to renew the Hegelian commitment to the rationality of reason (the title of his last chapter, "The Cunning of Reason," is borrowed from Hegel), "simply," as Toulmin suggests, stripped of its progressive and providentialist aspects.[13] In the process of this act of disciplinary renewal, that is, the "anti-metaphysicalizing" revision of Hegel, Toulmin is forced to abstract from human history a guarantee to rationality and inscribe it within the evolutionary, or revisionary, enterprises of professionalized disciplines—all despite his asserted belief in the social activity of human beings as the agency and subject of history. That is to say, Toulmin has an even less material and less adequate theory of human activity than does Hegel.

The effect of these contradictions, and especially of the inscription of the rational in disciplines, is an overly abstract and therefore self-legitimating conception of the disciplinary practices of modern social organization. Necessarily occluded in this doubling and self-revising model are the effects of interest and conflict (that is, error) located within disciplines as essential features of their survival and their roles within larger complexes of power and knowledge in modern societies dominated by extended states and the international order of capital. Put crudely the questions are these: Who determines the new just way? Who sets out the strategic problems? Who puts in place the new terms and how do they acquire the power and position to do so? Marx taught us the dangers of Hegel's abstractions. But Toulmin, like many of his colleagues, abstracts even from Hegel.

His account of human action at the frontiers of reason fails to theorize any form of ideology. He has not considered the notions of mystification and self-interest which can be found in Marx's *The German Ideology*, to say nothing about more complex formulations developed, for instance, by Louis Althusser and Gramsci. Toulmin's ideological and conceptual inability to consider the complexity of the factors that make up the decisions of intellectuals is a mark of both the disciplinary illiteracy of Philosophy in the United States and of the self-confirming representation of intellectuals which implicitly underlies his work. For who will read this text? Only those willing and able to accept affirmation of the rationality of the intellectual and the state institutions that they justify. Whatever interests professional intellectuals have, Toulmin narrowly circumscribes. In other words, he carries out a radical ascesis to maintain his theory:

> At such points, a Supreme Court Justice can no longer speak for the law as it is; instead, he must pass judgment in the light of a longer-term vision, both of what the law has been and is, and of what it should become. . . . Cases of this kind take us to the "rational frontier" at which fallible individuals, acting in the name of the human enterprise that they represent, have to deal with novel and unforeseen problems by opening up new possibilities; and, at this frontier, we can no longer separate the rational procedures of law from the judicial purposes of the men who are reshaping them, or from the historical situations in which these men find themselves. (HU, 240)

In the best construction that can be put on the matter, these intellectuals accept their responsibility to bet on the future, to risk being wrong despite their best-educated (here we deal with *Bildung*, not just professional training) judgments, and escape the risks of quietism and defeat. There are weak and strong objections to be made to this position. One could easily argue that representative intellectuals have no expertise that can guarantee the accuracy of their judgments or the priority of their values and decisions. But Toulmin already has an answer to this: rationality offers no such guarantees, only the best possible chance. In fact, such objections are uninteresting not only generally but also particularly because Toulmin has developed models to preempt any critique calling for either absolute standards of reason or any commitment to relativism.

But five stronger objections, I think, can be made: first, Toulmin ignores the role that ideology plays in the cultural sphere—general talk about historical situations won't do it; second, his atomistic genealogical evolutionary model ignores the importance nondiscursive contexts have upon the regulative development of any one institution or discourse; third, he rarely reflects on his own reasons for vaporizing individuals and their uniquely informed, rational decisions as the basis for the deeper rationality of disciplines—a rationality that must be thought of as social, especially given the legal and populational models; fourth, nowhere does Toulmin reflect on what I will call the underlying humanism that is the self-confirming condition for the possibility of his project; and fifth, nowhere does he consider that jurists act, even in the law, on the basis of more than their judicial purposes. Even insofar as they are judges, factors other than their position within the law, no matter how broadly this is taken (unless it is so broadly taken as to be absurd), modify, indeed constitute, their judicial purposes.

Human enterprises exist within larger contexts of economic and social life than Toulmin grants. Even highly professionalized individuals, acting as experts, occupy positions crossed by many social, intellectual, political, and cultural vectors. Toulmin, like those who make much of interpretive communities, undertheorizes the complexity of what used to be called "context." If we take the case of academic literary study, the issue becomes clearer: its emergence was not simply the result of decisions made by representative intellectuals; rather, at least in the United States, it must be seen within the context of larger discursive formations as they produced and altered the subject, imagination, and "aesthetic autonomy."[14] Of course, the academic study of literature is part of the general professionalization of middle-class life and social dominance.[15] It is also part of the rise of functionalism to

ideological prominence in the United States.[16] Furthermore, within
the disciplines themselves much more consideration must be given to
the effects that instrumentalism and self-interest have upon the revisionary decisions made by these intellectuals. Toulmin does admit (but
does not theorize) the fact that older generations, as he puts it, always
resist the changing of the guard, but that finally the disciplinary appeal
to reason, proof, expertise, and public argument guarantees the success
of the better ideas—even if not at the time of their first conception,
when, for a variety of reasons, their time might not be ripe.[17]

One can only conclude that Toulmin is a weak reader of Darwin. At
no point does he begin to think of the relationship between instrumental reason and self-interest, on the one hand, and what we might call
"self-preservation," on the other. But Toulmin is not only a weak reader
of Darwin; he is also a weak theorist of modernity, as a contrast with
Horkheimer and the Frankfurt School suggests. In modernity, Horkheimer argued, reason placed itself at the disposal of the powerful.[18]
Foucault revises this to say (and Adorno would agree in part) that
instrumentalized, disciplinary reason provides power and is one crucial site of power. Following Nietzsche, these critics of modernity
discover there the collectivization of the Lockean notion of reason as
the satisfier of self-interest. Horkheimer's material analysis leads him to
conclude in part that those who enjoy what he calls a "life of abun-
dance" are free to choose.[19] But, in effect, their freedom is hollow. This
is a point Adorno pursued in his critiques of mass culture.[20] More
important, however, is Horkheimer's demonstration that this ability to
choose is purely abstract, always conditioned by the need to survive as
a group (or class):

> For them [those who enjoy a life of abundance] it was possible to
> select among the so-called cultural goods, always provided that
> these goods were in harmony with their interests of dominion.
> This was the only pluralism of values that materialized. . . . The
> perpetuation of privileges was the only rational criterion which
> determined whether one should fight against or collude with
> other interests and groups. . . . The great historic decisions differed
> from one another in being farsighted or nearsighted, not in the
> nature of their ends.[21]

It is not necessary to recapitulate the Frankfurt School's complex
judgment on the totalitarianism of the Enlightenment to concede the

cogency of this remark about the bourgeois's self-interested consumption and production of cultural alternatives. The virtue of Horkheimer's analysis for our purposes is that it does not demarcate as rigidly as does Toulmin's practice distinct political, intellectual, and social spaces for cultural and disciplinary production. As a result, Horkheimer's comment seems apropos on at least two levels: Toulmin talks of his disciplinary analysis as an analogue for an analysis of all society— he operates as if we were still living in a classically liberal social order— especially in his discussion of the common law and the competition among ruling ideas (note: not ruling classes or groups) in a society; furthermore, even though Toulmin fails to consider or acknowledge it, the global operations of rationality in a culture inscribe all disciplines so these cannot, except arbitrarily and with great violence, be treated individually or internally, as it were. Without tracing the marks of this inscription across the institution and through the culture itself, any analysis must be reductive. Above all, this tracing must have a material component. Ideas do not come to the field of battle disembodied, unarticulated, and undisseminated. How they progress, why some do not, and how they take hold must be re-marked.

In effect, then, Toulmin reverses the necessary procedures for studying the role of reason in society. He postulates the rationality and verdicality of concepts and the institutionalized procedures that produce them by virtue of their pragmatic efficacy. He does not examine how these concepts become established within regulative structures of discourse, nor, more important, how these regulative structures themselves come to be except, implicitly, as the result of the rational activities within already given institutions and discourses. Furthermore, Toulmin's move reasserts the traditional intellectual's claim to superiority over others. Specifically, it transfers from sociology into Philosophy the classic abstract formulations of sociology of knowledge which first emerged in Karl Mannheim.[22]

In his trenchant critique of Mannheim's work, Adorno demonstrates that attention to the material foundations of reason and its modern forms of practice requires that the commonsensical model of rational efficacy be suspended and brought itself under examination:

The thesis of the primacy of being over consciousness [this is a reassertion of the thesis of *The German Ideology*] includes the methodological imperative to express the dynamic tendencies of reality in the formation and movement of concepts in accordance with the demand that they have pragmatic and expedient features. The sociology of knowledge has closed its eyes to this imperative. Its abstractions are arbitrary as long as they merely harmonize with an experience which proceeds by differentiating and correcting.[23]

Toulmin's common-law model attempts to rationalize this process of differentiation and correction. In his hands, History and the Philosophy of Science itself becomes an instance of instrumental reason as it legitimates the processes of struggle which take place within disciplines: the controls and intentions that circumscribe those struggles both guarantee and mark their rationality.

We are, after Feyerabend, accustomed to charges that the Philosophy of Science has as its major institutional purpose the legitimation of capitalist science and technology.[24] What we are perhaps not quite so used to hearing, however, is the charge that the sort of model Toulmin proposes also legitimates disciplinary elites and their social and professional privileges as institutions of the extended state. Yet this is precisely Toulmin's function in high intellectual culture: to obscure the irrationalities of social life by ensuring the rationality of strategic thinking; and to occlude the difficulty societies and institutions face in preserving themselves within contradictory social orders.

Equally essential to an understanding of Toulmin's function are the intellectual elites whose gifts, training, and social position make them the supports of the reason of not only their own disciplines but also the social order as a whole. Such an attitude is itself an echo of Mannheim's mistaken insistence upon the free-floating nature of intellectuals as well as the prolepsis of Alvin Gouldner's lapse into pre-Gramscian categories: Gouldner came to believe that traditional elite intellectuals provide the best hope for rational social life in late capitalist society.[25] Toulmin's failure to consider how these intellectual elites come into being, in relation to which other social groups, and to perform which social functions typifies his refusal to come to grips with the material problems of power and privilege in society. In place of critical and historical thinking about these questions, Toulmin replicates the worst of liberal thinking, offering us only a neohumanist explanation of the goodwill and values of the elites. He reduces matters of normativity and social reproduction to the following scene of bureaucratic benevolence, to trust in the "men" who, properly trained and connected, know what to do:

> Strategic uncertainties take us to a "rational frontier," where men must deal with novel types of problems by developing whole new methods of thought; and, at these frontiers, we can no longer separate entirely the rational processes of a science from the intellectual purposes of the men who are reshaping them, or from the historical situation in which they find themselves. . . . Any profound redirection in the strategy of a discipline thus has to be justified by appeal, not to any previously established patterns of argument, but to the overall experience of men in the entire history of the rational enterprise concerned. (HU, 241)

The very grounds for appeal which justify the rationality of disciplines and their society have material workings, but Toulmin does not pursue them. What this quotation offers is an idealizing reification and fetishization of the intellect and of the value of social memory and tradition as the guarantee of rationality beyond the reach of already known procedures. (For Toulmin, no rational professional ever wagers on the future.) In contrast, Adorno remarks about elites in capitalist societies that "whoever does not fit in is kept out. Even the differences of conviction which reflect those of real interests serve primarily to obscure the underlying unity which prevails in decisive matters."[26]

After Nietzsche, Foucault helps us see that Toulmin's fetishization of disciplined, humanistic reason not only prevents the intellectuals's examination of the real social and material interests at work in the struggles within disciplines (and over the positions they occupy in society) but also blocks all critical reflection upon the nature of intellectual agency: above all, the agents of these rationalized structures are themselves functional elements in discursive and nondiscursive structures which deny autonomy to the agent and may well be said to have emptied out in advance of any deconstruction the concept of the autonomous subject in a postmodern society.

Toulmin's liberal model implies a harmony between individual agents as autonomous subjects and the discourses and institutions that inscribe them as intellectuals. Toulmin's concept could not withstand a Gramscian critique of the intellectual when he argues that this harmony itself depends upon the continuity of human experience as internalized and preserved (as canon and tradition) by the leaders of a culture. In other words, this continuous experience (in an otherwise amnesic society) belongs only to Philosophers and other professionals. When we recall such early modern texts as Nietzsche's *On the Genealogy of Morals*, which is a demonstration of the dissolution of the liberal subject, and Baudelaire's elaborate salon celebration of Delacroix as the sole aesthetic appropriator of the great tradition in modernity, then we must marvel at the dispassionately self-assured ease with which Toulmin and other neohumanists assert that this appropriation—the ground of intellectual assurance and legitimacy—is always already there for us in the given institutions of our culture. As Jake says to Brett in *The Sun Also Rises*: "Yes. Isn't it pretty to think so?"

Unlike Toulmin, Foucault begins with the very question of the cultural and political status of both knowledge and reason, on the one hand, and of the institutions, discourses, and empowered elites that deploy and embody them, on the other. Foucault follows Canguilhem in questioning the "normativizing" moves of the Philosophy of Science and expands his research to examine the disciplined society itself. The result of this approach is to trace the irrationality of practice in professions and among institutionalized intellectuals.

In *On the Normal and the Pathological*, for example (a text introduced by Foucault), Canguilhem analyzes how the very existence of physiology as a science depends upon the phenomenological experience of sick men which is itself rationalized into a high intellectual discourse that comes to be disseminated and institutionalized in society. Of course, this study can be read as prefiguring Foucault's work on prisons, clinics, and sexuality, and as a useful point of entry into the contrast between Toulmin's legitimating practice and Foucault's and Canguilhem's critical genealogical approach.

Canguilhem focuses his analysis upon the question of the norm in scientific discourse and how it comes into being: "*Normative*, in Philosophy, means every judgment which evaluates or qualifies a fact in relation to a norm, but this mode of judgment is essentially subordinate to that which establishes norms. *Normative*, in the fullest sense of the word, is that which establishes norms."[27]

Canguilhem and Foucault have a different approach to the rational and discursive than does Toulmin. A reader of Foucault, for example, will recognize that this move in Canguilhem prefigures Foucault's entire theorizing about "power/knowledge" which is the controversial center of his work. In addition, though, Canguilhem's move indicates that both of these writers, like Nietzsche, are interested in the irrationality of the moves made by intellectual and cultural discourses as these are written over and around the phenomenal everyday experience of human beings in society. Furthermore, they focus this interest on the ways in which this experience comes into being and acquires cognitive and cultural status by virtue of being taken up within already existing objective categories and processes of disciplinary practice. We can see, after Foucault and Canguilhem, that discourses constitute and emerge from new experience just insofar as within them this experience becomes sensible.[28] In other words, it is possible (but inexact) to say that new experiences change institutions only because this constitutive power of discourses has the institutional power to make ontic whatever experiences they represent. Above all they prevent noninstitutionalized, nonprofessional, nontraditional figurations from gaining access to the cultural means of communication and reproduction. This structuring of knowledge has brought about a permanently institutionalized society; it would be merely naive or utopian to imagine as an alternative a noninstitutionalized or nonprofessionalized apparatus for producing knowledge; rather, what needs to be thought through more clearly is the relationship between any apparatus and the hegemonic forces in a particular society: this, after all, is the central focus of Foucault's notion of the regime of truth.

What Foucault finds in Canguilhem to develop his Nietzschean critique is a relentless assault on positivism. Canguilhem directs his attack against Comte's insistence that the priority of science as a means to truth (based on laboratory experimental procedures) justified therapeutic interventions into the sickness of men who had already identified themselves as sick. But the attack on positivism is itself only a way into the critique of the fetishization of science as the reification of reason. Canguilhem's analysis is an ideological critique that exemplifies how one should study the relationship between knowledge and (in the broadest sense) political institutions. For our purposes here, it is the second aspect of Canguilhem's work which is of the greatest interest both because it sharpens our sense of Toulmin's inadequacies as a Philosopher of disciplines and because it suggests an important source of Foucault's work.

Canguilhem focuses on Comte's adoption and adaptation of Broussais's thesis. As we read Canguilhem, we see that his text writes out for us the double movement that takes place in all revisionist modifications of the canon. Comte's interpretation of science took Broussais's thesis from the limited realm of physiology and, for Comte's own purposes, so to speak, extended its applicability to other spheres and so re-authorized it. For reasons largely independent of Broussais's intention, then, Comte's rereading of physiology's founding discourse exemplifies how the material and institutional networks of authority and power establish what is rational and legitimate within the intellectual disciplines and across an entire spectrum of representations, opinions, rumors, and common sense. Comte's assumption of Broussais's thesis has a significant institutional intellectual function: it extends the space of rationality from the region of physiology to those newly state-related areas of politics and the positive social sciences. More precisely, Comte's revisionary move exemplifies how irrationally a concept is appropriated; no ideal procedures regulate Comte's revision; no humanist memory of a precedent guarantees the efficacy, rationality, or benevolence of such appropriation or its inscribing systems of representation. For reasons of social and political power, Comte's agency extends a concept into areas for which it has no scientifically justified immediate applicability and no certain progressive value. It is significant that Comte has extended this concept into discourses and institutions much less scientifically organized than either natural science or the law. At least one result of this move is that these other discourses then aspire to fix the notions of science to their practice and theory to acquire legitimacy and social position within the consensus that is the regime of truth, while at the same time assigning leading roles to the dominant intellectuals of their disciplines.

Canguilhem shows that this process succeeds because Comte derives his already enormous intellectual authority from his role as ideological representative of the new hegemony that is grounded in positive science. Comte's strategy is paradigmatic: appropriate a concept by dialectically emptying and overfilling it and so turn it into a functional trope. In this case, a metaphor becomes an ideological tool or weapon in the political battle to empower systems of representation and align them to the socially dominant forces of the economic and cultural order: what Foucault calls "the regime of truth." Canguilhem nicely summarizes the process:

By stating in a general way that diseases do not change vital phenomena, Comte is justified in stating that the cure for political crises consists in bringing societies back to their essential and permanent structure, and tolerating progress only within limits of variation of natural order defined by social statics. In positivist doctrine, Broussais's principle remains an idea subordinated to a system, and it is the physicians, psychologists, and men of letters, positivist by inspiration and tradition, who disseminated it as an independent conception.[29]

Canguilhem shows us how the positivists join the cadre of free-floating traditional intellectuals who, like clerics, rearrange systems of representation as if there were no historical limits to or consequences of their actions, no resisting "otherness" to whatever they revise: free-floating intellectuals are revisionists who are free to rip concepts from context and rearrange their tropes to whatever end they like; they are doing the bidding of the hegemony that the newly configured representations create and support; and, most important in this case, they legitimize and make constitutive *revision* as the fundamental practice of modern intellectual life. Such a discovery lets us see Toulmin's defense of the putative rationality of disciplines for what it is: a reflection of the self-conception of traditional intellectuals and an occluding of the role of such intellectuals in the production and dissemination of the regime of truth.

Canguilhem and Foucault offer one useful technique for clearing away this darkness and for controlling the modern intellectual practice of arrogant and self-interested (because self-creating) revision—and that is genealogy. This involves a peculiar stance toward the relationship of the present to the past and to historical study itself.

Canguilhem notes that his suspicions of the deployment of reason in modern science led him to look for its genetic origins. He tries to learn how the present configuration of political and cultural forces has positioned theory, science, and method in modern structures of knowledge. More suspicious and reflective than Toulmin, Canguilhem proposes a method for investigating the past's production of the present and the present's self-production out of its revision of the past (using Comte as an instance) which is perhaps most fully developed in Foucault's *Discipline and Punish*:

It may be surprising to see than an exposition of Comte's theory has turned into a pretext for a retrospective study. Why wasn't a chronological order employed at the outset? Because a historical narrative always reverses the true order of interest and inquiry. It is in the present that problems provoke reflection. And if reflection leads to a regression, the regression is necessarily related to it. Thus the historical origin is really less important than the reflective origin. . . . What is certain in any case is that even in the milieu of medical culture, the theories of general pathology originated by Bichat, Brown, and Broussais were influential only to the extent that Comte found them advantageous. The physicians of the second half of the nineteenth century were for the most part ignorant of Broussais and Brown, but few were unaware of Comte or Littré; just as today most physiologists cannot ignore Bernard, but disregard Bichat to whom Bernard is connected through Magendie. By going back to more remote sources of Comte's ideas—through the pathology of Broussais, Brown, and Bichat—we put ourselves in a better position to understand their significance and limits.[30]

In his Nietzschean insistence that the present promotes reflection, Canguilhem displaces conventional genetic histories of science and establishes the importance of what he calls the "reflective origin." The realities of the present provoke not a revision of the past, not the sort of history of science Foucault rejects in "The Discourse on Language"; but a critical genealogy that discovers how in light of the issues pressing in the present and so reflected back into the past, the past must be read to account for the present configuration of forces which, itself, emerged at that reflective origin. This is a powerfully delegitimating method that is itself a form of resistance (often taking the form of narrative) to the courses of things as they have led, so to speak, to the present moment of reflection.

Toulmin cannot write such critical history. Despite his insistent claim that practice forms disciplinary knowledge and its categories, his specific assertions remain empty. They can have no content because the revisionist disciplines he defends constitute themselves by Comte's method of dialectically overloading and emptying out concepts; the result is that they produce a vacuous rhetoric that cannot reflect their origins, that is, their coming into being within the spaces first defined by their own and affiliated discourses and institutions. The critical genealogical model (which Foucault describes as the attempt to write the history of the present) always asks what is at stake in the individual events that constitute the disciplines and their discursive regularities, and how one can tell the story of their transformations and constitutive relationships to the regime of truth. Critical genealogy allows, among other things, for consideration of both the discursive structures in which or out of which an intellectual/political event emerges and the real material interests in which it may be inscribed. Also, it creates one of the conditions for theorizing how intellectual discourses and practices stage cultural and political conflicts. After Canguilhem it offers the terms *normal* and *pathological* as binaries through which the regulative ideals of cultural production can be reflected.

At this point one might adapt a generally Althusserian line to Toulmin's model of historical continuity. Such a reading would show that the common-law argument cannot rationalize fundamental historical contradictions of Toulmin's own moment; indeed, it would usefully see Toulmin's attempt as in itself a symptom of those contradictions.[31] Canguilhem's work, however, lets us see something more important and more general: that Toulmin can make no convincing claim that his evolutionary model of disciplines is demonstrative. On the contrary, it suggests how narrow and simple Toulmin's model is.

In the 1940s Canguilhem worked out a conception similar to Toulmin's which used populational models to describe how medical practice (as opposed to physiological science) creates norms and normatives. But Canguilhem's model is not only much more elegant and powerful, it is also more flexible: it genealogically figures each moment in a structure not as part of an assumed continuum of reason itself produced by a continuing commitment to rational disciplinary ideals held and acted upon by reasonable and disinterested men; rather it sees each event and its place within the site of a discipline (as well as the stability of a discipline itself) as much more tenuous, confused, and disharmonious than might appear on an unreflected surface.

The differences between Canguilhem's and Toulmin's adoptions of Darwin let us see, to put it in terms reminiscent of Adorno's critique of Mannheim, that Toulmin takes appearance for essence. Since Toulmin misreads Darwin as assuring evolutionary success, his revisionist model becomes a machine representing "normal" disciplinary practices as everywhere ensuring stability and harmony, rationality and disinterest. In literary criticism, Toulmin's model surely does not hold, despite Stanley Fish's propaganda for the regulative force of interpretive communities. (The significance of Fish's parallel interest in the law needs to be worked out elsewhere.) Criticism is surely an "unformed science," despite the great allure of Northrop Frye and his followers; but it is also the case that "inside" the field, "professional intellectual interests" are self-consciously implicated in relations of power among "generations" and "elites" of literary study. Revisionism is the only regulative ideal to be found at the top of the heap.[32] Furthermore, despite the recent "boomlet" in literary studies marked by the attempts of a number of elite universities to attract the best and brightest of a new generation,[33] Toulmin's model cannot account for the economic and cultural factors that threaten the very survival of advanced literary study in the United States.

But literary criticism is a perfect example of Canguilhem's version of the Darwinian scheme: a period of stability marked by the dominant New Criticism's supervention of other conflicting elements in criticism, followed by open conflict over disciplinary identity and attempts at revision necessary for the survival of the profession. Canguilhem schematizes the process around the figure of compensation:

> It would not express a specific stable equilibrium but rather the unstable equilibrium of nearly all equal norms and forms of life temporarily brought together. Instead of considering a specific type as being really stable because it presents stable characteristics devoid of any incompatibility, it should be considered as being apparently stable because it has temporarily succeeded in reconciling opposing demands by means of a set of compensations. A normal specific form would be the product of a normalization between functions and organs whose synthetic harmony is obtained in defined conditions and not given.[34]

Canguilhem's figure of compensation translates politically into Gramsci's notion of hegemony, that is, the dominant, which gives its identity to the stable moment, achieves its position by virtue of the set of concessions it offers to the conflicting groups it directs and leads. In other words, compensation is a political process in the creation of intellectual and disciplinary stability. It is not rational in the disinterested sense Toulmin hypothesizes. Figuring politics as practical reason is the traditional intelligentsia's ideological defense of its own privilege, a privilege provided by the dominant groups that benefit from its caste practices.

What Toulmin takes away from reason is the element of "critique" which Marx, for example, in *The German Ideology* insisted separated him from Feuerbach: a recognition that all discursive practice is part of class warfare and that mere skepticism, the mere demystification of religious visions, always forgets the primary task of critique—to join in the political battle (not, as Richard Rorty would have it, just "the conversation") of cultural, economic, and national conflicts.

As a genealogist interested in disclosing the history and structure of power from the point of view of the present, Foucault learns his basic lessons from Nietzsche and Canguilhem: he learns what we should call "the lesson of error." Accident or chance, Canguilhem argues, lies at the biological basis of life, in the genetic materials themselves. Errors in genetic coding always occur. For Foucault, and all genealogists, this implies that error and not reason is "at the root of what makes human thought and its history."[35] Not only does Canguilhem guide Foucault in studying genealogically how power/knowledge has grasped the body, but Canguilhem's positioning of biological error as an unavoidable feature of genetic information systems grounds (especially in *The Birth of the Clinic*) Foucault's own insistent claims for historical discontinuity and the role of power in the relationship between thought and history:

> The opposition of true and false, the values we attribute to both, the effects of power that different societies and different institutions link to this division—even all this is perhaps only the latest response to this possibility of error, which is intrinsic to life. If the history of science is discontinuous, that is, if it can be analyzed only as a series of "corrections," as a new distribution of true and false which never finally, once and for all, liberates the truth, it is because there, too, "error" constitutes not overlooking or delaying a truth but the dimension proper to the life of men and to the time of the species.[36]

We might say that Toulmin's expansion of reason is one of the latest forms of error, that always found among traditional intellectuals as they tell stories about and to themselves and their masters. Of course, error marks Toulmin's texts, and so like all humanistic texts they are inscribed within death, if I may extend Foucault's own reading of Canguilhem's figure of the origin of clinical medicine.[37] Toulmin's own thinking leads us nowhere near these questions, for as a traditional intellectual there is no reflective origin to be found in his work. He makes no effort to understand his own position within the regime of truth, that is to say, the space within which he practices is taken for granted, assumed to have natural status within the discourses of truth and judgment. The result, in part, is that his work goes on untroubled by any implications it might have within the apparatus of power/ knowledge, especially as this affects those less empowered by this very apparatus. In effect, I take Toulmin to exemplify intellectual irresponsibility, a disregard for extension of the regime of truth across society and national borders, and a carelessness toward interrogating one's own intellectual function within such an apparatus.[38]

We can conclude that Toulmin is genealogically unselfconscious; his model errs in its theory of practice. Yet Toulmin is interesting because his is a form of error necessary to the truth apparatus of modern intellectual practice itself. We can see in Toulmin's work the extent of a particular problem that I have discussed elsewhere:[39] established liberal humanistic discourse, even when it claims to be historical and concerned with institutions, always effectively blocks entry into the workings of irrationality, desire, interest, and will within the professionalized disciplines. More important, it always substitutes its own normalcy and familiarity for the strange and difficult task of genealogically looking into the history and position of intellectuals and their work in the current regime of truth. Seen in this way, Toulmin appears as an exemplary instance of how institutionalized discourses in our regime of truth substitute abstract analytics for the complex genealogical narratives needed to recall our own history.[40] A more thorough critique of Toulmin would be necessary to fulfill the two primary aims that should motivate such criticism: to negate the very thingness, the ontic naturalness, the givenness, as it were, of Toulmin's kind of practice, but more important again, to exemplify in itself the kind of genealogical critique that takes seriously both the historical specificity of its subject and contemporary problematics: to write a history of the present which best accounts for the coming into being of the current regime while also recalling those few moments of alternative practice and discourse the present regime would rather have forgotten. Such a genealogical practice would recover for itself—and for others who take up that practice as a tool in their own struggles—the very critical impulse that amnesic liberal discourses misappropriate and deaden.[41]

Without such a genealogical critique, humanistic institutions will maintain the regime of truth even while engaged in reform. Humane motivation is not an adequate defense against mistakes that further the replication of the current regime. Without critical knowledge there can be no awareness of the pitfalls that confront the reforming or even revolutionary consciousness. If one hopes to avoid some of these pitfalls, one must recall a wide-reaching tradition of critical anxiety and responsibility that includes Benjamin and Adorno as well as Blackmur and Jameson,[42] that is, a tradition that insists upon difficulty, slowness, complex, often dialectical and highly ironic styles as an effective antidote to the uncritical professional prejudices of the current regime of truth: speed, slogans, transparency, and reproducibility. Although there are critical histories everywhere—indeed, even histories of these histories—they are variously positioned and nothing seems more definitely to mark their differences than their relative commitment to the tradition I have just mentioned. The further such a history is from this tradition both in its style and its problematics of reading, the closer it is, so to speak, to that institution Toulmin so clearly represents.[43]

8

......

Reclaiming Criticism:
Willful Love
in the Tradition
of Henry Adams

Society was bound for quick success and cared only for enough intelligence to go on with.—R. P. Blackmur on Henry Adams

R. P. Blackmur's impressive critical sympathies remained focused on the work of Henry Adams during his entire career. From his apprenticeship at *The Hound and Horn* until his death as a professor at Princeton and a guru to foundations and publishers, Blackmur never long let his attention stray from Adams's life and writing. Blackmur was unable to finish the often and long-promised magnum opus on Adams, just as he was unable to finish a number of other book-length projects he considered and sometimes announced. The Adams project was more important to Blackmur's life and critical imagination than any of his other often transitory concerns. Certainly Henry James was a crucial longtime preoccupation; we might regret that Blackmur never made the promised sustained study of that novelist. Yet, as Denis Donoghue has argued very convincingly, one can, in some detail, trace Blackmur's changing attitude to James and come to the conclusion that he finally put the novelist behind him.[1] There was no such resigning of Adams.

Blackmur's constant return to Adams seems to be of no particular interest to contemporary criticism. With a few notable exceptions, Blackmur has not been a very powerful or overt influence on our most celebrated theoreticians and practicing critics. Nor has Adams—with his anti-Semitism and ambiguous positions in the history of feminism and American imperialism—been an exemplary figure for modern intellectuals nor a particularly privileged figure in the recent histories of

U.S. literature; and history students tell me they no longer take him seriously even in that discipline. So Blackmur's concern with Adams would seem today little more than a conundrum of literary critical history and one perhaps best left behind.

There are, though, small signs of critical interest in these writers. Norman Podhoretz, for example, makes Adams a figure behind the anomie of modernism and postmodernism; others—like Donoghue or Robert Boyers—try to blood the ghastly Blackmur as the antagonist of theory. Although the critics who make these gestures are on the margins of the great debates and central movements of contemporary literary criticism, there are reasons to take them seriously even though I cannot now give them detailed analysis. Suffice it to say that these critics emerge from the cultural reaction around the Reagan-Bush administrations and from the often equally conservative "against theory" elements of the contemporary academy. At times, of course, "progressive" critical figures, such as Edward W. Said and Jim Merod, invoke Blackmurian standards and defend some of his procedures; they sometimes write, in part, under his influence.[2] But these progressive critics are a minority of those who bother with Blackmur these days.

We have been warned of the dangers to the critical mind posed by the twin attractions of "system" and "culture."[3] The former narrows criticism to the boring, repetitive, and predictable act of representing texts and other cultural objects or events according to some pseudo-scientific methodological standard; the latter shapes critical production according to the often unseen but always ready-made molds of a hegemonic culture.[4] Within the complex discourse of literary studies, as in all other formally developed disciplines, there are, in addition to these broad cultural molds, various more-specific linguistic and institutional codes that mark the special knowledge and authority of the initiated professional. As various as these might be, however, they commonly affect the knowledge, the representations, produced by the professionals precisely in that they largely determine what can be taken as knowledge within the guild-consciousness of a discipline's practices. To a very great extent, professional critics cannot escape the positive determinations of these codes. Upon them rests not so much the communicability of representations, but the very possibility of having certain positions upon and through which even ironic and oppositional representations can circulate.

System builders succumb to the allure of science as the alternative to cultural determinations, and the "culture critics"[5] attack them for their illusions in so doing; but criticism must be carried out in another space of intellectual performance that is not constrained by the narrow determinations of this opposition. Criticism should not be predictable or mechanistic; criticism is or should be more than producing insight into privileged literary texts and cultural events. Arnold, to take a high example, or William Bennet or Alan Bloom to take two lower ones, would, in part, have us assume the task of elaborating information and values out of and about the monuments of our supposedly unified or dominant culture; Nietzsche has helped us see the dangers in such monumentalism.

Indeed, in his tradition, other types of criticism can develop. We recall, for example, Edward Said's programmatic assertion, after Foucault and Gramsci, that criticism or critical consciousness must have a more worldly set of aims:

> Is [not the task of criticism] to occupy itself with the intrinsic conditions on which knowledge is made possible? For in order to see what it is that we can know as students of texts, we must be able to understand the units of knowledge as functions of textuality, which itself must be describable in terms dealing with not only the agencies of culture but also the requirements of intelligible method and the material form of knowledge which, if it is not of divine or supernatural provenance, is produced in the secular world.

This extraordinarily admirable project reclaims for criticism many of the duties abandoned by philosophy and social science and leads to the development of "culture studies" programs in institutions throughout the country.[6]

As severe, though, as Said's critique is of the weaknesses in both system and culture, it is not quite severe enough in its critique of the current state of critical practice in the United States. The great upsurge in criticism that began in the 1960s has lost a good deal of its momentum. In part this is due to the death of figures like de Man and Foucault and to the changed cultural and political circumstances of the 1980s. In part it is also due to a reaction within the profession "against theory," a reaction that insists upon recapturing some of the putatively lost capacity to deal pragmatically with texts.[7] Yet, in another way, the impulse to original and rigorous critical work has died down into its own success.

Foucault taught us that power is significant not as repression but as production. In fact, the movements of contemporary criticism have, for the most part, been so successfully institutionalized that an observer as astute as Gerald Graff can argue that the competition among various schools has resulted in a new tolerant and pluralistic democracy in literary study.[8] Indeed, the profession *has* changed in that academic critics can now march, in a relatively unimpeded way, to the beat of any programmatic drummer and stride right up to any problem or text and deal with it according to the critical categories that seem most useful in explaining or getting around it. This is certainly different than it used to be just fifteen years ago when, we recall, J. Hillis Miller needed to defend theory and deconstruction from the exclusionary attacks of a Meyer Abrams or Wayne Booth. Above all, we have internalized de Man's insistence that criticism is crisis and institutionalized some of its implications so that we almost all have permission to do whatever kinds of criticism we feel the need to do. Of course, this situation produces better and worse criticism.

The direst institutional effect of this state of affairs is the all-too-common tendency among younger scholars especially—but not exclusively—to clothe their work in one of the many recognizable positions practiced by those with a definite posture in the profession. Such a tendency commodifies thought and harms criticism as it imposes on the young the obligation to develop a name in already known and circulating terms.

Of course, the institutional reality that brings about this situation is precisely the academic equivalent of the process of commodification: critical theories and positions get reified into transmissible codes; what were perhaps once real vehicles for critical work appropriate to a time and place get transformed by pedagogy, guidebooks, and the reduction of ideas inevitable in professional circulation into easily learnable gestures that do not so much enable critical work as identify their bearers with a recognizable position on the spectrum of authorized postures.

So powerful and troubling is this process that even as resolutely an anti-systemic and self-critical a writer as Said finds his own insistent interrogation of the worldliness of literature and culture, his own rigorous theory of critical consciousness, can be made into an authorized discourse, elements of which can be borrowed by other, sometimes younger critics and attached to criticism, carried out, so to speak, in "Said's tradition." Yet if one of Said's undesired ephebes were to take

Said seriously he or she would realize that the very essence of Said's stated program is that it not be adopted by disciples. Critical conscious-ness, as Said speaks of it, is highly individual; for him it depends upon the worldly status of the practicing critic whose work is not meant simply to provide another set of terms to authorize more "literary criticism." (Of course, there are problems with this anticommunitarian discourse and I don't mean to be seen as endorsing Said's position without qualification.)

Let me be clear on what I mean by this: Said's work, like that of any powerful intellectual, will have influence; that is another and inescap-able problem. I am talking about something different than influence here; I am talking about the current historical situation in literary crit-icism, one that has, as I see it, degenerated into such a sorry ethical and intellectual state that, for the most part, unbeknown to its practitioners, a series of postures, gestures, and positions have come to displace just the kind of critical consciousness someone like Said promotes—of course in part this may be a result of the profession's continuing em-phasis on the individual as the privileged and, indeed, only site of criticism. Said's essay on system and culture has little to say about this process; with the exception of certain feminist critical writings,[9] there simply is very little critical work being done today with the original force and inventive, self-critical authority of several years ago—and what there is is mostly the development of projects set into place back then.

These are large claims that cannot be demonstrated fully. One exam-ple will have to indicate the nature of the problem. The so-called New Historicism associated most prominently with Berkeley, the journal *Representations*, and the work of Stephen Greenblatt has set out to institu-tionalize itself as a movement, as a set of recognizable gestures and concerns. And indeed it has done so quite brilliantly. The new Univer-sity of California Press series of New Historicist texts that extends the "genre" out of the Renaissance to other areas is only its most recent success. The New Historicism has produced interesting, enabling, and stimulating work and the effort to disparage it by making the common claim that it is merely the old historicism dressed up is a weak one. What is worth remarking, though, is the New Historicism's success in getting itself on the map of professional legitimacy and with such effect that an older theoretical paradigm and its journal, *Diacritics*, sends out one of its most authoritative figures, Dominick LaCapra, to do battle with it.[10]

Effectively, to be a younger scholar in the Renaissance today means having a position on the New Historicism, perhaps even encoding one's work in such a way that it sounds like or unlike the classics of that school produced by Greenblatt or another leader of the group. This process seems to me all too common today and not just among younger scholars. At conference after conference one finds critics speaking to each other in coded gestures that have the effect of placing the speaker somewhere in a recognizable constellation of positions and earning him or her applause or hostility as a consequence. Too often even the hostility is not real; one distinguished critic has been heard to say: you attack me and I attack you and we both get famous.

Said has identified Foucault, Derrida, Raymond Williams, Gramsci and some very few others as part of a tradition of worldly criticism, but in a recent essay on R. P. Blackmur he reminds us that, in this great American critic, we have a true rarity:

> Critics write, of course, in order to be read; to change, refine, or deepen understanding; to press evaluation and revaluation. Yet rare are the critics for whom criticism is its own justification, and not an act for the gaining of adherents or for the persuasion of larger and larger audiences. Rarer still are critics whose work at its center cradles the paradox that whatever criticism urges or de-livers must not, indeed cannot, be replicated, reproduced, reused as a lesson learned and then applied.[11]

In projecting his own critical ideal, Said has gotten at the center of Blackmurian criticism.

Blackmur, it seems, found his own great original on just this matter in the figure of Henry Adams. While Said tries to understand Blackmur's characteristic stance in terms of style and gesture—terms absolutely appropriate to Blackmur's project—he himself went at this matter in Adams in a different way. Said, like Blackmur, belongs to a tradition of critical exile, an issue which Said, following Auerbach, has made into a critical ethics. For Blackmur, too, the critic must be in exile. The pathos of literal exile from one's national home that everywhere tinges Auer-bach's and Said's work Blackmur—before Said—turns into a universal category of modern critical intelligence, into a category of aesthetic, moral, and political distance essential to the skeptical mind placed eccentrically within an inhospitable society.

Blackmur's terms for these matters appear in his 1930s writings on

Adams which are roughly contemporary with his first lovingly comba-
tive comments on academic literary criticism. Writing of Adams as one
of "many great men"[12] who appear as "either sports or parasites upon
the society that produced them," Blackmur speculates on the qualities
that forced this position upon him:

> They stand out too much from their native society: all outsiders
> from the life they expressed and upon which they fed, . . . it only
> accented their own sense of eccentricity and loneliness. That is
> how Adams stood out . . . but within him, as within the others in
> their degrees, was an intelligence whose actions were direct,
> naked, and at their best terrifyingly sane. (HA, 6)

Blackmur's point is forceful: the humanistic ideal that sees the work
of these "great men" as expressive of their and our society and as
providing the connective tissues of our culture depends upon the
critical work of after-the-fact interpretation that establishes the links
between their work and the culture. But the intelligence of these "great
men" never feels, acts, or lives in such a connective or expressive
mode; and the reason why not is clear. Blackmur insists upon the sanity
of the great eccentrics as the very mark of their difference from their
cultures. For Blackmur, intelligence is the highest of qualities—as it was
for Adams—and its possession foregrounds a figure against a relief of
the commonplace and normative.

Of course, The Education of Henry Adams is the great allegory of the fate of
intelligence in modernity as a product and opponent of both nature
and history. Intelligence can take many forms for Adams; it can be
political, administrative, diplomatic, scientific, or merely technological
skill. In its highest forms, however, it involves the mind as a capacity to
deal with the sensorium of experience. Needless to say, in The Education,
the allegory of such intelligence is the history of its failure. Blackmur
lets that story give basic form to his own critical fears and desires:

> Surely the dominant emotion of an education, when its inherent
> possibilities are compared with those achieved, must strike the
> honest heart as the emotion of failure. The failure is not of knowl-
> edge or of feeling. It is the failure of the ability to react correctly or
> even intelligently to more than an abbreviated version of knowl-
> edge and feeling: failure in the radical sense that we cannot con-
> sciously react to more than a minor fraction of the life we yet

deeply know and endure and die. It is the failure the mind comes to ultimately and all along when it is compelled to measure its knowledge in terms of its ignorance. (HA, 4)

Of course, this states a High Modernist critical ideal and its pathos. I suggest, however, that in the face of what we have been taught recently to accept as postmodern pastiche[13]—which in the academic critical arena equates with the tendency to posture and position described above—Blackmur's derivation from Adams of a critical ideal that tries but fails intelligently to respond to the complexity of life has a more than corrective value.

Indeed, Blackmur's image of a critical mind that measures its knowledge by its correspondingly greater ignorance has political and ethical import. In The Political Unconscious,[14] Jameson warns against critics being duped by the seductive heterocosms produced by High Modernist writers; he warns us also against mistaking the ideology of High Modernism that generates these heterocosms in images of the isolated and self-sufficient individual body. But unlike Blackmur's image, derived from a reading of Adams, Jameson's sense of critical Marxism depends upon, among other things, an image of critical warfare derived most immediately from Gramsci and so from the technologies of World War I. When Jameson insists, for example, that Marxism alone can extend its reach far enough to match the expanse of capital, he is invoking Gramsci's metaphor of a war of position. He is also trying to make the military and party metaphor do duty for the practice of individual critics in an America that has no such party structure. More important, he makes this claim as part of an effort to develop a fourfold theory of interpretation that, in a manner echoing Kant more than Marx, will oblige each and every cultural artifact and event to account for itself in certain specific terms. In the preface to the second edition of The Critique of Pure Reason,[15] Kant identifies the lesson of science: reason only has insight into "that which it produces after a plan of its own." As a result, Kant argues, man must not be led to understanding by nature, but must constrain "nature to give answer to questions of reason's own determining." "Reason," Kant goes on to say,

holding in one hand its principles, according to which alone concordant appearances can be admitted as equivalent to laws, and in the other hand the experiment which it has devised in conformity with these principles, must approach nature in order to be taught by it. It must not, however, do so in the character of a pupil who listens to everything that the teacher chooses to say, but of an appointed judge who compels the witnesses to answer questions which he has himself formulated . . . while reason must seek in nature . . . it must adopt as its guide, in so seeking, that which it has itself put into nature.

Of course, historically minded critics are more likely to invoke Vico than Kant in justifying putting insistent questions to historical realities. The form of the issue is the same though, no matter if the original figure be Kant or Vico: the text, if we speak in literary rather than scientific terms, is obliged to answer questions put to it authoritatively and with the weight of coercive force behind them—as an ungenerous critic might say of Jameson's determination to make genre answer his historicized questions. By contrast, and more in the spirit of Foucault, we might suggest that such questioning belongs to an age when the leading intellectual worked on the model of the sovereign, juridical ideal.

Adams and Blackmur suggest something still more. Ethically, they suggest the need for a scruple[16] about posing such coercive questions; they worry about the illusion of gaining knowledge, no matter of history or reason, by obliging the text or life to answer. In language that belongs to a Western tradition as old as Herodotus, Adams insists that an authentic failure is easy to recognize: "For great failure we want the utmost unrelenting imagination and the impersonal agony of knowledge searching the haven of objective form. Most failures come too easily, take too little stock of the life and forces around them. . . . A genuine failure comes hard and slow, and, as in a tragedy, is only fully realized at the end" (HA, 4).

Failure of this sort occurs in the relationship between intelligence, morality, and power. Henry's ancestors had never given in to the temptations of power, but balanced a claim to power with a scruple that eventually brought their careers to premature but accomplished ends. Henry, however, had a scruple that kept him from power altogether, and, as far as Blackmur is concerned, that fact in itself condemns American democracy.

Blackmur makes the strongest possible claim for the ethical and political value of this quality in Adams's mind. In a passage that recalls Nietzsche's retrospective reconstruction of his own origins as a "philosopher,"[17] Blackmur, from Adams's "scruple," generalizes the conditions for critical intellectual resistance to a dominant and illegitimate society:

> If, as I think, it was the scruple of his mind that made Adams an outsider and that at the same time gave precise value to his eccentricity, then the scruple should be defined both for itself and in terms of Adams. It is what I have been deviously leading up to: as it represents the single heroic and admirable quality of the modern and skeptical mind as such; and a quality not called for by the occasion but crowning it, even when disastrously.
> Scruple, generally speaking, is the agent of integrity, what keeps action honest on the level of affairs, or on the level of imagination when actuality or truth is the object. . . . It is scruples that compel attention to detail and subordinate the detail to an end. When excess atrophies the mind, whether of scruples or the lack of them, it is because either an impossible end or no end was in view. In science the adjudication of scruples is called method and taken for granted; but the whole test of the democratic process is whether or not the seat of power attracts the scrupulous intelligence and gives it rein. . . . [Politics, for Adams, was] a game . . . played impersonally with, as ultimate stake, the responsible control of social energy. Since ultimate value was never sure, every move ought to be made with the maximum intelligence and subject to every criticism your experience provided. (HA, 6–7)

That the citizen-critic needs to be skeptical and open-minded might account for Blackmur's life-long admiration of Montaigne. But Blackmur's skepticism paradoxically needs to rest upon something: not a sense of the absolute; we cannot be confident of any ultimate. For him, skepticism must be in the service of an end, but the end itself must always be open to question, and the means to accomplish it must always be under suspicion. This set of values prefigures what Said calls "critical consciousness." For Said criticism is always responsive, always occasional and he simply calls "will" whatever it is that allows for this responsiveness. For Adams, as Blackmur figures him, this skeptical "critical consciousness," in politics and letters, needs itself to be firmly enabled in a way that skirts the typically American consequences of the individualized will: a "scruple," is, then, as it were, Adams's condition for the occasional, reflexive, and suspicious skeptic. Indeed, "scruple" is just what makes a critic more than a self-interested American; it is just what makes the exile into a critic—whatever it might be. But no matter what it might be, it is precisely that which preserves the occasional critic from the temptation to power and from the consequent danger that endless self-revision, endless self-making, endless repositioning can result in a hypostatized, hypervalorized abstract will to critical self-authorization.[18]

Blackmur's representation of the "scruple" as the motive for attention to detail is most important. Kant, we recall, would have the intellectual seize upon whatever is rational in nature and coerce it to respond to already given questions and methods; just as some critics insist in relation to culture. "Scruple," however, makes possible a different attitude, one more attentive to the complexity and difference that Kantian questioning tries to overwhelm, and one more aware and tolerant of the inevitable ignorance out of which and against which all desire for knowledge as well as all positively produced knowledge actually appears. We are reminded of Keats's "negative capability" and of Foucault's critique of the "regime of truth" of any Western scientific society. In literary critical terms, such a "scrupulous" attitude turns the critic toward the text not armed with a series of postures, gestures, and methods, not with a series of determinant and determining questions, but with a desire to do as well by the text as possible: in Blackmur's terms, with a desire to "react to more than a minor fraction of the life we yet deeply know and endure and die." What keeps a critic a critic in different occasions when there is no determining ultimate value and when there is active resistance to the institutionalized commonplaces of academic, political discourse? Blackmur's answer is the scruple as what he calls "the agent of integrity."

The scruple is not a cause of critical passivity, but a principle of agency and will. It does not promote a quietistic phenomenology. Blackmur repeatedly notes that in the face of recalcitrant social realities, Adams would become willful and stubborn: "But acts of will or stubbornness are merely the last resorts of minds compelled to act scrupulously against the unintelligent or the unintelligible" (HA, 6). But Blackmur recognizes and, in fact, demonstrates that the scrupulous skeptic must have a will that directs its affection in encounters with whatever is less intelligent and less complex.

In "A Critic's Job of Work" (1935), Blackmur defines criticism in such a way that at first it makes the will seem uninvolved:

Criticism, I take it, is the formal discourse of an amateur. When there is enough love and enough knowledge represented in the discourse it is a self-sufficient but by no means an isolated art. It witnesses constantly in its own life its interdependence with the other arts. It lays out the terms and parallels of appreciation from the outside in order to convict itself of internal intimacy; it names and arranges what it knows and loves, and searches endlessly with every fresh impulse or impression for better names and more orderly arrangements. It is only in this sense that poetry (or some other art) is a criticism of life; poetry names and arranges, and thus arrests and transfixes its subject in a form which has a life of its own forever separate but springing from the life which confronts it.[19]

It is to overstate the case to insist that for Blackmur criticism is an end in itself. Criticism is, as we say, semiautonomous, but it is not "an isolated art." The amateur's love continually records criticism's links with other discourses and acts, in effect, like the poetry it knows so well. Criticism is a form of intelligence that tests the names it assigns to what it loves and tries to understand and preserve. Like Adams's desire for political order as opposed to society's relish for chaos or tyranny, the critic's love obliges the critic to help find and preserve the order in what is loved and to save its place in a larger network of interdependencies. The aim here, like all erotic aims, is to preserve and produce new life, to generate, if not reproduce, the energies that, by giving form, give life to the complex sensorium of experience that the poet or critic embraces.

Most important of all Blackmur's thoughts in this passage is his rehearsal of the role of will in love. For the amateur, who knows his beloved intimately, must have the scruple that obliges the lover to attend to the details that make up the beloved's integrity. But this knowing means forming; it means, as Blackmur says of Adams's scruple, seeing the details in light of an end; it means reacting to the detail with a sense of all one's experience of complexity. Above all, in terms made possible both by the ideal and specificity of such a complex end, it means aligning the details into a form that shows both the lover's noncoercive erotics and the lover's willful desire to know and preserve the beloved other while trying to be energized, to maintain one's own integrity in the act of love. There is, in other words, a wide space for the action of will in a love that insists on knowing in light of ignorance, mystery, and desire.

In this essay itself, Blackmur gives considerable evidence of this structure in the way in which he works through the insufficient but energizing academic criticism of I. A. Richards, S. Foster Damon, and Kenneth Burke. Blackmur does not simply dismiss these critics; their writing essentially enables the development of his own work. When we reconfigure his encounter with these critics as part of the erotics of this essay, we see that[20] Blackmur's own critical work acquires shape, form, and clarifies its interrelationships in its working against what he calls in discussing Adams the "unintelligent and unintelligible." Blackmur, however, unlike Adams, does not stiffen his will into stubbornness; he reflectively modifies it in light of the tentative end of his work. That he draws energy from the critics he lovingly reshapes and delimits he nearly says explicitly in his approach to Burke: "The writer of whom he reminds us, for the buoyancy and sheer remarkableness of his speculations, is Charles Santiago Saunders Pierce; one is enlivened by them without any *necessary* reference to their truth; hence they have truth for their own purposes, that is, for their own uses. Into what these purposes and uses are it is our present business to inquire" (LG, 392).

Blackmur finds the original of his critical stance in Adams. When Adams insists, for example, that Albert Gallatin is the most admirable of American statesman and not Thomas Jefferson, Adams represents values that essentially prefigure Blackmur's critical ideal. Jefferson, Adams tells us, was unable ever to approach a matter tentatively. Inevitably, he was always bound by the consequences of his acts and decisions. At once opposed to the centralization of power in Washington—he assisted in the writing of the Virginia and Kentucky resolutions of nullification—and the first imperial president inaugurated in Washington, Jefferson bound himself and his government in untenable contradictions. We might say he held his end(s) too firmly:

> This doctrine [of the *Notes on Virginia*] was not original with Jefferson, but its application to national affairs on a great scale was something new in the world, and the theory itself clashed with his intellectual instincts of liberality and innovation . . . political power had established precedents inconsistent with their object.[21]

By contrast, Adams represents Albert Gallatin as possessing all the qualities of skeptical, loving suspicion, of a self-correcting but directed intellect missing from Jefferson's "philosophy." Gallatin used his talents in politics, but they were, as we see throughout Adams's work, the talents appropriate, especially in post Civil War America, to the artist and critic:

> Gallatin's celebrated financial policy carried into practice the doctrine that the powers of government, being necessarily irresponsible, and therefore hostile to liberty, ought to be exercised only within the narrowest bounds, in order to leave democracy free to develop itself without interference in its true social, intellectual, and economical strength. Unlike Jefferson and the Virginians, Gallatin never hesitated to claim for government all the powers necessary for whatever object was in hand; but he agreed with them in checking the practical use of power, and this he did with a degree of rigor which has often been imitated but never equaled.[22]

Adams's concern was always that the institutionalized results of intellection would destroy not only the effects of the original work, but, by solidifying the institution and burdening the mind with the history of its own decision, weaken the chance for criticism, self-criticism, and further imaginings. For Adams, the problem, as Blackmur nicely saw it, was always a question of how intelligence would deal with power—including the consequences of its own empowerment. Gallatin's achievements emerge from a central strength, a strength of doubt that suspects doctrine of lurking everywhere, even in its own most tentative and lovingly generous formulations.

What we know of Adams is that with the corruption of American government after the Civil War and with the obvious unwillingness of republican governments to make use of him, Adams increasingly represented this severe doubt as an achievement of art and faith. In The Education of Henry Adams, he proposes that we see this strength in its positive potential for artistic production in the figure of John La Farge. The text of The Education works by contrasting implicitly Gallatin, Hay, and La Farge. Despite Hay's monumental achievements in forming the Atlantic system and the "open door" policy, he finally is a defeated figure. Adams was a friend of James Bryce whose monumental two-volume work, The American Commonwealth, appeared in 1888. While Bryce's study reasserted his faith in the people, as Adams's Gore had done in Democracy (1880),[23] he also held that the friction in the U.S. system of government combined with its incapacity to attract the best minds, threatened its ability to act successfully in the modern world. That even Hay could not repeat Gallatin's success turned Adams to the aesthetic in search of an area of social life where the same talents of the critical mind might have success. We might say, as a kind of shorthand, that while professionalism destroyed Hay, La Farge, as the epitome of the critical mind in aesthetics, was saved by his eccentricity. For Adams, both were gifted amateurs, but since Hay is forced to become professional in the operations of power, to become an "office holder," he is, as Adams says, "lost to friendship." Adams insists repeatedly that friends are always lost when they acquire power. Hay is only a unique and partial exception to the rule; his sense of humor—which shows during their long walks together and lets Adams sometimes see his old friend once more—declines rapidly during his days as secretary of state and its decline marks the parallel approach of his imaginative and physical deaths.

In *The Education*, then, I would argue, one should see La Farge as ultimately the foil to Gallatin, a role he plays but passes through in relation to Hay, the obvious hero and victim of the public sphere. La Farge, we recall, appears rather abruptly in the "Indian Summer" chapter of *The Education* as the alternative to Jeffersonian regret and decline. To appreciate the weight Adams gives La Farge we must remember that it is La Farge who initiates Adams into the mysteries of glass in Chartres cathedral. In essence, he becomes a muse, certainly one of the conditions for the possibility of all the late work done by Adams in *Mont St. Michel* as well as in *The Education*, itself.

La Farge, Adams tells us, belongs to another time, the era of the great Gothic cathedrals. He is not only a latecomer but both Adams's alter ego and his complement:

> Of all his friends La Farge alone owned a mind complex enough to contrast against the common-places of American uniformity, and in the process had vastly perplexed most Americans who came in contact with it. The American mind,—the Bostonian as well as the southern or western,—likes to walk straight up to its object, and assert or deny something that it takes for a fact; it has a conventional approach, a conventional analysis, and a conventional conclusion, as well as a conventional expression, all the time loudly asserting its unconventionality. The most disconcerting trait of John La Farge was his reversal of the process. His approach was

quiet and indirect; he moved round an object, and never separated it from its surroundings; he prided himself on faithfulness to
tradition and convention; he was never abrupt and abhorred dis-
pute. . . . To La Farge, eccentricity meant convention; a mind really
eccentric never betrayed it. True eccentricity was a tone,—a
shade,—a *nuance*,—and the finer the tone, the truer the eccentricity.[24]

La Farge is a disconcerting eccentric; his method one of indirection.
Blackmur perhaps credited Adams with too little capacity for "indirection," while insisting himself too much on it as the premier capacity of
criticism.

For Adams, La Farge's complex mind has a simplicity about it that
gives him unique access to whatever underlies the complex figure of
imaginative power Adams calls "the virgin." For Blackmur, Adams, with
his scrupulous intelligence that holds in abeyance all threats to its own
suspicions—especially its own suspicions of itself—represents the ca-
pacious desire of the rational imagination to remain in contact with its
own sources.

In "A Critic's Job of Work," Blackmur early on insists that Freud is
"the classic contemporary example of use and misuse" of the rational
imagination. That is, the easy institutionalization of Freud's work in
"Freudian psychoanalytic" criticism distorts what Blackmur likes to
think is "the provisional, dramatic character of his speculations." The
problem posed by Freud is not unlike the one faced by Jefferson: "the
impetus of Freud was so great that a school of literalists arose with all
the mad consequence of schism and heresy and fundamentalism
which have no more honorable place in the scientific than the artistic
imagination" (LG, 374).

That Blackmur singles out Freud for this discussion becomes most
important when, at the end of this essay, he defends both his own
nonprogrammatic criticism and the qualities of art to which it hopes to
preserve access. We are accustomed to seeing Blackmur as a critic
endlessly worried about the fatal consequences of institutionalizing his
or any critical method. We see him as a consummate ironist intent on
deferring any regularization of his writing. And we are accustomed to
this as a matter of style as much if not more than as a matter of content:

My own approach, such as it is, and if it can be named, does not tell
the whole story either; the reader is conscientiously left with the

poem with the real work yet to do; and I wish to advance it—as indeed I have been advancing it *seriatim*—only in connection with the reduced and compensated approaches I have laid out; and I expect, too, that if my approach is used at all it will require its own reduction as well as its compensations. Which is why this essay has taken its present form, preferring for once, in the realm of theory and apologetics, the implicit to the explicit statement. It is, I suppose, an approach to literary criticism—to the discourse of an amateur—primarily through the technique, in the widest sense of that word, of the examples handled. (LG, 396)

In other words, unlike the commonplace American who prefers the direct approach, Blackmur, like Adams's La Farge, circles around his object, always keeping his end in view, testing the intelligence of each move with the fullest wisdom brought by an experience of life's complex sensorium.

But what is the end to which this mass of complex irony is disposed? The force of the discussion of Freud becomes clear after he tells us that criticism aims "to find understandable terms to fit the composition of the facts" (LG, 397). For the "mixture" of words, images, and notions that make up both poetry and the laborious apprehension of poetry is carried out in the "preconscious" (LG, 398). Mere technical analysis of the mixture of facts must be supplemented by "direct apprehension," what he also calls "intuition" (LG, 397–98). Criticism is always worldly, as Said would have it, but for Blackmur it not only produces the categories in and by which poetry or facts are apprehended and theorized, but it also accounts for the principles according to which these processes take place: "It may be that there are principles that cover both the direct apprehension and the labor of providing modes for the understanding of the expressive arts." But Blackmur's concern for the preconscious as the site for factual mixing leads him to repeat a fundamental concern: "If so, they are Socratic and found within, and subject to the fundamental skepticism as in Montaigne" (LG, 397). There is a psycho-poetics of a sort here; the "seed" of poetry and criticism are found within both the self and poem, within the word especially insofar as this is in itself a mixture with the image and notion. In each such "seed," as Eliot tells us about each poetic rhythm, there is, "at least prophetically, the whole future growth, the whole harvested life" (LG, 398).

What emerges finally in Blackmur's critical theory of this period is a poetics that is the base of criticism. Criticism, in its privative forms, resists cautiously all the seductions of intelligence. It tries to be as intelligent as possible, but fails always in order to humble the reason, to teach it humility as the objective correlative to ignorance and failure. The capacity for poetry is greater than the capacities of reason and so, strangely, reason must be used, in its most self-aware, ironic, and skeptical forms, to protect the poetic from reason in its degraded as well as most skeptically refined form. The end which the reason must keep always in mind is its own humiliation for the sake of the preconscious that is the condition of life and love, the condition for turning away from the abuses of reason in politics (Stalinism, fascism, and capitalism) and in science ("Freudianism, practical criticism, and rhetoric").

In a passage that recalls some of the debates between Benjamin and Brecht over the archaic, Blackmur, having circled around and circled around, finally, cautiously, approaches his object, the "end" of all his irony:

> The mixture, if I may start a hare so late, the mixture, even the fresh use of an old word, is made in the preconscious, and is by hypothesis unascertainable. But let us not use hypotheses, let us not desire to ascertain. By intuition we adventure in the preconscious; and there, where adventure is, there is no need or suspicion of certainty or meaning; there is the living, expanding, *prescient* substance without the tags and handles of conscious form. Art is the looking-glass of the preconscious, and when it is deepest seems to participate in it sensibly. Or, better, for purposes of criticism, our sensibility resumes the division of the senses and faculties at the same time that it preens itself into conscious form. Criticism may have as an object the establishment and evaluation (comparison and analysis) of the modes of making the preconscious *consciously* available. (LG, 398)

This is a defense of poetry that, in the late twentieth century, has the eccentric value of asking all direct critical approaches that make up the pluralistic academy both to judge their own results and efforts by the demanding standard Blackmur proposes and to question if the structure of academic criticism in its currently institutionalized forms has the capacity to make the preconscious available or to evaluate the various efforts to do so. Blackmur adopted Adams's line and sometimes called himself a conservative anarchist. In this context, the phrase is double-edged. In the face of the occasional needs of contemporary society and the defined paths to professional success, a defense of poetry seems to be a "retrocriticism," just one of the many nostalgias of the Reagan/Bush era when we travel "back to the future." But anarchy is the central term here: the eccentric defense of what Blackmur struggles to name, tentatively, as the preconscious: the capability for creation, judgment, and love that stands as the always-threatened corrective to both the abuses of reason and the highest intelligence.

The critic must always act with the most "provisional skepticism," but not perhaps as Said would have it, for the sake of criticism itself; rather for the sake of whatever it is (tentatively named the preconscious) that makes criticism possible—whatever it is that makes poetry, love, and all the expressive arts possible as a defense of life against the fatal consequence of "doctrine." "Poetry," in this broad sense, is a "beacon not a life-raft" and its tragedy is its inevitable rigidity (LG, 376). It seems hardly coincidental that Blackmur insists upon relighting this beacon in the 1930s, in the face of "Caesarism in Rome and Berlin" (LG, 374) and the "stereotyped vision . . . of conservative capitalism" (LG, 378). In a way that recalls Adams's Gore and his friend Bryce (and perhaps reminds some of us of Gramsci's writings on the universality of intellectual capacity), Blackmur insists that "like walking, criticism is a pretty nearly universal art." The problem is that both activities are hard to do well; especially since, for complex reasons, most prefer the easy to the hard path. Perhaps in the era of Reagan and Bush and a terroristic but declining imperialism, we need to recall Blackmur's concerns for critics at another time of imaginative need:

> For either [criticism or walking] a new terrain is fatiguing and awkward, and in our day most men prefer paved walks or some form of rapid transit—some easy theory or outmastering dogma. A good critic keeps his criticism from becoming either instinctive or vicarious, and the labor of his understanding is always specific, like the art which he examines. (LG, 378)

9

......

Paul de Man:
Critic against
Consensus

Paul de Man published "The Rhetoric of Temporality" in 1969.[1] (One likes to think of him writing it in 1968.) It is one of his most highly regarded essays. In the introduction to his edition of de Man's *Critical Writings, 1953–1978*, entitled "Paul de Man: Life and Works" (1989), Lindsay Waters says that " 'The Rhetoric of Temporality' is rightly (I think) felt to be his most fully achieved essay."[2] Daniel O'Hara, in "Paul de Man: Nietzsche's Teacher" (1985), lets "The Rhetoric of Temporality" occupy the center of his own meditation on the erotics of de Man's writing.[3] In *Critical Genealogies*, Jonathan Arac twice notes the importance of this essay, once as a moment in contemporary criticism's rewriting the history of Romanticism; and once as an instance of Benjamin's importance for contemporary criticism.[4] "The Rhetoric of Temporality" is also important in Donald Pease's revision of Matthiessen's construction of the "American Renaissance." Pease's accomplishment depends in large measure upon his reading of Poe as the allegorist of Hawthorne's loss of cultural memory, a reading which draws on "The Rhetoric of Temporality" to help establish its own conclusions.[5] One could, of course, name other critics who have dealt with this essay— some more and some less sympathetic to de Man and deconstruction.

Lindsay Waters makes clear that he feels this essay deserves its high reputation because, in "The Rhetoric of Temporality," de Man "had the tools he needed to achieve what he knew was impossible before."[6] Like Arac and others, Waters takes note that in this essay de Man has occasion to make use of his readings in Benjamin's book, *The Origin of German Tragic Drama.*[7] For Waters, Benjamin allows de Man "to reapproach the question of history that had always been central to his work" and get beyond the Heideggerean discourse on temporality. He puts "the language of rhetoric in the place of that of temporality."[8] And with this displacement, as Waters reads it, de Man takes on Benjamin's project: "In the end he rejected the notions of interiority and inwardness as tools of analysis and he also rejected the inner/outer dichotomy that he had derived from the tradition of German idealism."[9] The Benjaminian turn in "The Rhetoric of Temporality," in Waters's opinion, lets de Man attend to the materiality of literature as a ruin that "bears the imprint of the progression of history inscribed within it."[10] Of course, de Man's essay so troubles the very possibility of history under the sign of "anteriority" that to accept Waters's reading we would first need to deconstruct his own dualistic rhetoric of inside/outside. Pointing out this small slip in Waters's writing about de Man's movement away from these dualisms does not single out Waters for having made an "error" in reading. As de Man himself would no doubt have it, Waters could not write of these matters without reinscribing what we might call, in the context of "The Rhetoric of Temporality," a symbolist rhetoric and position, a language of identity, of commensurability between language and a nonlinguistic "history" "inscribed" "within it."

"The Rhetoric of Temporality" is a remarkably complex essay; it is de Man at his performing best. The two parts of the essay on allegory and irony respectively bring preliminary historicizing into contact with theoretical writing that subverts its needed historicism and they do so in such a way as to enact a "truth" or "understanding" that could not appear in the concept alone. This last sentence is a dense (hopefully not simply unclear) and abstract statement about some important aspects of de Man's essay. As we recall, the essay's first part seems to recount historically how romanticism's production of a symbolist aesthetic in a rhetoric of subjectivity parallels or is accompanied by the development of a new rhetorical mode that de Man, after Benjamin, calls "allegory." De Man goes on to tell us that the nineteenth century forgot "allegory" in its valorization of a subjectivist, symbolist aesthetic and that, in part, his essay aims to recover the lost rhetorical form and, in the process, rewrite the history of romanticism. Along the way of this history, de Man encapsulates understandings of the Germans, particularly Goethe, Schiller, and Schlegel; of the English, especially Coleridge; and of the French, especially Rousseau. He also makes a number of what we would call theoretical remarks about the nature of language, allegory, and the symbol, emphasizing their relation to time, history, the self, and difference.

The second part of the essay is in a disjunctive but complementary relation to the first. The second section is on irony and is insistently non- or even anti-historical; it insists that irony has history as its enemy and can never be historicized; indeed, as a trope, irony can account for the production of selves some of which, we might say, are narrativized in allegorical duration. But the structure of de Man's essay does not result in a simple "inversion of hierarchies" or "subversion" of itself. De Man's insight is always of such a kind that only on the level of his own performance can one begin to see (or could he begin to make visible) the "truth" of his own "understanding." Were we to read the essay very closely—and there is not space to do so here—we would be able to write many things about the interwoven structures of truth/error, blindness/insight, etc. that are all caught up in what we now call the materiality of the sign.[11]

It would be extremely interesting and important to rewrite de Man's writing here, to follow his own "purpose," as it were, in working out the impersonal, often, "inhuman" nature of language at the level of the conditions for the production of meaning and value. One can justifiably defer this project in part because Carol Jacobs has already done a powerful rewriting of de Man's essay and done so in such a way that it lets others begin to talk about not only de Man's concern for but his actual authority within the profession.

Jacobs opens her rewriting of de Man with the sort of paragraph many of those who take de Man seriously must write whenever trying to write about him:

> There is no way to say adequately what the significance of de Man might be. It could not be otherwise, for he himself linked death to the impossibility of defining man as presence and with man's perpetual transgression of his own sense of self as totalized. And, given that the transgression is perpetual, it took no literal death to both upset and set the task, that of reading the man, which is to say, writing about him.[12]

Just what are the expectations fulfilled by this remarkable paragraph? One wants to begin by saying that the paragraph is allegorical in that it is allusively figural as de Man describes Julie's garden to be: that is, as Rousseau's language alludes to and derives from *The Romance of the Rose*

and *Robinson Crusoe*, Jacobs's language is itself formulaic, borrowed almost "whole cloth," as a "*doublure*," we might say, from the texts that
carry de Man's signature. Of course, we immediately notice the characteristic joke, the pun on "reading the man," the sort of move that marks
the "grim rigor" of de Man's own work. Also, there are many familiar de
Manian ideas here; Jacobs finds she cannot begin to write "about" de
Man, as it were, except from within his own problematic, from within
what *Yale French Studies* has taught us to call "The Lesson of Paul de
Man."[13] What we note, too, is a characteristic dialectic of the sort that
Said once called "authority" and "molestation."[14] In other words, we
see how de Man has enabled Jacobs's own essay: without de Man's
writing of the link between death (and rhetoric) and the transgression
against the totalized self, Jacobs, we might say, could have mistakenly
written about the dead de Man in some way other than "reading the
man"—an authorization that itself guides her through a powerful rewriting of one of the most complex and insightful essays of the past
twenty years. So de Man saves Jacobs from mistakes whenever she
writes; at least, he saves her from the conventional and never banished
forms of mystification, if only by raising her struggle with and against
them to a higher plane where the fatality of theory provides understanding, even if no alternative to the entrapments it reveals, reworks,
and reinscribes.

Yet, de Man's authority is also a "molestation" because Jacobs cannot
begin her writing on de Man—given the rigor of her own reading—but
from within de Man's lesson. To be enabled and constrained by consequences: this is a difficult thing to understand or to say. Said would have
it that "molestation" is simply "a consciousness of one's duplicity, one's
confinement to a fictive, scriptive realm."[15] Perhaps de Man has helped
us more than Said to understand this "confinement" as a state of
language; from a point of view like de Man's, Said's formulation is naive
because it speaks of a consciousness that senses its own confinement to
a fictive realm on the basis of its sense of a difference from "reality," a
difference that, in Said's view, leads the molested author to feel herself
to be confined to a realm of illusion. De Man, of course, is always more
precise when he speaks of such things, so, in "The Rhetoric of Temporality," he writes of "a disjunction between the way in which the
world appears in reality and the way it appears in language" (191). What
Said calls "molestation" is, then, only a weak interpretation of the
incommensurability of language and human experience, and is, as

such, a historicization of an ahistorical, indeed, inhuman structure that in part underlies the production of history, of narrative.

To put the matter another way, we might say that the dialectic of Jacobs's relation to the lesson of the master is caught by the figure of allegory itself. With Nietzsche we might call it the dialectic of belatedness, or, of the structural relation between priority and anteriority. Jacobs, after all, is in a consequent position for, as Michael Hays is wont to remind us, de Man is dead.[16] To be as true to the lesson of de Man, then, as Jacobs would have herself be, this consequent relation can only be, as de Man says in writing of allegory, "a relationship between signs in which the reference to their respective meanings has become of secondary importance." It becomes, to use a shorthand, an act of reading. De Man's teaching and his death become signs postulated as being "in the past" or even "at the origin" in Jacobs's, of course, self-conscious allegory. The never present, transgressed, and now dead de Man has become a repetition of a sort de Man, himself, has theorized:

> But this relationship between signs necessarily contains a constitutive temporal element; it remains necessary, if there is to be allegory, that the allegorical sign refer to another sign that precedes it. The meaning constituted by the allegorical sign can then consist only in the *repetition* (in the Kierkegaardian sense of the term) of a previous sign with which it can never coincide, since it is of the essence of this previous sign to be pure anteriority. The secularized allegory of the early romantics thus necessarily contains the negative moment which in Rousseau is that of renunciation, in Wordsworth that of the loss of self in death or in error. (207)

In a performance like Jacobs's, then, the relation between master and apprentice can only be repetition; and so wherever there is or has been a strong teacher the student can only be an allegorist: allegory, the story of ruin, can be the ephebe's only form.[17] Jacobs knows this, of course, and in a full repetition of de Man's most brilliant performance, "ends" her essay, by ironizing her ironic play with de Man's dialectics:

> After this long digression [into the performative aspects of "The Rhetoric of Temporality"] which was, of necessity, both a definition and transgression of de Man's text, we might return to the original crises, that of saying not only what de Man means but also what we mean when we say de Man. No doubt this essay, I confess,

in de Man's words, produces "a darkness more redoubtable than . . . [any] error . . . it might dispel." To be sure, this is no excuse. But, whatever I have done in reading his text, if the reader will forgive the rhetorical question, would it not still be possible to assert that it is "Ah! encore de Man"?[18]

Rewriting de Man means turning to the master for the authority to write, to use certain figures, without reverting to an unproblematic—or pre-de Manian sense of language and its nonrelation to death, history, experience, etc. Jacobs, we should say, writes without losing sight of de Man's lesson; she writes—and can write—only by virtue of positioning herself in relation to a pure anteriority that de Man has become in the allegory of his students. Jacobs's first reminder to her own readers is that the self is always transgressed by death: in this allegory, however, death is the pure anteriority that defines the ephebe's authorized position, or, to put it another way "the man" is death, the transgression of the self. (Can we say this is an allegory of the ephebes's "murder" of the master?)

This is the sort of reading of de Man that many object to. Some of de Man's students—those who are merely ephebes[19]—object because it is a reading that lacks rigor and—dare one say it?—sympathy and understanding. It is also the sort of reading that makes many of deconstruction's right- and left-wing critics politically, ethically, and professionally unhappy with de Man and his influence: the ephebes—if not the master—seem to be paralyzed, spinning their wheels within a repetition that has become old news, that has no effective politics, that has hardly transformed even the profession except, for the cynical, by too easily making some too quickly distinguished careers.

Rather than attempt to propose an entirely different way of approaching de Man—as others are now trying to do—I want to draw attention to a few aspects of "The Rhetoric of Temporality" that, as far as I know, have received little attention. Other commentators have made much of irony, allegory, anteriority, symbolism, rhetoric, and other key terms of de Man's developing rhetorical criticism in this essay. Of course, any serious commentary on the essay must do so. But were one to read the essay with slightly different emphases, were one to see it in a slightly different tradition, perhaps the importance of these terms would take on a slightly different sense, a tactical sense.

I want to propose a look at this essay that begins with a recollection and a repetition of my own. De Man tells us that the relation of the present to the past in allegory is repetition in a Kierkegaardian sense. Kierkegaard, we should remember, insisted that repetition is recollection forward, that it is a structure that ensures futurity as anteriority, a futurity marked by difference, that is, distance from equally figurative pasts and presents. Of course, such a notion lets us argue that the ephebes' allegory of their own derivative and perhaps murderous authority can be just such a futurity. There are at least two things interesting about this allegorical moment: that the profession allows or allowed it to be institutionalized; and that de Man's work so clearly—as Jacobs's brilliantly troubling immanental readings show—enables and authorizes that allegory of professional authorization. Ezra Pound's *Cantos* give us one language to say this: the ephebes enter the enchanted realm of authority, the space where one can come to be known.[20]

Ought one not consider if de Man's text offers other "futurities," as it were, and if it might be, in a way, a most clever—and he was nothing if not clever—analysis of the professional and ideological realities that form this powerful nexus of authority, professional privilege, and death? "The Rhetoric of Temporality" came to me—or I came to it—in graduate school in the 1970s from the tradition of Nietzsche—a claim which I suppose shocks no one—and from the tradition of Marx—a claim that others will, perhaps find somewhat more surprising or even foolish.[21] But coming on the essay, and on de Man generally in these ways, lets me say, if you will, that there are certain oppositional and even historical movements in the essay that some other readers choose not to discuss.

R. P. Blackmur once wrote of how a good critic, like a good poet, will always produce a "cumulus" of meaning in a "conjury" of words, a cumulus that, like a symbol as Blackmur understood it, always had social implications and emerged from social realities.[22] Looking at part of de Man's essay in light of Blackmur's thought suggests different emphases than those common to many of de Man's students' readings of his work.

Most obviously, de Man is criticizing what he sees as the ideological, intellectual, and academic dominance of the discourse of the symbol. The critique is part and parcel of his ongoing struggle with Hegel and the institutionalization of his thought, his philosophy, his figures; de

Man makes clear some of what is at stake in this critique as he discusses the symbol:

> The valorization of [the] symbol at the expense of allegory coincide[s] with the growth of an aesthetics that refuses to distinguish between experience and the representation of this experience. The poetic language of genius is capable of transcending this distinction and can thus transform all individual experience directly into language; the world is then no longer seen as a configuration of entities that designate a plurality of distinct and isolated meanings, but as a configuration of symbols ultimately leading to a total, single, and universal meaning. This appeal to the infinity of a totality constitutes the main attraction of the symbol as opposed to allegory, a sign that refers to one specific meaning and thus exhausts its suggestive potentialities once it has been deciphered. (188)

"The Rhetoric of Temporality" is as much concerned with the discursive and institutional establishment of the symbol as it is with the linguistic or, if you will, "inhuman" structures that betray themselves in—and betray us into—the abysmal dialectics of allegory and irony. De Man's critique—in his discussion of allegory and irony—is a critique of the totality, as it is in his early essays on Nietzsche, perhaps most explicitly in "Genesis and Genealogy in Nietzsche's *Birth of Tragedy*."[23] It is above all a critique of the nineteenth century's forgetting of the tense relation between symbol and allegory in Goethe, Coleridge, and others. It is, if you will, as much a critique of the "Professors" as it is a critique of an inhuman linguistic structure. For example, to read Hölderlin symbolically is not only a mistake, but it is an act that displaces Hölderlin's metaphors by the synecdoche of the organic symbol; and it is an act the burdens of which de Man tries to make explicit and to deconstruct.

The target of de Man's weapons are equally the Professors and their discourse—in this case, Abrams and Wasserman and the discourse on romanticism. De Man draws attention to the academic consensus that is the institutional counterpart, the empowered figuration, of the ideology of the organic symbol—the desire for "totality." When he writes of the Professors he says such things as "The main interpretative [sic] effort of English and American historians of romanticism has focused on . . .";

as well as: "recent articles by . . . Abrams and . . . Wasserman . . . make use of very similar, at times even identical material. The two interpreters agree on many issues, to the point of overlapping" (193, 194). Indeed, although de Man the historian finds evidence of the valorization of the symbol in Coleridge, it is the Professors who forget Coleridge's ambiguities—the "allegory" of his texts—and reimagine him as someone who succumbs to the temptations of the symbolic aesthetic: "This strategy [of borrowing nature's stability for the self] is certainly present in Coleridge. And it is present, though perhaps not consciously, in critics such as Abrams and Wasserman, who see Coleridge as the great synthesizer and who take his dialectic of subject and object to be the authentic pattern of romantic imagery" (197). De Man goes on to point out the same consensus-formation in the study of French and German as in that of English romanticism. It is that discursive, ideological, and intellectual solidification—that orthodoxy, that consensus-building—against which de Man directs the efforts of this essay. He repeatedly tells us that it is the "priority," the "superiority," the empowerment, if you will, of this set of intellectual judgments, this set of values, that must be displaced—presumably by driving it or them into abysmal oscillations, the insane vertigoes that he tries so hard to authorize as their replacement in the Professors's talk. Of course, the project is mad and failed. But ought we not see it as directed, historical, tactical, and the purposive act of an agent? Ought we not see it as, above all, an act that warns its beholders of its worst dangers—madness, death, and repetition?

But why must this orthodoxy be displaced? The Professors's commitment to the "symbol's" priority involves an inseparable commitment to totalization, to forms of history writing penetrated by the drive to totalize. Of course, given what has come to light about de Man's wartime involvements with fascism, we understand in a newly personal way why he would have been so sensitive to the equation between discourses that totalize and totalizing practices and totalitarian politics. It would be an exaggeration to say that the Professors are "totalitarians," but not to insist that both their discursive and ideological commitments to the symbolist aesthetic and its historical narratives, on the one hand, and their institutional consensus forming, their willful amnesic "misreadings," on the other hand, exist as one cultural manifestation of an arrangement of "knowledge" and "language forms" that incontrovertibly exists in a continual relation with the politics of totalitarianism. Nothing less than this argument emerges in "Genesis and Genealogy."[24]

In that essay, de Man shows that organic models of literary history are analogous to Hegelian discourses of circular totality, of closure that marks an inescapable identity between "beginning" and "end": " 'Das Resultat,' " de Man quotes Hegel from the introduction to The Phenomenology of Spirit, " 'ist nur darum dasselbe, was der Anfang, weil der Anfang Zweck ist.' "[25] As de Man shows in "The Rhetoric of Temporality," the Professors of romanticism tend to repeat the structures of romanticism in the very act of writing its history. For de Man, one way to consider evading this duplication would be to imagine a nonorganic history of romanticism. There is, however, one problem that must be dealt with prior to the effort to make this move: the fact that most historians of romanticism are themselves still "pre-Hegelian," that is "caught in a nondialectical notion of a subject-object dichotomy."[26] There would be real reason, then, to carry out a study that would trace the organic model in romanticism and its history. Of course, that model finds its latest literary critical articulations in the Professors's works mentioned in "The Rhetoric of Temporality." Without following de Man through his readings of Nietzsche, it is nonetheless apparent what is "wrong," as it were, with the practice of these Professors, even in their Hegelian duplications of romanticism. Like those much greater dialecticians, Auerbach and Benjamin, the Professors emulate Hegel in "bypass[ing] . . . the contemporary moment entirely."[27] Indeed, even deconstruction does not guarantee that organic totalizing history can be avoided; genetic history would merely redeploy itself. Deconstruction disrupts linear sequences so "that no sequence of actual events or no particular subject could ever acquire, by itself, full historical meaning." These events and subjects remain, however, "moments" within a process: "since the movement consists of their totalization, they can still be said to share in the experience of this movement."[28]

De Man's general point is clear; equally important, however, are the implications of this theoretical insight for the institutionalized practices and discourses of the Professors: for the most part, their work is "pre-Hegelian," simply "Hegelian," or, even when "deconstructed," stubbornly "Hegelian." It totalizes by virtue of sharing the organic, genetic model of the "idea," "romanticism," of which it claims to write the history. De Man's challenge to the Professors' history takes the form of a question: what if "the Romantics came closer than we do to undermining the absolute authority of this system"? "The ultimate test or 'proof' of the fact that Romanticism puts the genetic pattern of history in question would then be the impossibility of writing a history of Romanticism."[29]

De Man's criticism of the Professors and their institutions takes the form of delegitimating the forms of historical discourse that ground their knowledge production. De Man's readings clearly show that he aims not just to reveal the "abyss" over which all language "hovers," rather, he clearly aims to undermine authority, claims to originality, to knowledge, and institutional legitimacy. This constellation of contentions is clearest perhaps at the very end of "Genesis and Genealogy." There he shows, first, that he is interested in "consequences"; second, that the Professors do not know how to read; third, that they rest unaffected by the fact that such texts as Nietzsche's, when taken seriously, should indeed have consequences on the ways in which one thinks and works; and, fourth, that in this "resting" the Professors are, like all of us, the products of the "absolute authority" of systems, of "exemplary models."[30]

Returning to "The Rhetoric of Temporality," we can see that de Man's effort—to displace his predecessor Professors and their politically dangerous, naively inherited discourses—requires Benjamin's theory of allegory: the romantic allegorizers and the Professors are all pure anteriority for a discourse that needs them to be such, to have no meaning of their own so they can be most effectively displaced. It is a move, however, that authorizes, indeed, demands of his students a similar dialectical allegory of murderous reverence—but against whom should it be directed? There is a danger in this demand, though, for that way lies not only new authority and its questioning, but necessarily death, madness, and redundant repetition: "absolute irony is a consciousness of madness, itself the end of all consciousness; it is a consciousness of a nonconsciousness, a reflection on madness from the inside of madness itself." Absolute irony is a double movement: stabilizing itself in a linguistic self, a masked production, a doubling from which one can—the ironist, whoever he or she might be, hopes—come to see the writing's madness. But this double reflection is not good enough; it could be mistaken for a real form of life, for sympathy and care. The absolute ironist must observe, disinterestedly, the temptation to care: this de Man sometimes calls theory. But theory is a moment of redundancy, redundancy of the very worst sort, knowing now what we know about collaboration and resistance:

> Technically correct rhetorical readings may be boring, monotonous, predictable, and unpleasant, but they are irrefutable. They are also totalizing (and potentially totalitarian) for since the structures and functions they expose do not lead to the knowledge of an entity (such as language) but are an unreliable process of knowledge production that prevents all entities, including linguistic entities, from coming into discourse as such. . . . They are, always in theory, the most elastic and dialectical model to end all models and they can rightly claim to contain within their own defective selves all the other defective models of reading-avoidance, referential, semiological, grammatical, performative, logical, or whatever. They are theory and not theory at the same time, the universal theory of the impossibility of theory. . . . Nothing can overcome the resistance to theory since theory is this resistance. The loftier the aims and the better the methods of literary theory, the less possible it becomes.[31]

The New Critics, with their understanding of absolute irony, felt irony's great value to lie precisely in its making the authority of its speaker, its writer, invulnerable to irony, to all accusations of being incomplete, of inadequate complexity and knowledge, of having produced only a partial simulacrum of the universe.[32] De Man's warning about irony is that it always is tempted to collaborate, most especially at those moments when it is most dominant, most impervious to the humanity of other weaker, partial, less-satisfactory positions and perspectives. Irony and theory can resist this Professorial temptation to consensus, but their unique specularity ties them to a fatal repetition of their enemies's errors—albeit on a higher, more powerful level. Theory and irony—these are valued only as the sites of struggle, not as the site of victory; indeed, their victories end as collaborations no matter how they begin as resistance. Allegory and irony: the one leaves us with ruins while the other "recapture[s] some of the factitiousness of human experience" (226).

In his essay, "The Tiger on the Paper Mat," which functions as a foreword to The Resistance to Theory, Wlad Godzich recovers something of the social origins of *theoria*, not as pure anteriority, but as a sign of theory's social existence as an authorized "bearing-witness-to" which alone gives evidence, which alone allows entities to enter into discourse as existing and "true." With some irony of his own, Godzich leaves us with the reminder become obligation that de Man has left us with the problem of praxis.[33]

10

......

Dante,
Gramsci, and
Cultural
Criticism

Antonio Gramsci produced several brief but important remarks on Dante. The most important of these are to be found in a letter mailed from prison to his sister-in-law, Tatiana, in which Gramsci theorizes about "political leadership" in relation to the figural problematic of "paternity" and "pedagogy." A close reading of these remarks illustrates not only the importance of culture (and cultural history) in Gramsci's politics, but also his readers' obligation to give careful and precise attention to language in retheorizing his thinking, his activity, and his writing. Attention to language is important because it suggests that efforts to "conceptualize" Gramsci, to think abstractly about his putative "concepts"—such as of "leadership" or "party"—will always over-simplify, always reify and academicize the positionality, the tactical, interventionary character of his intellectual production and political struggle. Such "conceptualizing" also portrays Gramsci as a systematic political philosopher, as a "mind," in the neo-Kantian or Cassirean mode; in addition, such a procedure narrativizes Gramsci's work either in terms of figures of "development," "maturation," or "deepening." In sum, it pictures Gramsci as a "high modernist" intellectual, supremely confident in his "vision," instantaneous in his apprehension of truth, and stylistically self-identified in his writing. In other words, it either aestheticizes Gramsci as a political visionary or normalizes him as a systematic philosopher thinking conceptually and abstractly about matters that can be represented unproblematically in instrumental language.

In contrast to such a conceptualizing model, a reading of Gramsci's

writings on Dante reveals some of how Gramsci reflects upon the problems of representation—semiotic and political—and also how these
troubling theoretical reflections find their place in the linguistic, that is,
rhetorical and literary, formulations of his writing. Such a reading indicates that those commentators who ignore these concerns misunderstand Gramsci, misunderstand the cultural politics of representation
within and about which Gramsci writes, and misunderstand the importance of the problematic of representation to political thought and
action. Of course, that Gramsci's writing is marked by the problematic
of representation does not mean that Gramsci is a politically inactive
"meta-theorist" of the sort that some critics feel (perhaps partly un-
justly) can be found among so-called "deconstructors." It means, rather,
that Gramsci should be seen as a political man who takes seriously not
only culture and its institutional forms and traditions, but also the
politico-theoretical consequences—for action and thought—of culturally burdened, culturally enabled, culturally "inscribed" forms of verbal
representation. Seen in slightly different terms Gramsci appears as a
political writer producing interventions into culture which themselves
carry the inescapable traces of political, cultural history—traces within
the effects and systems of genealogically burdened representations—
traces that need to be acknowledged and dealt with in the very interventions the political person makes within culture. Gramsci's struggles,
that is, take place partly and necessarily within the field of representation—and it means he needs to be read in light of this fact of his writing.

Reading Gramsci in this way has consequences: he would no longer
be "read" conceptually, as a writer (or "activist") uninterested either in
the consequences of language for political expression or in the burdens
of culture inscribed within the language culturally aware political activ-
ists and theorists inherit from their pasts. His writings would have to be
read as themselves central places for engaging in a political battle in the
politically central sphere of culture. His writings would have to be read
as contesting for the politically appropriate deployment of the culturally central resources of a tradition that could either constrain or free
the future. In other words, and more specifically, Gramsci's writing on
Dante must be read as an inventory of the historical, cultural, and
political burdens and possibilities haunting and enabling his own
thinking about leadership, the party, the intellectual, fatherhood, and
cultural teaching—as well as the real chance for significant political
action in these areas of culture.[1] Indeed, working through some of the

entanglements within the problematic represented by the nexus of figures in his reading of Dante—paternity, party, pedagogy—shows Gramsci's testimony to the cultural and historical complexities that inscribe his thinking about matters central to his politics. It also shows that this "thinking through" is, itself, within the sphere of cultural politics, a politically significant battle against ideological enemies as well as the hegemonic constraints of tradition in the idioms of cultural, critical, and political discourse.

The force of Gramsci's commitment to make present, to confront, to exploit, and to overcome the various traces of this specific political cultural history can be seen by contrast with other powerful modern readers of Dante, specifically T. S. Eliot—whose readings of Dante define the international high modernists' use of his work—and Croce—whose book on Dante presents the most important immediate politico-cultural adversary for Gramsci: Croce's text both gives Dante a certain ideologically and culturally material position within fascism and it sums and perpetuates (or redeploys) a tradition of Dante commentary whose historical material role within the culture Gramsci confronts in the critical, political agon staged by Gramsci's reading of the *Inferno*'s tenth Canto.

II

Gramsci's revision of what he calls the pedantic criticism of Dante's great poem is important. The pedants, as it were—the highly specialized and academic critics of the academy and other high cultural institutions, that is, teachers, journalists, priests—constitute the material, institutional nexus, the memory and political effectivity of a certain image of Dante's value within both the high culture and the common sense of the Italian tradition. Gramsci, however, directs his efforts to revise that tradition against Croce, rather than the anonymous pedants. Although Gramsci's intellectual work provides a crucial model for the detailed study of the detailed materiality of culture, politics, and tradition, it must be pointed out that his own writings often stage political contests with the leading figures—in both the biographical and rhetorical sense of that word—of the traditions, the discourses, the ideologies, and the parties with which he and his allies must contend. And that is just the case here. Gramsci turns his remarks into not only a critique of Croce, the most important intellectual of his time, but also against the empowered and enabling tropes central to the maintenance of the dominant cultural tradition he hopes to exploit and oppose. In such of his writings as the early political journalism, in various specific notes throughout the *Prison Notebooks*, but especially in the essay on "The Southern Question," Gramsci offers remarkably important insights into the workings of cultural materiality in its most specific and often anonymous forms. Especially the essay on "The Southern Question" exemplifies how that sort of analysis might be done. But the remarks on Dante show Gramsci at a different sort of work, one meant to drive at the source, as it were, of the cultural system sustained by the anonymous pedants. The critique is of Croce, himself, of course, for his errors and against his influence, but, so to speak, it is also a critique and struggle against his functionality, his positionality, against the kind of figure and position represented by Croce and the tradition to which he belongs. In trying to think through the politically fraught question of the nature of leadership in a democratic political movement, Gramsci critiques and struggles to displace a certain functioning notion and positionality of (especially intellectual) leadership and some of the kinds of cultural production upon which the maintenance of that implicitly antidemocratic kind of leadership rests. So the critique of Croce is not merely a debate about the "correct" way to read even a culturally traditional text; it is also a revelation of that unacceptable positionality, of its powerful inscription within the dominant culture—or in the way the then-dominant culture takes its tradition—and that inscription's traces within even the oppositional language and practice of Gramsci himself. It is an essay on the nature of tradition and its inescapable conflicts, burdens, and empowerments. It shows the oppositional intellectual's awareness of how traditions, coming to individuals different by virtue of their class, their region, their language, their knowledge, and their politics nonetheless compel conflict both within those individuals and their languages—to arrange the traditions' forces to the desired ends—and between individuals and their positions within the empowered culture to bring about the desired social ends. Class-based political struggles cannot be carried out without struggles over and within the cultural effects of tradition. On one level, these are struggles over who will "control" or "interpret" or "inherit" a tradition, indeed, over what of the past will come to make up the "dominant tradition." But on another level, these are struggles that also show how profoundly "molested" even powerful opposi-

tional leaders are by the absolutely inescapable genealogical obstacles—as well as opportunities—already established traditions create
even within the very words of the oppositional, critical, political resistance itself. It is within the space of this awareness that Gramsci's
notes contend with Croce now taken quite precisely as the figure of the
entire problematic of cultural burden within and against which the
oppositional political leader must contend.

III

Gramsci focuses his reading of Dante around Canto X of the *Inferno*. In
this canto, Dante the pilgrim encounters two dead souls, Cavalcante
and Farinata, both heretics and both politicians prominent in the violence that rent Florence for about thirty years or so. Farinata, the leader
of the Ghibellines, and Cavalcante, one of the important Guelf bourgeois, are punished in the same way: locked forever in tombs of fire,
unable to know the present, and destined, when the future ends, to
have no knowledge at all. The canto explicitly involves Dante the
pilgrim in the politics of Florence, in the struggle between the imperialist and middleclass factions, and does so in a way that depends upon
the particular fate of these damned. Cavalcante must ask Dante about
his son, Guido, precisely because this heretic is damned to know
nothing of the future. It is around this necessary question, arising from
paternal love, that Gramsci builds his reading of Dante—as had most
important commentators in the past.

   In his reading, Gramsci specifically refutes Croce's then authoritative
claim that, in Canto X, the drama is Farinata's. Croce has it that after
Cavalcante's disappearance from the scene, Farinata's role changes to
what Croce calls "structure": he loses his "poetic" status. Gramsci reads
the canto differently, insisting that the drama is Cavalcante's and that
Farinata's "pedagogic" remarks after the former's fall back into the
tomb are necessary to Dante's representation of the punishment appropriate to this circle: Dante's silence in response to Cavalcante's
shock at Dante's "ebbe" comes from his not understanding Cavalcante's punishment and so his ignorance of Guido's fate. Farinata's
explanation that, as epicurean heretics, they are punished with no
knowledge of the present, lets Dante see why Cavalcante responded
with such horror to Dante's use of the past tense. More important,
however, Gramsci's reading stresses that Dante's art is one of action:

Cavalcante is the one punished in the circle. No one has observed that if the drama of Cavalcante is not taken into consideration, one does not see the torment of the damned in that circle being *enacted*. The *structure* ought to have led to a more exact aesthetic evaluation of the canto, since every punishment is represented in act.

The crucial word in the line "Forse cui Guido vostro ebbe a disdegno" is not "cui" or "disdegno," but only "*ebbe*." The "aesthetic" and "dramatic" accent on the line falls on "ebbe," and it is the source of Cavalcante's drama, interpreted in the stage directions of Farinata. And there is the "catharsis." Dante corrects himself and takes Cavalcante out of his torment. In other words, he interrupts his punishment in *action*.[2]

In these and other remarks on Canto X, Gramsci clearly revises and displaces Croce's dualistic aesthetic that divides a poem into poetry and structure and, in so doing, as in the following quotation, equates poetry solely with the lyrical:

Since the structure that we have briefly delineated arises from a didactic and practical rather than poetic motive, research does not serve either to indicate the particular poetic character, assuming that there is one, of each canto, or the passage from one poetic situation to another, but can yield only what is in its nature to yield, namely, things which are external to the poetry and determined by structural connections. As Croce would have it, every effort made to convert structural reasons into artistic reasons is a sterile waste of intelligence.[3]

Gramsci's reading of Canto X is a direct response to Croce's conclusion; as he says in his letter of 20 September 1931 to Tatiana: "This interpretation should completely undermine Croce's thesis about poetry *versus* structure in the *Divina Commoedia*. Without structure there would be no poetry, thus structure itself has a poetic value."[4]

Many critics claim that Gramsci does not completely escape the Crocean categories in his reading of this canto.[5] By contrast, Frank Rosengarten argues in an extended essay that Gramsci's remarks on Canto X dialecticize Croce's terms, Dante's poem, and the role of the critic.[6] Gramsci's critics nonetheless object that he errs in preserving Croce's idealistically derived terms. Such objections, however, miss the fact that Gramsci must necessarily contend with and within the most powerfully authorized terms for the discussion of this politically active and important literary political figure of Italian culture, one who, of course, must be given a newly central place in the culture of the fascist state—and precisely by Croce's efforts.

The political and intellectual importance of Gramsci's remarks appears clearly if Gramsci's difference from much important modern critical commentary on Dante is kept in focus. Unlike nearly every other modernist critic of continuing importance, Gramsci did not try to make of Dante a representation of his own intellectual status and function. Perhaps the two most telling examples of critics who used Dante as part of an economy of intellectual self-authorization are T. S. Eliot and Erich Auerbach.[7]

T. S. Eliot represented Dante so that he epitomized the imagination and culture of a not-yet modern society. With the famous "dissociation of sensibility," Eliot identifies the "split" between mind and emotion, the division of personality and culture, as a "fall into time," into history, into modernity. Of course, the politics of this figure brings Eliot into conflict with Gramsci in a double way. This conflict, however, exists only because Gramsci and Eliot have common and traditional ground in their readings of Dante. For Gramsci, Cavalcante's experience in Canto X is, among other things, paradigmatic of Dante's expressive poetics, his representation of intensity in act and drama. For Eliot, similarly, from the first "deciphering" of Dante's language comes "some direct shock of poetic intensity." "Nothing but laziness," says Eliot, "can deaden the desire for fuller and fuller knowledge."[8] Like Eliot, Gramsci also tirelessly ridicules Dante's unresponsive pedant-critics for failing to explore his work fully and for accepting historical, aesthetic clichés in lieu of serious intellectual work. Gramsci, for example, commenting in The Notebooks on Vincenzo Morello's (Rastignac) comfortable assurance that scholarship has solved all the problems in any reading of Dante, writes the following: "How nice to be so easily satisfied. And it is very convenient to work on this kind of assumption: it lets one off the tiring task of individually filtering out and looking closely at the results reached by historical aesthetic criticism" (157).

Eliot and Gramsci also both take Dante as a test case for critical intellectual acumen and, more important, as a site of utopian, visionary, political energy. Eliot, for example, often speaks of how the shock of Dante's imagination inspires desire for knowledge of more. As Frank Rosengarten's work usefully suggests something very similar is at work in Gramsci's interest in Canto X: his reading is personally motivated because there are significant parallels between his situation and that of Cavalcante. Rosengarten shows how Gramsci stresses the human, personal value of Dante's achievement in representing Cavalcante's paternal suffering. Indeed, one effect of Gramsci's efforts is traditionally humanistic: his reading of Dante preserves a transhistorical capacity for human suffering that, in its various historical manifestations, foregrounds something like a universal human quality.[9] Of course, an attentive reading of Gramsci's remarks in the context of his own hopes for a different socialist future suggests that this sort of horrendous suffering might become something of the prerevolutionary past; but in these comments on Dante there is nothing to suggest that after any change in socio-political realities will a father's sufferings change or be any less appropriately veiled as a representation of human nature. These are among the few somewhat surprising common grounds between Gramsci, the Communist worker, and Eliot, the archconservative Anglican classicist.

But, of course, the differences are what matter. Eliot can make Dante into a prelapsarian figure because he identifies the dissociation of sensibility, in part, with the development of nationalism. That Eliot can read Dante as coming before the emergence of nationalism is an act of misprision that requires some explanation (202). Even though Gramsci's remarks do not enter into the complex details of Florentine politics his treatment of Dante places him in the factional divisions of the communal warfare of that city as a political intellectual hoping to find some agent that can restore a sort of peace, a status quo ante. As Gramsci sets up his reading of Dante, in contrast to Eliot's representative interpretation, it is quite specifically the case that Florentine politics require a nationalist solution and are already tending in that direction when Dante writes his poem, a poem that both emerges from the defeat of his desires and intervenes in the national development—even though a national solution is not reached, as Machiavelli's efforts testify.

Eliot, by contrast, needs a Dante who is not only a reactionary but a latecomer, a last link with the state of grace represented by the myth of a universal middle ages and its universal language, Latin: "medieval Latin tended to concentrate on what men of various races and lands could think together." Dante's Italian, for Eliot, is valuable because it can represent and share in this mind of Europe: "and the localization ('Florentine' speech) seems if anything to emphasize the universality, because it cuts across the modern division of nationality.... Dante, none the less an Italian and a patriot, is first a European" (201).

Eliot's linguistic idealization and universalization of Dante gradually makes him over—not only from a specific historical political figure involved in concrete cultural political practice but also from the mythicized heroic figure of the lost communal past—into an articulation of what Eliot desires in the present and for the future. Dante, Eliot claims, is "easy to read." It is not that Dante's language is simple or his thought or representations less than complex; rather, Dante is "easy to read" because Eliot sees him as a stylist in a way that, despite Eliot's own conservative politics, has a potentially progressive ideological tendency:

> The style of Dante has a peculiar lucidity—a *poetic* as distinguished from an *intellectual* lucidity. The thought may be obscure, but the word is lucid, or rather translucent. In English poetry words have a kind of opacity which is part of their beauty. I do not mean that the beauty of English poetry is what is called mere "verbal beauty." It is rather that words have associations, and the groups of words in association have associations, which is a kind of local self-consciousness, because they are the growth of a *particular* civilization.... The Italian of Dante ... is not in this way a modern language. (201)

It is progressive that Eliot should note the historical, material embeddedness of modern European languages; what is modernist—and so to many unacceptable—about this is his projection of a lost origin (through a restatement of the myth of the fall) upon a premodern and prelapsarian Dante. Eliot's Dante marks the end of old Europe and the onset of modernist nationalism which fulfills itself, for Eliot, in the Treaty of Versailles. Not only is this treaty the calamitous conclusion of modernization and nationalism, but for Eliot, it is also the harbinger of their necessary overcoming by those (poet/critics) who, like Eliot, so to speak, learn well from the Dante who is "so easy to read."

For Eliot, only those who can read this Dante—only those who are summoned to their own identity as poets—can begin the cultural and political change that will overthrow modernism and nationalism in favor of a new, but traditional, aristocratic order. It is not difficult to uncover the rhetorical tactics at work in Eliot's essay. "Reading" Dante in this way is to be taken as an act of "recognition" in which the reader and the poet set each other off—on the one hand as (benevolent) father and on the other as (equally benevolent) son; each is inspirited by the violence of this fantastic recognition:

> The experience of a poem is the experience both of a moment and of a lifetime. It is very much like our intenser experiences of other human beings. There is a first, or an early moment which is unique, of shock and surprise, even of terror (*Ego dominus tuus*); a moment which can never be forgotten, but which is never re-peated integrally; and yet would become destitute of significance if it did not survive in a larger whole of experience; which survives inside a deeper and a calmer feeling. (212)

Terror is the ephebe's experience of the sublime master's integral alterity by contrast with which his own need for inspiration, power, and completion compels the ephebe's ritual return to the divine and yet natural source of energy in the master.[10] Of course, all this is a dialectic of self-making, or, if you will, god-making, in the process of which and in the representations that are produced in *processu*, the ephebe makes himself in the heroic "afterimage" of the projected image of the master.[11] In Eliot's terms, this is allegory: "*clear visual images. And clear visual images are given much more intensity by having a meaning*" (204). According to Eliot then, and in terms not far from those of recent literary and linguistic theory, allegory is a diachronic elaboration of the synchronic; but, for Eliot, its possibility depends upon the hypothetical and residual existence of a premodern imagina-tive mode, namely, "vision."[12] Dante has, Eliot tells us, "a *visual* imagina-tion" because "he lived in an age when men still saw visions." We have lost the trick: "We have nothing but dreams, and we have forgotten that seeing visions—a practice now relegated to the aberrant and unedu-cated—was once a more significant, interesting, and disciplined kind of dreaming" (204).

Eliot's remarks importantly limn the critical allegory in and by which Dante becomes for a number of authorized poets and critics a pro-jected image of anti- and ante-modernist authority, a figure, a persona, or a "mask" reconstructed to resonate with their unhappy but powerful energies, repressions, and desires.[13] In this long essay on Dante, dis-tilled from the longer and still unpublished Clark lectures, Eliot creates retrospectively his own genealogy; but it is as a representation of a particular modern use of Dante, and in contrast to Gramsci, that it has its importance.

Like Vossler, Auerbach, and Croce, Eliot privileges his master with the capacity of fully developed humanity, what Eliot calls "The system of Dante's organization of sensibility" (235). This phrase, which momentarily can be taken to epitomize Eliot's poetics as an expressive theory of individual vision dependent upon and represented by the unique bodily organization of the individual poet's integral nervous system—this phrase is so ideologically burdened as to lead to Jameson's mocking rejection of the authoritarian heterocosms of high-modernist writing.[14] In Eliot's expressive poetics, the poem projects the poet's sensibility thus organizing the sensorium of experience in a wholeness, complete and entire: "The smell of steaks in passageways/ Six o'clock."

Yet there is a progressive moment in this modernist poetics that Jameson's focus on the totalitarian demands of the putatively privileged sensibility cannot consider; it is perhaps best described abstractly as a hermeneutic model of readerly openness, that is, self-abnegation in interpretation. Allegorically, the poetics of sensibility can lead to a hermeneutics of generosity, a suspension of critical apparatus and judgment in the name of empathy. R. P. Blackmur has it that the critic must always judge and that the road to judgment must always be slow and filled with failures. "What we need," Eliot writes in a similar way, "is not information but knowledge: the first step to knowledge is to recognize the differences between [the poet's] form of thought and feeling and ours" (237). This hermeneutics is dialogic at best, not historicist; nonetheless, it calls for respect for the otherness of the text and a (perhaps momentary) concession of right to the text: it requires, again in Blackmur's vocabulary, a moment of critical humility, of self-abnegation in reading and judgment.[15] Of course, there are moments in Eliot not so generous as this; true to his poetic projection of heroic, originary mastery—which obliges readers to forget the desire to be inspirited by the imagined and projected other[16]—Eliot crystallizes this "self-abnegation" as a foundational moment in the birth of the poet. It becomes the law of critical reading and a moment akin to faith: "We have to learn to accept their forms: and this *acceptance* is more important than anything that can be called belief. There is almost a definite moment of acceptance at which the New Life begins" (237).

IV

That part of Gramsci's visionary and utopian energies are at work in his readings of Dante bears upon his politics, especially upon his understanding of the relationship of political leaders to their followers—just as it does upon his so-called "aesthetics." Indeed, a reading of some of his remarks on Dante suggests that some of the conventional ways for discussing these matters in political and philosophical circles—is he a Leninist? an anti-Leninist? a Hegelian? etc.—might better be put aside in favor of an approach that treats his writings as dramatized formulations of matters not given to abstract conceptualization and nominalization.

Gramsci allegorizes a formative response to Dante and this act aligns him not just with (and against) Eliot but with a wide variety of modern poets and writers. Needless to say, Gramsci's energies do not produce a simulacrum of Eliot's allegory for they have different "imaginings" of that which might come to be. In Gramsci's correction of Croce (in the letter to Tatiana for Professor Cosmo, his old Dante professor), there is a revealing gambit on a set of what quickly come to be defining binary oppositions:

> De Sanctis, in his essay on Farinata, commenting on the harshness of the tenth canto of Dante's Inferno, attributes it to the fact that Farinata, after having been depicted as heroic in the first part of the episode, becomes in the last half a pedagogue. Using Croce's scheme, Farinata changes from poetry to structure.

And again, drawing the line between Farinata and Cavalcante, Gramsci writes:

> Here the difference between the two emerges. Farinata, upon hearing Florentine spoken, becomes once more a man of politics, the Ghibelline hero. Cavalcante's thoughts, instead, are directed toward Guido. . . . Cavalcante's drama passes subtly, but is marked by an unutterable intensity. (208–9)

By the end of this letter, Gramsci, of course, has overcome Croce's singularly dull distinction between poetry and structure, but he has left the other opposition "heroic"/"pedagogic" standing unchallenged. Why so? In La Poesia di Dante (1920), Croce uses the figure of the heroic Farinata not just as a representative instance of the political man, not just of poetry, indeed, not even just of their identity, but as a representation of the poet himself, of Dante in the most sublime incarnation of human completion. Croce's reference is to the scene at the beginning of Canto X:

The mind of Dante is full at this moment of his ideal journey, of images of men, of events, of struggles going on in his city. But the imagination no longer places before him images of hate; the new feeling is admiration for the great and strong men of Florence, which is no longer the sower of every vice, vituperated by Ciacco, but the "noble fatherland," of which it is his joy and boast to be a native, the fatherland that one curses and loves, for which one suffers and of which one is proud and which really does stand at the apex of the soul as a sacred thing. Farinata rises up, the figure in which this sentiment of poetic elevation expresses itself; Farinata the magnanimous, who like a true epic hero completely and wholly the warrior devoted to his cause, to his political ideal, to the city to which he belongs and which for that reason belongs to him; all other affection is foreign to him. Now he makes himself superior to the evils which surround him, holding his head high, with a look on his face as though he had a great contempt for Hell. He is careless of human loves and sorrows, and does not deign to pay attention to Cavalcante who is close to him; nor is he in the least moved by his solicitude and paternal affection. His first inquiry is that of the partisan and warrior.[17]

Cavalcante is contrasted to Farinata: "Then there arose to sight alongside of him a shade, visible to the chin: I think he had raised himself on his knees."[18] Cavalcante's unheroic self-presentation suggests that the guiding opposition of hero/pedagogue, if read through its displacing and doubling opposition—political/paternal—contrasts not just two moments in Farinata, but contrasts Farinata with Cavalcante and finally Dante with Croce, which means, of course, Croce with Gramsci. For Croce, heroism consists in the replacement of all other affections by the love of the fatherland and glory won in political struggle: Cavalcante, by the standard of the hero, is weak and so not an adequate representation of the poet's spirit sublimely full of its power and imaginings. Farinata becomes a "pedagogue"—the term is Gramsci's not Croce's—when he becomes structure, as Croce calls him, "a sop to the readers of the theological-ethical romance."[19] But Cavalcante is above all for Gramsci a father, a "pedagogue," *pedagogo*.

Pedagogo, of course, is from *paid-agein*, to lead or direct a child, usually a young boy. This etymology suggests part of how burdened the figure of Farinata is for Gramsci and the tradition in which he is working. Rosengarten studies some of the parallels between Cavalcante's relation to Guido and Gramsci's relations to his sons. He also makes the point that Cavalcante's punishment—an inability to see the present while being able to see the future, the ironically perfect punishment for the visionary poet—roughly corresponds to Gramsci's fulsome state in prison. Indeed, one of Gramsci's notes on Farinata supports this idea: in *The Prison Notebooks*, Gramsci writes that Dante "wants the knot which prevented him from answering Cavalcante to be untied" (153).

"Pedagogue" opens this personal level onto the political and suggests another reading of the "hero"/"pedagogue" binary. Farinata, of course, is the pedagogue designated in the text, but may we not see him as a displacement from the figure of Cavalcante as father? Etymology as well as established tradition bring the father and the pedagogue together in this context, rather than dividing them as, for example, would be the case with Philip's bringing Aristotle to tutor Alexander. In reading Gramsci's "*pedagogo*," we must recall how often he expresses his anxiety about his sons growing up without paternal direction and how, sometimes, he tries to provide guidance through his letters to Giulia. In personal practice and in his reading of Canto X, the father and the pedagogue are one for Gramsci. The pedagogue is Cavalcante whose veiled sufferings are *as a father*, the director of his son whose fate is unclear to him; this, in turn, suggests two political elements in Gramsci: first, the idea of the political leader as a director figured on the model of the paternal pedagogue; second, the idea of domination as both cultural and political hegemony.

In contrast to Croce, who valorizes Farinata only in a reading that figures him as a heroic sublime representation of the lyrical poet singing the politics of the noble fatherland; and in contrast to Eliot whose complex represents Dante as a father in the image of his own needs— in contrast to both of these moderns, Gramsci's representations of paternity, leadership, and hegemony in opposition to both "heroism" and "poetry" suggests something of the democratic vision of Gramsci's politics, of how this, in part, comes from personal experience; of how it implicitly involves a critique of representation on the level of text and political institution alike; and of how it involves critical interventions into the hegemonic culture of literary and critical traditions themselves. Croce asserts that Farinata is a mimetic representation of the lyrically ineffable sublimity of the Poet; Eliot, in a complex game of doubling projection, enacts a drama of authorization and legitimation. In both sets of moves these conservative intellectuals assign representative status to themselves and their authorized and authorizing representations; and both do this in the dynamics of sublime and privileged sensibility.

Gramsci, by contrast, emphasizes rather differently, rather somewhat less than heroically, the commonality of experience in pedagogy. (Its latent sexism is a larger and more important matter inviting discussion and critique.) It is not Farinata's sublime disdain that represents Dante, nor is Dante represented in a simple displacement by Cavalcante's paternal pedagogy. For Gramsci, Dante represents and comes to be represented, in a double displacement, by what he makes of Farinata as the representation of what Gramsci would have be outside representation altogether: the unseen suffering of Cavalcante, of a father, of a pedagogue, of (finally) a democratic leader whose heirs—those who make the future he hopes for—have a most uncertain fate. (This is, of course, a story on the verge of political defeat.) The nature of leadership in Gramsci's thought has been a problem for his interpreters precisely because, like the leader himself, "leadership" itself needs to be represented as outside representation: both to avoid nonorganic modes of representative politics and to avoid figuring the leader in either Eliot's or Croce's tropes of masterful fathers or vanguard political intellectuals.

A critique of representation—as ideology, language, and government—emerges from Gramsci's plaintive and enabling obsession with Canto X. His hope for a better future, for another polity of human relations requires that the disdain of a Farinata which is the desire of a Croce, be disempowered precisely by disempowering the authorizing and authorized workings of representation: indeed, even Eliot's self-consciously ironic allegory of representation, with its enabling figure of the privileged sensibility, fulfills the double logic of representation.

In sum, then, Gramsci's concern for a leadership that does not usurp the people's right and ability to struggle to make their own future (with the use of poets' visions) are continuous with his experience of paternal loss and his, at least, textual comprehension of the politics of representation.

I I

......

Madness,

Medicine, and

the State

Not only is *Madness and Civilization* important for its being the first book of Michel Foucault's to deal explicitly with matters of power and institutional function in ways easily seen as continuous with his work in the 1970s, but it also stands out as a peculiar instance of the materiality of "authorship" which, of course, was one of Foucault's central concerns. I am referring, of course, to the fact that *Madness and Civilization* has remained for over twenty-five years the only available English version of *Folie et déraison: histoire de la folie à l'âge classique*, despite Foucault's presence among English-speaking academics.[1]

Dreyfus and Rabinow, in their defining study, *Michel Foucault: Beyond Structuralism and Hermeneutics*[2] argue that in this book Foucault not only more explicitly discusses questions of causality and explanation than he does later—when he is more usually concerned to understand appearances and practices that produce the human sciences as we know them—but also that he develops the book around a basic opposition between reason and what they call "some fundamental form of Otherness" that grounds the possibility of reason and science (SH, 11). They also argue that "Foucault associated himself with those rare and special thinkers who had a glimpse of the 'sovereign enterprise of unreason'" (SH, 11). In this reading they perhaps follow Michel Serres's comparison of Foucault's work to Nietzsche's *Birth of Tragedy*.[3]

Dreyfus and Rabinow develop an extended but conventional analysis of this text, yet, in so doing, they point out an interesting direction for further study which they themselves do not develop. In the process of correctly insisting that Foucault grounds his later analyses in the body, they note how during this period he linked an understanding of ontology with the historicity of our human practices. They see this link as something better left behind for a more material method built around an understanding of the body as the object of discipline and ethics—"giving publicly accessible concrete content to whatever remained of his temptation to find the ontological basis of our historical practices" (SH, 11). Without adopting their point that Foucault gave up his "temptation" to ontological explanations, a discussion of which would lead us to Heidegger, we can take note of their perception that as early as 1961 Foucault hoped to study the basis of historical practices. This is important not because it is in any way an original perception, but because, in its very conventional correctness, it only partially illuminates Foucault's work of the time. Pursuing the question of ontology back to Heidegger's rethinking of "history" no doubt would more rigorously ground what must be simply described as a feature of Foucault's interest in *Histoire de la Folie* as well as *The Birth of the Clinic*.[4] In these two books from the early sixties, Foucault takes up a profound concern with the relationship between history—as historical consciousness, as history writing, and as a form of knowledge—and the state itself. Dreyfus and Rabinow note, apropos of *The Order of Things*,[5] that Foucault had an interest in the mid-sixties in matters of the state, specifically in the state's "control over its inhabitants . . . as working, trading, living human beings" (SH, 139).

What is not so clear in Dreyfus and Rabinow's book, however, is that Foucault's interest in the state in relation to the problems of history exists from the early 1960s. The topic, however, seems not to have had much treatment in the Foucault scholarship. Following Dreyfus and Rabinow, most of Foucault's sympathetic readers have until now treated the problem of the state primarily in terms of his later work on governmentality or bio-power.[6]

Foucault has had, however, usually from the disciplines of History and Philosophy, a number of hostile readers.[7] Some of this hostility comes from fairly overt ideological objections as, for example, when Gadamer decries Foucault as some sort of proto-fascist for being an antimodernist. More of it, certainly in the United States, results from disciplinary formations, from Foucault's challenge to given orders of disciplinary knowledge.[8] For this reason, it should not be unexpected that insight into Foucault's difficult relation to the problems of history might appear in the work of those who have the most severe reservations about his writings. Often these antagonistic readers cannot get beyond their ideological and disciplinary predispositions to attempt, sympathetically, a careful reading of Foucault's work, as it is said in English, "in its own terms." But the issue here is not the disciplines as such, not yet. The issue rather is Foucault's early investigations into the formation of history in the age of enlightenment, at the time of the emergence of the state with its doctrine of *raison d' état*.

Although it is an uninteresting book, J. G. Merquior's *Foucault* conveniently instantiates the troubled insight that marks most of Foucault's Anglo-American trained enemies.[9] Merquior interestingly carries out his critique of Foucault's *Madness and Civilization* with reference to his essay, "Nietzsche, Genealogy, History." Merquior heaps scorn on Foucault's praise for Nietzsche's contempt for "the history of historians," with its pursuit of a transcendental point of observation. Foucault, like Nietzsche, adopts a genealogical model that blatantly accepts its perspectivism and its "injustice." Merquior's scorn arises from deep within his own enlightenment commitment to questions of determinate truth, to empiricism, and to conventional forms of historical judgment. Tired of being told that one misunderstands Foucault when one asks "does Foucault get his history right," Merquior, like other historians— and he quotes Alan Megill on this point[10]—makes a conventional move against Foucault, one similar to that made on occasion by philosophers. This ploy involves asserting that despite Foucault's "intent" or "plan" his work "actually is" history or philosophy or whatever, and so libel to indictment for being a failed or bad version of what it claims not to be.[11]

Merquior's version of this gambit is noteworthy only because it makes central to the discussion of *Madness and Civilization* the problem of Foucault's writing's relation to "history." Merquior typifies the common view that Foucault's work is "anti-historical" but that *Madness and Civilization* is a failed and immature effort that does not get beyond "counter-history" (M, 26). Foucault's project, Merquior would have it, was purely historical, an attempt to get at madness before it fell victim to psychiatry.[12] "It is true," says Merquior, "that later Foucault came to deny he was aiming at a reconstitution of madness as an independent historical referent—but there is no gainsaying that, *at the time*, he had a 'normal' historiographic purpose in mind when he wrote *Madness and Civilization*" (M, 26).

Approaching Foucault's problematic indirectly, that is, by looking at

some of the combined ideological, disciplinary, and rhetorical moves
that characterize a "normal" or "disinterested" professional's response
to the writings of the early 1960s—approaching Foucault's problematic
indirectly reveals fairly clearly, albeit only as a sketch, a set of issues at
stake in those texts—without attempting to judge, for better or worse,
their "success" or "efficacy." Merquior, for example, is at haste to establish, like professional historians and those of a liberal ideological bent,
that Foucault is writing history so that his work can be dismissed and so
his critique of enlightenment discredited, *tout court*, by an appeal to
what is already known and to the mechanisms for legitimating what is
already known as it spreads itself to include "new knowledge." Merquior has rushed to deny the charge that one should not ask of his texts,
"does Foucault get his history right," by asserting that, in *Madness and
Civilization* at least, Foucault's efforts were those of a standard historian:
to set the record straight about madness. Merquior, however, also
covers himself against a charge from some who might not find his
assertion convincing by "arguing" that even if Foucault, like Nietzsche,
is writing a " 'presentist' history," he is not released "from his empirical
duties to the data. On the contrary: in order to prove their point,
present-centered *histoires à thèse* must try and persuade us of the accuracy of their reading of the past" (M, 26).

Having made these gestures to reinscribe Foucault's work into the
disciplines of history where it can be judged and, of course, dismissed—along with its author—as uninformed and prejudiced, Merquior feels free to appeal to precisely the standards of historical knowledge and judgment which, by his own actions, he admits that
Foucault's work puts in jeopardy. What is it that is put to risk? What
does Merquior typically rush to defend? The short answer is the enlightenment—whatever we take that to mean. For Merquior, it seems
to mean a commitment to rational inquiry, tested by empirical research, embodied, preserved, and deployed in and from bibliogra-
phies, footnotes, and the rest of the material apparatus that marks the
existence of history as a discipline and established form and depository
of knowledge and its reproduction.

Merquior goes on to show that Foucault gets his facts wrong, especially in comparison to a series of "splendid" books by historians such
as Sedgwick, Midelfort, and Doerner: "Sedgwick pulled the carpet from
under several key assumptions in Foucault's historical picture. . . . Midelfort has assembled a number of historical points which further under-

mine much of the ground of *Madness and Civilization*. . . . He also evinces a formidable command of an impressive literature on the history of both madness and psychiatry [Midelfort's book is not "splendid" but "brilliant"]. . . . Indeed, since 1969, we have the natural corrective to Foucault's Manichaean [sic] picture in Klaus Doerner's well-researched 'social history of insanity and psychiatry' " (M, 28–30).

There is something interesting in all this far beyond Merquior's personal inability to read Foucault carefully. What is at work is a defensive response to Foucault's strong challenge to the stories told of the histories of madness by those employing techniques which the "enlightenment" legitimates. Merquior cannot simply ignore Foucault: not only because of Foucault's "influence"—no doubt unjustified to someone of Merquior's predispositions—but also because that "influence" casts a critical eye on both the "content" of histories and also on the very embedded legitimation processes within the practices of "history," itself. Indeed, in both *Madness and Civilization* and *The Birth of the Clinic*, Foucault extends Canguilhem's critical ideas about the normal and pathological[13] to discuss some of the ways in which the production of historical knowledge can be seen as linked to the production of certain sorts of state formations, certain "regimes of truth," as Foucault later would teach us to call them, and, of course, certain procedures of subject and truth formation. Doerner's book "naturally" corrects Foucault's, for Merquior, because it shows that Foucault is not only wrong, having failed to consider such substantive and specific phenomena as "the spread of preromantic sensibility," but that he "offers 'too one-sided' an account—one where the dialectics of Enlightenment is 'unilaterally resolved in terms of its destructive aspect' " (M, 31). The interest in this passage is obvious: putting Foucault into a sort of "Frankfurt School" context, it becomes possible to condemn him, as Habermas does on occasion, for being an "irrationalist," to deal with him, in other words, as an already known quantity, and thereby to extend the reach of a legitimated way of judging "knowledge" to disarm one of its most severe critics. Curiously, Merquior, claiming to be an heir and defender of enlightenment and reason, would have the workings of thought stand still, would have the activity of critique suspended for the sake of the status quo within knowledge procedures—suspended within, to put it bluntly, stories that history tells about how important and beneficial certain forms of knowledge production are, especially as they have come to be called "enlightened."

Merquior represents, in other words, a betrayal of enlightenment as a critique of and engagement with the present—a turning away from Kant's efforts to answer the question, "What is Enlightenment?", an effort replicated by Foucault; and as such a betrayal it calls to mind, most ironically in the context of Foucault's critique of dialectical thinking, a certain passage from Hegel's preface to The Phenomenology of Spirit, which perfectly represents the kind of static knowledge and knowledge-producing apparatus one finds defending itself in Merquior's typically thoughtless work. It is "typical" just in that it instantiates the characteristically repetitive and formalist nature of "historical" inquiry:

> Regarding the contents, the others certainly sometimes make it easy enough for themselves to have great spread. They drag a lot of material into their field, material that is already familiar and well ordered. And when they deal preferably with the queer and curious, they only seem that much more to have firm possession of the rest which knowledge has long taken care of in its way, as if their mastery of the unruly came in addition to all this. . . . But when . . . it becomes manifest that [this comprehensiveness] was not attained insofar as one and the same principle differentiated itself into different forms, but it is rather the formless repetition of one and the same principle which is merely applied externally to different material and thus receives a dull semblance of differentiation. The idea, true enough by itself, remains in fact just where it was in the beginning as long as the development consists merely in such repetition of the same formula. When the knowing subject applies the one unmoved form to whatever is presented, and the material is externally dipped into this resting element, this is not, any more than arbitrary notions about the contents, the fulfillment of that which is in fact required—to wit, the wealth that wells forth out of itself and the self-differentiation of the forms. Rather it is a drab monochromatic formalism that gets to the differentiation of the material solely because this is long prepared and familiar.[14]

In 1821, Hegel was worried about the various tendencies, in Schelling and others, to construct disciplines of knowledge which defined knowledge by the already known, by a repetition formalistic in its embrace of the "queer and curious" within orders of knowledge guaranteed as knowledge precisely by the fact that thought no longer moved within them. And despite the anti-Kantian moments in his preface to *The Phenomenology*, Hegel, in these critiques, can be seen to maintain the Kantian ideal of thought's engagement with the present as the essential characteristic of modern philosophy, of modernity, itself.[15] Hegel writes against precisely the "thought-lessness" girding the work of Merquior and other defenders of the knowledge/power apparatus Foucault calls the "regime of truth." And in their wide-spreading stasis, they point toward important movements of thought in the early Foucault which, as Dreyfus and Rabinow's work indicates, sometimes even his favorable commentators have not pursued.

II

Madness and Civilization rests upon not only an often-noted opposition between reason and unreason, but also a linkage of reason with state authority and so an opposition between the state and unreason. This implies as well an opposition between unreason and a certain set of notions of subjectivity as well as a certain linkage between that set and the state. Unpacking such a complex of issues thoroughly is beyond the ambition of this essay. Reading *Madness and Civilization* does, however, reveal some of these connections and complex binaries and so reminds us of the centrality of language to Foucault and, in so doing, points out why "readers" such as Merquior cannot deal with his works: in the most literal sense, they pay no attention either to his writing or to the problem of language as such in his writing.

For example, writing of the "imaginary landscape" which "reappears" during the Great Fear and its confinements, Foucault carefully links his emphasis on the workings of power in the construction of "fortresses" for the mad with the renewal of the problem of language; and he does this as preparatory to raising the problem of modernity itself: "Sadism appears at the very moment that unreason, confined for over a century and reduced to silence, reappears, no longer as an image of the world, no longer as a *figura*, but as language and desire" (MC, 210). While this moment represents an important step in what has been described as Foucault's effort to bring madness back from silence, to "free" or "recover" its voice—and as such it has been objected to by Derrida who sees in it a certain transcendence[16]—it should also be read in context. When it is placed over and against the powerful "historicizing" remarks that follow, we see that it is primarily an instance of Foucault's concern with the understanding of modernity:

This awareness, however, has a very special style. The obsession with unreason is a very affective one, involved in the movement of iconographic resurrections. The fear of madness is much freer with regard to this heritage; and while the return of unreason has the aspect of a massive repetition, connecting with itself outside of time, the awareness of madness is, on the contrary accompanied by a certain analysis of modernity, which situates it from the start in a temporal, historical, and social context. (MC, 212)

The Merquioran misprision depends, in one sense, upon not being able to read this passage. Foucault seems to be saying that "madness" returns and that he himself follows on a movement of the rediscovery of madness—only, in his work, against the medicalization that forecloses a listening to unreason as an essential part of its work. It is not the case, however, that this departure from a "modernizing" tradition exemplified by medicine commits Foucault to either an essentialist or transcendent position regarding such a thing as "madness in itself." There are more complex positions, one of which he takes here.

It is clear, for example, that Foucault denies that the return of madness he is discussing is a "repetition." He will not accept the essentialist ideal that there is an identity of "madness" across time nor an identity of cultural productions for the representation of "madness." Furthermore, Foucault has already completely denied that the return he means here is "figural."[17] Language and desire replace figura as the modes of cultural production and embodiment: in modernity, language displaces figuration.[18]

These taken together link Foucault's work to the problem of history within modernity, or, to put it another way, indicate that in modernity history is a problem in a new way, in a way inseparable from the problems of language. "Figura" had maintained itself upon a religious basis, specifically the Catholic notion of the incarnation which, interestingly, provides a basis for a certain notion of repetition, especially as imagined by Kierkegaard. The problem of language within modernity is a movement away from the Christian cultural structures—or perhaps a displacement—and toward a modern schema of time that involves the simulacrum of repetition within modernity's endless iteration of the new—which, of course, involves as well the endless political, cultural production of "discrete subjects" or "individuals" as agents and authors.

Foucault finds in the awareness of madness not merely a sign or element of modernity—although that is certainly there—but also that which characterizes modernity as a form of historical knowledge production, as a cultural, political project determining to produce secular and so finite knowledge as its legitimation.[19] Indeed, it is relatively clear that in this passage Foucault's concern is not with "madness," or even with the "representations of madness," but rather, most importantly, with modernity: attend to the awareness of madness because that awareness is "accompanied by a certain analysis of modernity." And, further, if we recall the striking originality of Kant's insistence that enlightenment is marked by philosophy's becoming a critical concern with the present—the very point Foucault reiterates in his own comments on Kant's essay—then the force of Foucault's comment appears more fully: it is the fact that an analysis of modernity accompanies the awareness of madness "which situates it from the start in a temporal, historical, and social context." *Figura*'s historical force always requires that the present—for example, Christ's incarnation—be seen as both a fulfillment and an anticipation of another event at some other time: this commits history to its meaning outside time. The rejection of figural interpretations or structures of history newly involves history within temporality and so language as discourse: language as the embodying figuration of figural history's timeless patterns had nothing problematic about it. Strangely, language had no inherence in time; its temporality was a stasis fulfilled outside time in spatial repetition. Foucault's work here marks the demise of that sort of spatial repetition and, we might say, the emergence of the problematics of modernity as the philosophical, literary problem of temporality which, at least potentially, subverts, from the start, the postulated enlightenment discrete subject:

> In the disparity between the awareness of unreason and the awareness of madness, we have, at the end of the eighteenth century, the point of departure for a decisive movement: that by which the experience of unreason will continue, with Hölderlin, Nerval, and Nietzsche, to proceed ever deeper towards the roots of time— unreason thus becoming, *par excellence*, the world's *contratempo*— and the knowledge of madness seeking on the contrary ever to situate it ever more precisely within the development of nature and history. It is after this period that the time of unreason and the time of madness receive two opposing vectors: one being uncon-

ditioned return and absolute submersion; the other, on the contrary, developing according to the chronicle of a history. (MC, 212)

In a footnote to this passage, Foucault makes clear that the problem
he discusses exists in the different forms time takes in the literary as
opposed to scientific writings of madness/unreason. The awareness of
unreason abrogates scientific time—the time which aims to contain it
within the histories of madness and the sciences of nature—but it does
not empty out time altogether. On the contrary, it "deepens" time: "it is
not the absolute collapse of time. . . . It is a question of time turned
back" (MC, 297).

Modernity, we might say, affects two forms of time but as science
takes only one as its paradigm. That is, Foucault's work does not
merely, as critics have often argued, merely prefer the time of poets to
that of scientists, but it marks the profound emergence of the fact of
time's agonistic being as a template for cultural existence as a fact of
modernity itself. And, in so doing, it forms a fundamental challenge to
the basic knowledge-regimes whose beginnings are roughly corollary
to the awareness of unreason in the enlightenment. It forms a special
challenge to the history-writing of those disciplines which, it becomes
clear, are constitutive products and producers of that modernity. At the
beginning of the disciplines's efforts to produce scientific knowledge,
to intervene in the world, to form subjects—in this case by medical
means—and to write the record of the "attempt to do these things,"
that is, to write the history of disciplines themselves as they are being
established as legitimate—at the beginning, there is a necessary analysis
of modernity itself. These disciplines are, as it were, aware of the
traditionally ungrounded nature of their being; of their part in the
revolution against traditional cultures; and, as well, of their being written into time and history in newly problematic ways not grounded on a
secure figural foundation.

The disciplines' awareness of their own problematic stature, of the
confusion of their origins, has often been forgotten by those disciplines
themselves—as the Merquioran misunderstanding exemplifies. A
symptom of that confusion is history-writing. Finding themselves in "a
temporal, historical, and social context," the disciplines in general—no
matter whether they study time or nature—develop, as Foucault says,
"according to the chronicle of a history." That is, they write the story of
their existence as a development understood as "history"; or, to put the

matter in a way that reverses apparent priorities, they invent history writing as a way of grounding their being in a context that has as given neither linguistic nor traditional societal legitimacy. Within a finite world, modernity demands its disciplines produce history—not merely to avoid the corollary temporality of unreason as part of the political, cultural struggle embodied on the level of general material epistemology, but also to produce authoritative knowledge, institutions, and political order within the society and within the new individual subjects they create.

In his rewriting of those analyses of modernity science carries out in studying its objects, Foucault does more than debunk the liberal or whiggish myths generated as the story by modernity's secularizing, but progressive finitude; he also notes how the disciplines cannot legitimate themselves without producing histories of themselves which, as it were, always link the stories they tell to the central project of the state:

> Increasingly, a political and economic explanation was sought, in which wealth, progress, institutions appear as the determining element of madness. At the beginning of the nineteenth century, Spurzheim made a synthesis of all these analyses in one of the last texts devoted to them. Madness, "more frequent in England than anywhere else," is merely the penalty of the liberty that reigns there, and of the wealth universally enjoyed. Freedom of conscience entails more difficulty than authority and despotism. "Religious sentiments . . . [Foucault's elision] exist without restriction; every individual is entitled to preach to anyone who will listen to him," and by listening to such different opinions, "minds are disturbed in the search for truth." Dangers of indecision, of an irresolute attention, of a vacillating soul! The danger, too, of disputes, of passions, of obstinacy: "Everything meets with opposition, and opposition excites the feelings; in religion, in politics, in science, as in everything, each man is permitted to form an opinion; but he must expect to meet with opposition." Nor does so much liberty permit a man to master time; every man is left to his own uncertainty, and the State abandons all to their fluctuations. (MC, 213–14)

Foucault concedes that when Spurzheim was writing, reactionaries found it easy to blame liberalism for all the world's ills. He prefers to draw our attention to the fact that Spurzheim's critique of liberty is less important than "its very employment of the notion that designates for Spurzheim the non-natural milieu in which the psychological and physiological mechanisms of madness are favored, amplified, and multiplied" (MC, 214–15). This "non-natural milieu" clearly includes the state—even if, for Spurzheim, it is a state which abandons its charge to preserve order. More important is Spurzheim putting madness in relation to state politics at all. His formulations—despite their ideological antiliberalism—emerge from and exist within a set of discourses in which a conjunction between regulation, structures of knowledge, the "free agency" of the bourgeois subject, the need to prevent and treat madness, and so on gather at the intersection of the state and time.

In 1961, Foucault's work intersects that of Lefort, which rigorously draws attention to the global cultural, political changes achieved by "democracy." Indeed, Spurzheim's antiliberalism sounds at moments like de Toqueville when the latter tries to formulate his sense of the power's new regime emerging in so-called "American democracy." The momentary intersection of Lefort and Foucault suggests some of the importance of Foucault's statement that Spurzheim's antiliberalism is not his primary concern. Given that Foucault is himself a staunch radical critic of liberalism, conservative antiliberal appeals to regulating state authority could seem neither new nor important. Yet Spurzheim's critique of democratic liberalism is also, as Lefort helps us specifically to understand, a critique of modernity, or, better, it is itself a mark of modernity as precisely part of the societal turn from traditional toward democratic political organizations with all that this portends for cultural institutions, languages, and subjects in modern societies.[20] When Lefort discusses the relation between modernity and democracy in terms of overt political philosophy, he notices that, for the most part, conservative thinkers—such as Heidegger—who call democracy into question also call into question modernity. The point for Lefort is that "*From a political point of view, the questioning of modernity means the questioning of democracy.*"[21]

Since, for Foucault there can be no writing about madness without an analysis of modernity, there cannot, in turn, be writing about either which does not exemplify and/or analyze the antitraditional nature of democratic societies. Unreason clearly cannot be merely a return or simple repetition (to the traditional or "premodern," as it were), but it is a deepening of time as modernity is an opening into temporality which enlightenment—as we may now call it—deals with by means of history. Throughout the early sixties Foucault is concerned to show that the nexus of relations within modernity reveals history to be not a natural form of knowledge even though it is a necessary mode of political and cultural legitimation and identity formation for secular modernity itself—and perhaps never more often than when it is appealed to as that which has been lost in whatever the newest movement of modernity might be.

The Birth of the Clinic is often more explicit on these points than is Madness and Civilization. Perhaps because modern medicine, as we call it, writes its histories compulsively from its beginnings. There is one moment in The Birth of the Clinic in which Foucault gathers all of these strands of modernity in terms of the state, the subject—especially as the "gaze"—and history itself:

> What now constituted the unity of the medical gaze was not the circle of knowledge in which it was achieved but that open, infinite, moving totality, ceaselessly displaced and enriched by time, whose course it began but would never be able to stop—by this time a clinical recording of the infinite, variable series of events. But its support was not the perception of the patient in his singularity, but a collective consciousness, with all the information that intersects in it, growing in a complex, ever-proliferating way until it finally achieves the dimensions of a history, a geography, a state.[22]

The fact of totality, of a regulating socius, of an order of already known knowledge—and here Foucault intersects doubly with the Hegel who criticizes such modernist "spread" and who embodies a version of it in his dialectical "system"—of the state itself, all this makes up the story of the regime of truth that is modernity. Above all, it should make uneasy all historical thinkers, writers, and scholars. It should make uneasy all those uncritically committed to their training within the disciplines whose reproductions—racist, sexist, orientalist, and so on—both produce and make known the total consciousness of humanity, the study of which, we recall, is the task of humanism itself. This last idea we find not only in Nietzsche, but also in The Order of Things. How foolish then the naive return to the given in the work of someone like Merquior! How utterly inane a form of repetition! How completely failed a piece of criticism to hurl the charge that the critic violates the rules of the game! And by implication, of course, how foolish to attempt to make Foucault "available," to have him "make sense" to the philosophers, to the historians! They know him too well when they criticize and reject him. Foucault should not be "explained" and "justified" by being brought into the folds of normal secular enlightenment thought—for how little that effort has thought about the way in which its own enterprise had its beginnings in a world fleeing into madness from unreason.

Critics, one hopes, will not easily work the word "history" like a mantra, take up the charge "against theory," or naively press the case for "progressive politics." If there is hope that marginal groups might, in their life-forms and life-experiences, produce new cultures and politics, the critics and scholars who putatively hope to join, to assist, or to work in parallel to those efforts—they cannot simply take up the enlightenment tools "progressive politics" seem to offer. For they are tools which, as we have seen over and again, are themselves the machines to maintain dominance, to keep the marginal down: Edward Said on the great literatures and scholars of Europe—all shown within the rubrics of Orientalism[23]—Cornel West on the racism of European enlightenment aesthetic philosophy.[24] To paraphrase a great contemporary critic, one can't tear down the master's house with the master's tools!

Madness and Civilization is part of that once immensely powerful work of serious critics to join the efforts of emergent subjects to strike against the massive authority of a Western project of modernity that, despite its internal cultural complexities, often operated on the colonized world as a univocal force—just as it had operated to destroy the traditional Western societies upon which it follows or the emergent subcultures which it absorbed. In a recent essay on Bakhtin and Kant, Wlad Godzich indicates that the Bakhtin circle understood modernization to be the issue of the Russian revolution.[25] Godzich's complex essay makes inescapable the truth of Foucault's claims that history, modernity, modernization, and political democracy are inseparable areas of thought circulating always around the nexus of state and subject. A fuller reading of Foucault's work along these lines would show, I suspect, that it has not yet received the *political* reading it deserves. It would show that the critique of disciplines, of representation, of the state, and of the subject are fragments of a complex effort to rewrite the tools of intellectual political work made possible by the enlightenment. It would prove, ironically, the truth of what Habermas took to be his worst charge against Foucault, namely, that he was an antimodernist. It would also show Habermas insisting on the obvious—like Merquior—as if the "normal" had some bite on an intellectual project that extends its own critique to the very beginnings of the rules of knowledge that underlie modernity, itself.

Notes

......

Preface

1 For an important discussion of this issue and its consequences from a political rather than a literary theorist, see Barry Cooper, *The End of History* (Toronto: Univ. of Toronto Press, 1984).

2 Wlad Godzich's forthcoming book, *The Struggle for Theory* (Cambridge: Harvard Univ. Press), contains the most telling writing about this topic. Indeed, Godzich has more consistently attended to the importance of Hegel's work than any critic who has given much attention to the United States critical scene.

3 See Gayatri Spivak, *In Other Worlds* (New York: Methuen, 1987).

4 "From Restricted to General Economy," *Writing and Difference*, trans. and introduced by Alan Bass (Chicago: Univ. of Chicago Press, 1978), 259; originally published as "De l'économie restreinte à 'économie générale: Un hegelianisme sans réserve," *L'Arc* (May 1976). Derrida goes on to identify discourse with the Hegelian *Aufhebung* itself and points out that to "exceed" Hegel one cannot just go, as it were, to the logical end of the system for that is to remain within "discourse." Such tactics, we might say, are not "transgressive enough," remain with the dialectic, and cannot tear apart the discursive movements established by the *Aufhebung*.

5 We should remember that "praxis" belongs to a Greek verb that means, in part, to pass through or pass along.

6 The basic point of reference here is, of course, Hegel's discussion in *The Phenomenology of Spirit*. But I am also referring to Foucault's critique of the figure of the political or intellectual "master" throughout his work of the 1970s and to Bataille and Derrida's persistent critique the figure. One should also see behind these readings of the figure of Kojève. See also my previous discussion of this problem in *Intellectuals in Power* (New York: Columbia Univ. Press, 1986), especially chapter one.

1 Introduction: Discourse

1 See, for example, Fredric Jameson, *The Political Unconscious* (Ithaca: Cornell Univ. Press, 1981).
2 See chapter 6 this volume, "Agriculture and Academe."
3 Antonio Gramsci, *Selections from the Prison Notebooks* (New York: International Publishers, 1971), 323f.
4 Michel Foucault, *The History of Sexuality*, vol. 1 (New York: Pantheon Press, 1978), 58–67.
5 See Michel Foucault, *Discipline and Punish* (New York: Pantheon Press, 1977).
6 See Michel Foucault, "The Discourse on Language," in *The Archeology of Knowledge* (New York: Harper Colophon, 1976), 235–37.
7 Edward Said, *Beginnings* (New York: Basic Books, 1975), 351–52.
8 See Gilles Deleuze, *Nietzsche and Philosophy* (New York: Columbia Univ. Press, 1983); Michel Foucault, *Language, Counter-Memory, Practice* (Ithaca: Cornell Univ. Press, 1977).
9 See Michel Foucault, *The Use of Pleasure* (New York: Pantheon Press, 1985); and *The Care of the Self* (New York: Pantheon Press, 1986).
10 *Language, Counter-Memory, Practice.*
11 Michel Foucault, "The Subject and Power," in Herbert L. Dreyfus and Paul Rabinow, *Michel Foucault: Beyond Structuralism and Hermeneutics*, 2nd ed. (Chicago: Univ. of Chicago Press, 1983), 220.
12 See Barry Smart, *Foucault, Marxism, and Critique* (London: Routledge & Kegan Paul, 1983), 119–20.
13 "The Subject and Power," 223.
14 I should also mention the relation of genealogy to certain forms of philosophical pragmatism that are, in their own ways, prepared to admit a complicity between truth and power, but this issue is too complex to explore briefly—for some sense of the matter see Richard Rorty, *Consequences of Pragmatism* (Minneapolis: Univ. of Minnesota Press, 1982), 136–37, 203–8; and "Foucault and Epistemology," in David C. Hoy, ed., *Michel Foucault: A Critical Reader* (Oxford: Basil Blackwell, 1986), 48.
15 Rudolf Bahro, *The Alternative in Eastern Europe* (London: New Left Books, 1978).
16 See *Language, Counter-Memory, Practice*, 205–6.
17 Georg Lukács, *History and Class Consciousness* (Cambridge: MIT Press, 1971), 46–222.
18 Antonio Gramsci, *Letters from Prison* (New York: Harper & Row, 1973), 208–9.
19 See chapter 6 this volume "Agriculture and Academe."
20 R. P. Blackmur, *The Lion and the Honeycomb* (New York: Harcourt Brace, 1955).
21 "The Discourse on Language," 236.

2 The Penitentiary of Reflection

1 Kierkegaard, *Letters and Documents*, trans. Henrik Rosenmeier (Princeton: Princeton Univ. Press, 1978); *Two Ages: The Age of Revolution and the Present Age*, ed. & trans. Howard V. Hong and Edna H. Hong (Princeton: Princeton Univ. Press, 1978); *Kierkegaard's Pseudonymous Authorship: A Study of Time and the Self* (Princeton: Princeton Univ. Press, 1975), hereafter cited respectively in my text as LD, TA, and KPA.

2 See *Hateful Contraries* (Lexington: Univ. of Kentucky Press, 1966), 48, 100, 248. It is worth pointing out here that the type of reconsideration of Kierkegaard I am suggesting does not aim to reestablish either the modernist version of a writer torn between matters of faith and literature nor to reawaken any of the more sentimental, "subjectivist" existential versions of Kierkegaard.

3 "Cleanth Brooks and Modern Irony: A Kierkegaardian Critique," *boundary 2*, 4 (1976), 727–60; reprinted in *Destructive Poetics: Heidegger and Modern American Poetry* (New York: Columbia Univ. Press, 1980).

4 William V. Spanos, "Heidegger, Kierkegaard, and the Hermeneutic Circle: Towards a Postmodern Theory of Interpretation as Disclosure," *boundary 2*, 4 (1976), 455–88; reprinted in *Martin Heidegger and the Question of Literature* (Bloomington: Indiana Univ. Press, 1980); Edward W. Said, "Repetition," *The Literature of Fact*, ed. Angus Fletcher (New York: Columbia Univ. Press, 1976), 135–58; *Beginnings: Intention and Method* (New York: Basic Books, Inc., 1975), 85ff.

5 Stephen Crites, *In the Twilight of Christendom: Hegel vs. Kierkegaard on Faith and History* (Chambersburg: American Academy of Religion, No. 2, 1971): "Pseudonymous Authorship as Art and as Act," *Kierkegaard: A Collection of Critical Essays*, ed. Josiah Thompson (New York: Doubleday and Co., 1972), 183–229.

6 Sponheim, *Kierkegaard on Christ and Christian Coherence* (New York: Harper and Row, 1968).

7 For an elaboration upon the importance of this idea of "spatialized time," see William V. Spanos's seminal essay, "Modern Literary Criticism and the Spatialization of Time," *JAAC*, 29 (1970), 87–104. My essay largely assumes and builds upon the validity of Spanos's argument in this article.

8 *Discipline and Punish*, trans. Alan Sheridan (New York: Pantheon Books, 1977), 195–228.

9 Trans. Bernard Frechtman (New York: Harper and Row, 1965), 1222ff.

10 See the exchange between Said and Donato in *boundary 2*, 8 (1979).

11 (New York: International Publishers, 1963), 114–15.

12 *Discipline and Punish*, 170–94.

13 *Discipline and Punish*, 149.

14 See Geoffrey Hartman, "A Short History of Practical Criticism," *NLH*, 10 (1979), 495–509, who concludes by insisting that "It is a mistake to think of the humanist as spiritualizing anything: on the contrary, he materializes us; he makes us aware of the material culture (including texts) in which everyone has always lived." But Hartman goes on to say in a somewhat different spirit: "Only the passage of time spiritualizes us, that is, volatilizes and deracinates. . . ." Hartman's unwillingness or inability to see history as the medium of material existence rather than its antithesis is typical of contemporary criticism and reflects the same sort of bourgeois pessimism we have seen in Kierkegaard. This attitude allows Hartman to describe life as "a feast of mortuary riddles and jokes. . . ."

3   *Variations on Authority*

1 See, e.g., Barbara Johnson, "Nothing Fails Like Success," *SCE Reports*, 8 (1980), 7–16.

2 Brenkmann, "Deconstruction and the Social Text," *Social Text*, 1 (1979), 186–88;

Sprinker, "The Ideology of Deconstruction: Totalization in the Work of Paul de Man," paper delivered at MLA convention (1980) special session, "Deconstruction as/of Politics," 13.

3 (Chicago: Univ. of Chicago Press, 1979). See also my review of Graff, *Criticism*, 22 (1980), 77–81; Michael Sprinker, "Criticism as Reaction," *Diacritics*, 10 (1980), 2–14; Joseph Riddel, "What is Deconstruction, and Why Are They Writing All Those Graff-ic Things About It?" *SCE Reports*, 8 (1980), 17–29; and William V. Spanos, "Deconstruction and the Question of Postmodern Literature: Towards a Definition," *Par Report*, 2 (1979), 107–22.

4 See George Levine's review in *College English*, 43 (1981), 146–60. I want to thank Jonathan Arac for pointing this out to me.

5 "Repetition and Exclusion: Coleridge and New Criticism Reconsidered," *boundary 2*, 8 (1979), 261–74.

6 "The Genius of Irony: Nietzsche in Bloom," 109–75.

7 "Retrieving Heidegger's De-Struction," *SCE Reports*, no. 8 (Fall 1980), 30–53. On the spatialization of time, see especially "Modern Literary Criticism and the Spatialization of Time," *JAAC*, 29 (1970), 87–104.

8 See, e.g., M. H. Abrams, "The Deconstructive Angel," *Critical Inquiry*, 3 (1977), 425–38.

9 See Paul Bové, "The End of Humanism: Michel Foucault and the Power of Disciplines," *On Foucault, Humanities in Society*, 3 (1980), 23–40.

10 See also Joseph A. Buttigieg, "The Struggle Against Meta (Phantasma)-physics," *boundary 2*, 9 and 10 (1981), 187–208.

11 *The Well Wrought Urn* (New York: Harcourt, Brace, and World, Inc., 1947), 198.

12 See Frye, *Anatomy of Criticism* (Princeton: Princeton Univ. Press, 1957); Krieger, *The New Apologists for Poetry* (Bloomington: Indiana Univ. Press, 1963); Crane, "The Critical Monism of Cleanth Brooks," *Critics and Criticism* (Chicago: Univ. of Chicago Press, 1952), 83–107.

13 See "The Deconstructive Angel," 457–58; and "The Critic as Host," 217–26.

14 *The Verbal Icon* (Lexington: Univ. of Kentucky Press, 1954), 69–83.

15 See Daniel O'Hara, "The Genius of Irony," and Rodolphe Gasché, "Deconstruction as Criticism," *Glyph*, 6 (1979), 177–215.

16 Said, "The Problem of Textuality: Two Exemplary Positions," *Critical Inquiry*, 4 (1978), 673–714.

17 See Geoffrey Hartman, preface to DC.

4   *The Metaphysics of Textuality*

1 See, for example, Paul de Man's "Genesis and Genealogy in Nietzsche's *The Birth of Tragedy*," *Diacritics*, 2 (1972), 44–53, hereafter referred to in my text as GGN.

2 Jacques Derrida, "From Restricted to General Economy: A Hegelianism without Reserve," *Writing and Difference*, trans. Alan Bass (Chicago: Univ. of Chicago Press, 1978), 251–77; *L'écriture et la différence* (Paris: Editions du Seuil, 1967).

3 Trans. (Chicago: Univ. of Chicago Press, 1981), 35, hereafter referred to in my text as P.

4 F. Nietzsche, *Untimely Meditations*, trans. R. J. Hollingdale (Cambridge: Cambridge

Univ. Press, 1983), 57–123, cited in my text as UD; and Karl Marx, *The Eighteenth Brumaire of Louis Bonaparte*, trans. anon. (New York: International Publishers, 1963), cited in my text as EB.

5 For all their problems, Terry Eagleton's two recent books have helped shed some light on the crisis faced by the academy at this time: see *Literary Theory: An Introduction* (Minneapolis: Univ. of Minnesota Press, 1983) and *The Function of Criticism* (London: New Left Books, 1984).

6 This was certainly the majority opinion at the conference on "The Mediation of Received Values" which was held at the University of Minnesota, October 9–12, 1984.

7 I have made an argument similar to this in "Variations on Authority," *The Yale Critics*, ed. Jonathan Arac et al. (Minneapolis: Univ. of Minnesota Press, 1983), 3–19.

8 *The World, the Text, and the Critic* (Cambridge: Harvard Univ. Press, 1983), 1–30, 179–225.

9 Jacques Derrida, *Spurs*, trans. Barbara Harlow (Chicago: Univ. of Chicago Press, 1979), 59ff.

10 *Blindness and Insight* (New York: Oxford Univ. Press, 1971), 3, hereafter cited in my text as BI.

11 For some analysis of the history of this intellectual structure in American culture, see Sacvan Bercovitch, *The American Jeremiad* (Madison: Univ. of Wisconsin Press, 1978).

12 It is interesting that, from his very different political and critical position, Edward W. Said has recently reintroduced the term "critical consciousness," the same term de Man used to discuss what had been, he thought, irreversibly changed by the crisis. *The World, the Text, and the Critic* (Cambridge: Harvard Univ. Press, 1983), 1–30.

13 "Literature and Psychoanalysis: the Question of Reading: Otherwise." *Yale French Studies*, ed. Shoshana Felman, nos. 55/56 (1977); "The Pedagogical Imperative: Teaching as a Literary Genre," *Yale French Studies*, ed. Barbara Johnson, no. 63 (1982). It is significant that the second volume opens with an essay by de Man. "The Resistance to Theory," originally commissioned by the MLA for its collective volume, *Introduction to Scholarship in Modern Languages and Literatures*, but deemed inappropriate for that volume since it questions the basic terms and concepts of such reviews of scholarship and critical purpose. The MLA's reluctance to publish de Man's essay suggests how marginal to the most established bastions of the profession criticism and theory have always been; but it does not deny my larger thesis. The publication of this essay in the prestigious *Yale French Studies* simply indicates how complex the professional system of power and reward is. Furthermore, I am certain that by 1982 the reaction against critical theory marked by Michaels's and Knapp's essay, for example, had already gained the upper-hand.

14 The school has, of course, been in residence at Northwestern for some time and will be moving to Dartmouth College. An interesting essay could be written about the institutional and intellectual politics of the school.

15 See Paul A. Bové, "Variations on Authority," *The Yale Critics*, ed. Jonathan Arac et al. (Minneapolis: Univ. of Minnesota Press, 1983), 3–19.

16 One should keep in mind, for example, that Culler's *Structuralist Poetics* (Ithaca:

Cornell Univ. Press, 1975) won the MLA's Lowell prize and not Said's *Beginnings* (New York: Basic Books, 1975). See Frank Lentricchia, *After the New Criticism* (Chicago: Univ. of Chicago Press, 1980), 103f.

17 Abrams, "The Deconstructive Angel," *Critical Inquiry*, 3 (1977), 425–38; Miller, "The Critic as Host," *Critical Inquiry*, 3 (1977), 439–47.

18 See Rodolphe Gasché, "Deconstruction as Criticism," *Glyph*, 6 (1979), 177–215.

19 See Abrams, *Natural Supernaturalism* (New York: Norton Books, 1971), who makes precisely these contrasts between linear and circular form.

20 The influence of Derrida on the so-called Yale school has been well-documented. See Arac et al., *The Yale Critics*.

21 "Ariachne's Broken Woof," *Georgia Review*, 31 (1977), 59–60.

22 (Paris: Editions du Seuil, 1967), esp. 296ff.

23 I make this claim despite Derrida's occasional concern with institutional and political issues. One should take note of where these appear in English. See, for example, "The Principle of Reason: the University in the Eyes of its Pupils," *Diacritics*, 13 (Fall 1983), 3–20.

24 See "Criticism Between Culture and System," *The World, the Text, and the Critic*, 178–225.

25 *Revolution and Repetition: Marx/Hugo/Balzac* (Berkeley: Univ. of California Press, 1977), hereafter cited in my text as RR.

26 Trans. anon. (New York: International Publishers, 1963), hereafter cited in my text as EB.

27 *Marx devant le bonapartism* (The Hague: Mouton, 1960), esp. 50ff.

28 Isaiah Berlin, *Karl Marx*, 4th ed. (Oxford: Oxford Univ. Press, 1978) and Said, *The World, the Text, and the Critic*, 121–25.

29 *Karl Marx*, 50.

30 See *The World, the Text, and the Critic*, 4f.

31 Paul A. Bové, *Intellectuals and Power: A Genealogy of Critical Humanism* (New York: Columbia Univ. Press, 1985), esp. ch. six.

32 *Intellectuals and Power*, ch. six, esp. the pages on Kant.

5   The Ineluctability of Difference

1 See William V. Spanos, "The Detective and the Boundary: Some Notes on the Postmodern Literary Imagination," *boundary* 2, 1 (1972), 147–68, reprinted in *Existentialism* 2, ed. William V. Spanos (New York: Thomas Y. Crowell, 1976), 163–89; Ihab Hassan, *Paracriticism: Seven Speculations of the Times* (Urbana: Univ. of Illinois Press, 1975); Alan Wilde, *The Horizons of Assent* (Baltimore: Johns Hopkins Univ. Press, 1981); Joseph N. Riddel, *The Inverted Bell: Modernism and the Counterpoetics of William Carlos Williams* (Baton Rouge: Louisiana State Univ. Press, 1974). The work of all these critics goes beyond the polemical sketch I am offering here. Indeed, all their works have helped to define the space in which these issues can be raised, and they have ramifications well beyond the range of this essay.

Since I intend many of my comments as something of a self-criticism, see Paul A. Bové, *Destructive Poetics: Heidegger and Modern American Poetry* (New York: Columbia Univ. Press, 1980), in which I wrote too abstractly and ahistorically of "the radical

flux, disorder, alienation, and death which characterize the Postmodern world."
One other important theorist of the postmodern is Charles Altieri whose essay, "From Symbolist Form to Immanence: The Ground of Postmodern American Poetics," *boundary* 2, 1 (1973), 605–41, is fundamental. Altieri's work has developed in different directions since the mid 1970s and culminated in *Quality and Act* (Amherst: Univ. of Massachusetts Press, 1982); I cannot deal with the range of his work in this essay. See my review of *Quality and Act* in *Contemporary Literature*, 24 (1983), 379–86.

2 See, for example, Fredric Jameson, *The Political Unconscious* (Ithaca: Cornell Univ. Press, 1981).

3 Antonio Gramsci, "The Modern Prince," *Selections from the Prison Notebooks*, ed. and trans. Quintin Hoare and Geoffrey Nowell Smith (London: Lawrence and Wishart, 1971), 151.

4 See, for example, Daniel O'Hara, "The Romance of Interpretation: A 'Postmodern' Critical Style," *boundary* 2, 8 (1980), 259–84.

5 Stanley Aronowitz, *The Crisis in Historical Materialism: Class, Politics and Culture in Marxist Theory* (New York: Praeger, 1981); all further references to this work appear parenthetically in my text as CHM. See also Stanley Aronowitz, *False Promises: The Shaping of American Working Class Consciousness* (Durham: Duke Univ. Press, 1992), *Food, Shelter and the American Dream* (New York: Seabury Press, 1974), and *Working-Class Hero* (New York: Pilgrim, 1983).

6 Anthony Giddens, *A Contemporary Critique of Historical Materialism* (Berkeley and Los Angeles: Univ. of California Press, 1981), 156.

7 See Michel Foucault, "Intellectuals and Power," *Language, Counter-Memory, Practice: Selected Essays and Interviews*, trans. Donald F. Bouchard and Sherry Simon, ed. Donald F. Bouchard (Ithaca: Cornell Univ. Press, 1977), 207.

8 Adam Przeworski, "Proletariat into Class: The Process of Class Formation from Karl Kautsky's 'Class Struggle' to Recent Controversies," *Politics and Society*, 7 (1977), 343–402.

9 Paul Feyerabend, *Against Method* (London: New Left Books, 1975); Thomas Kuhn, *The Structure of Scientific Revolutions* (Chicago: Univ. of Chicago Press, 1962).

10 Larry Laudan, *Progress and Its Problems* (Berkeley: Univ. of California Press, 1978).

11 "Hubris" is not a very exact term, but it does, I think, get at the sense of arrogance and imperialism in intellectuals which is satisfied by generating master discourses. Of course, insofar as such models still constitute a measure of elite intellectual success, they are also socially a base of professional power.

12 Ernest Bloch, "Non-Synchronism and Dialectics," trans. Mark Ritter, *New German Critique*, no. 11 (1977), 22–38. This is also an important essay for Aronowitz's understanding of historiography.

13 Aronowitz's point of departure is Theodor W. Adorno's *Negative Dialectics*, trans. E. B. Ashton (New York: Seabury Press, 1973). On Adorno and poststructuralism, see the chapter by Rainer Nägele in *Postmodernism and Politics*, ed. Jonathan Arac (Minneapolis: Univ. of Minnesota Press).

14 Jürgen Habermas, *Knowledge and Human Interests*, trans. Jeremy Shapiro (Boston: Beacon Press, 1971), 198–209.

15 Jacques Derrida, *Glas* (Paris: Editions Galilée, 1974).

16 See Derrida's brilliant demonstration of the nonimmanence of the self in his critique of phenomenology, *Speech and Phenomena and Other Essays*, trans. David B. Allison (Evanston, Ill.: Northwestern Univ. Press, 1973).

17 Cf. Rudolph Bahro, *The Alternative in Eastern Europe*, trans. David Fernbach (London: New Left Books, 1978). Commenting on the system of economic regulation in Eastern Europe, Bahro writes that the system is socially unsatisfactory "because the party and state apparatus programme the economy in such a way as to transform every increase in productivity into a growth in production," 451.

18 Louis Althusser, "Ideology and Ideological State Apparatuses" (1970), in *Lenin and Philosophy*, trans. Ben Brewster (London: New Left Books, 1971), 156. For an examination of literary transformation that suggests the material nature of literary discourse, see Jonathan Arac, *Commissioned Spirits: The Shaping of Social Motion in Dickens, Carlyle, Melville, and Hawthorne* (New Brunswick, N.J.: Rutgers Univ. Press, 1979).

19 Alvin Gouldner also argues that advanced societies must find ideologically legitimate ways to restrict production, i.e., to limit the quest for satisfaction in commodities. See *The Two Marxisms* (New York: Seabury Press, 1980). This position is not simply the naive blindness of a powerful intellectual in a "post-scarcity, affluent society" with no regard for less-developed economies. It is rather a reflection of the recent recognition that ecological disaster is a worldwide product of capital and industrialization. See William Leiss, *The Limits of Satisfaction* (Toronto: Univ. of Toronto Press, 1978), 113–14.

20 Sigmund Freud, *Civilization and Its Discontents*, trans. James Strachey (New York: W. W. Norton, 1962).

21 It is not coincidental that the election of a reactionary government, the resurgence of antifeminism, and the rise of antiecological "deregulators" all take place at the same time as, or follow shortly upon, the publication of a series of "profamily," "common-sensical," and "antimodernist" books, which announce themselves as radical and even Marxist but can easily be seen as defenses of repressive social forms and partisan ideologies. See, for example, Christopher Lasch, *Haven in a Heartless World: The Family Besieged* (New York: Basic Books, 1977); *The Culture of Narcissism: American Life in an Age of Diminishing Expectations* (New York: W. W. Norton, 1978); and Gerald Graff, *Literature against Itself* (Chicago: Univ. of Chicago Press, 1979). Graff and Lasch have defended their work of the 1970s by suggesting that it was never meant to be conservative and has been seriously misread. Graff, for one, has certainly been sometimes unhappy with the "allies" his work has found. One must, therefore, accept the motives underlying their defense and point out additionally that their positions have indeed changed in important ways. Nonetheless, despite their intentions and after-the-fact apologies, one should also see that these texts functioned—and perhaps do still function—precisely in the manner I have suggested.

22 Foucault, "Intellectuals and Power." Aronowitz does not derive his theory of the radical intellectual from Gramsci's theory of the organic intellectual, but there are interesting relationships to be worked out.

23 For an example of this influential ideological position in literary criticism, see Wayne Booth, *Critical Understanding: The Powers and Limits of Pluralism* (Chicago: Univ. of Chicago Press, 1979).

24 See "The Romance of Interpretation."

25 Jonathan Arac, "The Criticism of Harold Bloom: Judgment and History," *Centrum*, 6 (1978), 42.

26 On Gramsci's refusal of doctrine, see Joseph Buttigieg, "The Exemplary Worldliness of Antonio Gramsci's Criticism," *boundary 2*, 11 (1982–83), 21–39.

27 Paul A Bové, *Intellectuals in Power: A Genealogy of Critical Humanism* (New York: Columbia Univ. Press, 1986).

28 See the introduction to *Postmodernism and Politics* by Jonathan Arac for an analysis of the problems with these models. See also Edward W. Said, "Response to Stanley Fish," *Critical Inquiry*, 10 (1983), 371–74.

29 See Booth, *Critical Understanding*, 34; and Linda Blanken, "A Good Citizen in the Republic of Criticism," *Humanities*, 2 (1981), 11–12.

30 Geoffrey H. Hartman, *Criticism in the Wilderness: The Study of Literature Today* (New Haven: Yale Univ. Press, 1980).

31 I would like to thank Joseph Buttigieg, Barbara Jetton, Karl Kroeber, and Cornel West for discussing this essay with me. I owe a larger than usual debt to Jonathan Arac and Dan O'Hara who generously gave of their time to read closely earlier drafts of this essay; they made valuable comments and asked necessary questions, many of which I am not yet able to answer.

6 Agriculture and Academe

1 Terry Eagleton, "The Idealism of American Criticism," *Against the Grain* (London: Verso Books, 1986), 49.

2 See Edward W. Said, "Reflections on American 'Left' Literary Criticism," *The World, the Text, and the Critic* (Cambridge: Harvard Univ. Press, 1983), 158–77.

3 See Donald E. Pease, *Visionary Compacts* (Madison: Univ. of Wisconsin Press, 1986).

4 *Parnassus on the Mississippi: The Southern Review and the Baton Rouge Literary Community, 1935–1942* (Baton Rouge: Louisiana State Univ. Press, 1984).

5 *The Fugitive Group: A Literary History* (Baton Rouge: Louisiana State Univ. Press, 1959).

6 See *Parnassus*, 185.

7 *The Republic of Letters in America: The Correspondence of John Peale Bishop and Allen Tate*, ed. Thomas Daniel Young and John J. Hindle (Lexington: Univ. of Kentucky Press, 1981), 45–46.

8 "What Does the South Want?," *Who Owns America?*, ed. Herbert Agar and Allen Tate (Boston and New York: Houghton Mifflin Co., at The Riverside Press, 1936), 181.

9 "Notes on Liberty and Property," *Who Owns America?*, 83.

10 "What Does the South Want?," 183.

11 See Grant McConnell, *The Decline of Agrarian Democracy* (Berkeley: Univ. of California Press, 1959), esp. 66–96.

12 "What Does the South Want?," 186.

13 "What Does the South Want?," 188.

14 "What Does the South Want?," 188.

15 C. Vann Woodward, *The Burden of History* (Baton Rouge: Louisiana State Univ. Press, 1960), 8–9.

16 "What Does the South Want?," 188.

17 "What Does the South Want?," 188.

18 "What Does the South Want?," 191.

19 Antonio Gramsci, *Selections from the Prison Notebooks*, trans. Quintin Hoare and Geoffrey Nowell Smith (New York: International Publishers, 1971), 242; hereafter cited as SPN.

20 *The American Jitters: A Year of the Slump* (New York: Charles Scribner's Sons, 1932).

21 *Letters on Literature and Politics, 1912–1972*: Selected and Edited by Elena Wilson (New York: Farrar, Straus, & Giroux, 1977), 209.

22 See Jonathan Arac, "F. O. Matthiessen: Authorizing an American Renaissance," *The American Renaissance Reconsidered*, ed. Walter Benn Michaels and Donald E. Pease (Baltimore: Johns Hopkins Univ. Press, 1985), 113–56; and Pease, *Visionary Compacts*, 246ff.

23 *Stonewall Jackson: The Good Soldier, A Narrative* (New York: Minton, Balch and Company, 1928); *Jefferson Davis: His Rise and Fall, A Biographical Narrative* (New York: Minton, Balch and Company, 1929); hereafter cited as SJ and JD.

24 *John Brown: The Making of a Martyr* (New York: Payson and Clarke, 1929); hereafter cited as JB.

25 "The Irrepressible Conflict," *I'll Take My Stand: The South and the Agrarian Tradition* (Baton Rouge: Louisiana State Univ. Press, 1980), 63; originally published, 1930.

26 "The Irrepressible Conflict," 67.

27 *The Tennessee: Volume I, the Old River, Frontier to Secession* (New York: Rinehart and Company, Inc., 1946); *The Tennessee: Volume II, the New River, Civil War to TVA* (New York: Rinehart and Company, 1948).

28 In *Memoirs and Opinions, 1926–1974* (Chicago: The Swallow Press, 1975), 111–12.

29 *Memoirs and Opinions*, 114.

30 *The Republic of Letters*, 35.

31 Tate's use of the word "character" here recalls Ezra Pound's similar use of the same figure in Canto XIII; see Paul A. Bové, *Intellectuals in Power* (New York: Columbia Univ. Press, 1986), 1–9.

32 *Memoirs and Opinions*, 152; cf. also 86.

7 *The Rationality of Disciplines*

1 Stephen Toulmin, *Human Understanding: The Collective Use and Evolution of Concepts* (Princeton: Princeton Univ. Press, 1971). Hereafter cited as HU.

2 See Michel Foucault, *Power/Knowledge: Selected Interviews and Other Writings, 1972–1977*, ed. Colin Gordon, trans. Colin Gordon et al. (New York: Pantheon, 1980), as well as his *Discipline and Punish: The Birth of the Prison*, trans. A. M. Sheridan Smith (New York: Pantheon, 1977).

3 I follow Richard Rorty in using the capital "P" to refer to the professional act of (and actors who do) thinking about certain problems like truth. See his "Pragmatism and Philosophy," in *Consequences of Pragmatism* (Minneapolis: Univ. of Minnesota Press, 1982).

4 Max Horkheimer, *Critique of Instrumental Reason*, trans. Matthew J. O'Connell et al. (New York: Seabury Press, 1974), vii.

5 I cannot discuss here either Toulmin's indebtedness to or differences from pragmatism. For Toulmin, however, the pragmatic becomes the instrumental.

6 Max Horkheimer, "The End of Reason," in *The Essential Frankfurt School Reader*, ed. Andrew Arato and Eike Gebhardt (New York: Continuum, 1982), 30–31.

7 A full discussion of Toulmin would have to include an investigation into the forces that, in part, account for Toulmin's decision to revise Darwin in this particular way.

8 See Michel Foucault, *L'Ordre du discours* (Paris: Gallimard, 1971), 73–74.

9 Space does not allow a complete reading of Toulmin's text against Darwin's. Suffice it to say that Darwin's own hesitations disappear in Toulmin's systematizing.

10 *L'Ordre du discours*, 73–74; translated as "The Discourse on Language" by Rupert Swyer in *The Archaeology of Knowledge* (New York: Harper and Row, 1976), 235.

11 Antonio Gramsci, *Selections from the Prison Notebooks*, trans. and ed. Quintin Hoare and Geoffrey Nowell Smith (New York: International Publishers, 1971), 323–33, 348, 419–25.

12 Rorty's "Pragmatism and Philosophy," xiii–xlvii, suggests how near and how far Toulmin is to pragmatic conceptions of rationality.

13 See *Human Understanding*, 329ff., and also Charles Altieri, *Act and Quality* (Amherst: Univ. of Massachusetts Press, 1982), esp. 318–31, for a similar attempt to revise Hegel.

14 See Paul A. Bové, *Intellectuals in Power: A Genealogy of Critical Humanism* (New York: Columbia Univ. Press, 1986).

15 See Burton J. Bledstein, *The Culture of Professionalism: The Middle Class and the Development of Higher Education in America* (New York: W. W. Norton, 1976).

16 For a few thoughts on this see John Fekete, *The Critical Twilight* (London: Routledge and Kegan Paul, 1977).

17 One can only say this does not correspond to anyone's sense of the profession of English studies.

18 In a way that is particularly apropos for Toulmin's assumption of an interest-free legal model, see on this point Roberto Mangabeira Unger, *The Critical Legal Studies Movement* (Cambridge: Harvard Univ. Press, 1986), 28–30. It is here that Unger discusses the privileges of certain groups within North Atlantic democracies.

19 "The End of Reason," 31.

20 See, for example, Theodor Adorno, "On the Fetish Character of Music and the Regression of Listening," in *The Essential Frankfurt School Reader*, 270–99.

21 "The End of Reason," 31–32.

22 See Karl Mannheim, *Ideology and Utopia: An Introduction to the Sociology of Knowledge*, trans. Louis Wirth and Edward Shils (New York: Harcourt, Brace and World, 1936), esp. 306–9.

23 Theodor Adorno, "Sociology of Knowledge and Its Consciousness," in *The Essential Frankfurt School Reader*, 459.

24 Paul Feyerabend, *Against Method* (London: NLB, 1975).

25 Alvin Gouldner, *The Future of Intellectuals and the Rise of the New Class* (New York: Continuum, 1979). See also *Intellectuals in Power*.

26 "Sociology of Knowledge," 455.

27 Georges Canguilhem, *On the Normal and the Pathological*, trans. Carolyn R. Fawcett (Dordrecht, Holland: D. Reidel Publishing, 1978), 70.

28 In this context, it is interesting that Fredric Jameson, writing on Sartre, should say

something that sounds so Foucaldian. Given Jameson's dismissive position on Foucault, Sartre's common influence alone can account for the coincidence: "What if the power of the revolutionary idea came fully as much from the new temporal reorganization of experience that it permits, as from any practical consequences which might flow from it as effects from a cause?" *Marxism and Form* (Princeton: Princeton Univ. Press, 1971), 258.

29 *On the Normal and the Pathological*, 28.

30 Ibid., 27–28.

31 See David Kairys, ed., *The Politics of Law: A Progressive Critique* (New York: Pantheon, 1982), esp. Edward Greer, "Antonio Gramsci and 'Legal Hegemony,'" 304–9, and Duncan Kennedy, "Legal Education as Training for Hierarchy," 40–61.

32 See *Intellectuals in Power*, and Daniel T. O'Hara, *The Romance of Interpretation: Visionary Criticism from Pater to de Man* (New York: Columbia Univ. Press, 1985).

33 See *New York Times*, March 16, 1986, sec. I, p. I.

34 *On the Normal and the Pathological*, 93.

35 Michel Foucault, Introduction to ibid., xix; see also *Intellectuals in Power*, esp. ch. six.

36 Foucault, "Introduction," *On the Normal and the Pathological*, xix.

37 See *Intellectuals in Power*, ch. six.

38 I am aware of Toulmin's recent book, *The Return to Cosmology: Postmodern Science and the Theology of Nature* (Berkeley and Los Angeles: Univ. of California Press, 1982), but do not believe that it any way invalidates my claim. On the contrary, one might say that even at its most postmodern moment when it evokes Heidegger and Keats (255–57), it continues to be nonreflexive. While worrying the relationship of the observer to the observed in true hermeneutic fashion, it never questions the position of the Philosopher or his discursive practice.

39 See, for example, Paul A. Bové, "Agriculture and Academe: America's Southern Question," this volume.

40 See *Intellectuals in Power*; see also Jonathan Arac, *Critical Genealogies: Historical Situations for Postmodern Literary Studies* (New York: Columbia Univ. Press, 1987).

41 It should be said that this critical impulse has positive as well as negative components, especially when positioned within the struggle for self-determination. See Bové, *Intellectuals in Power*, esp. ch. six. I should also point out that I make the argument for a positive element in criticism despite Foucault's own powerful critique of emancipatory rhetorics.

42 For examples of this tradition see R. P. Blackmur, *Language as Gesture* (New York: Columbia Univ. Press, 1981), esp. 396–99 and 410–12; and Jameson, *Marxism and Form*, xiii–xiv.

43 As so often in the past, I am indebted to Jonathan Arac for his extraordinary skills and patience as a reader and editor.

8   *Reclaiming Criticism*

1 "Blackmur on Henry James," *The Legacy of R. P. Blackmur: Essays, Memoirs, Texts*, ed. Edward T. Cone, Joseph Frank, and Edmund Keeley (New York: The Ecco Press, 1987), 21–43.

2 That Blackmur has been an influence on myriad important critical minds trained at Princeton needs not be said. One thinks of figures as diverse as Berryman, Said, Michael Fried, Daniel Javitch, Merod, and Joseph Frank.

3 Edward W. Said, "The Problem of Textuality: Two Exemplary Positions," *Critical Inquiry*, 4 (1978), 673–714; revised and reprinted as "Criticism Between Culture and System," *The World, the Text, and the Critic* (Cambridge: Harvard Univ. Press, 1983), 178–225. I shall refer to the later version of the essay.

4 Of course, with a fine enough empirical eye, one can always argue that the hegemonic doesn't exist; that there are always and everywhere slight variations and modulations that "make a difference." Such a commitment to a detailed empirical standard might itself be seen as a corrective to easy abstraction—and as such could be aligned with various dialectical theories of contradiction—but it might also be critically examined for its own place in the dominant values of intellectual discussion.

5 See Paul A. Bové, "Closing Up the Ranks: Xerxes' Hordes Are at the Pass," *In the Wake of Theory* (Middletown, Conn.: Wesleyan Univ. Press, 1991).

6 See, for example, the Program in the Study of Culture at the University of Pittsburgh; the Graduate Literature Program at Duke; the program in the Comparative Studies of Discourse and Society at the University of Minnesota. It is also true that as part of the reaction against theory and progressive criticism, as well as a result of normalizing professional practices, such programs are either being phased out or redefined in less oppositional directions.

7 See the introduction to *The Wake of Theory*.

8 *Professing Literature* (Chicago: Univ. of Chicago Press, 1987), esp. 247f.

9 See Marilyn Butler, "Feminist Criticism, late-80's style," TLS, March 11–17 (1988), 283–85, who writes: "The most typical feminist production of the 1980s is an article, once a lecture, directed at other women professionals, on how to achieve objectives from which no one publicly dissents" (283). Of the most noted feminist essays, Butler writes: "A flair for titles has helped to make some of these performances almost legendary."

10 See, for example, LaCapra's description of Greenblatt as a leading intellectual to be contested in "History and Criticism," an unpublished manuscript presented as a lecture at, among other places, Cornell in March 1987 and at the University of Pennsylvania on April 3, 1987.

11 "The Horizon of R. P. Blackmur," *The Legacy of R. P. Blackmur: Essays, Memoirs, Texts*, 99.

12 R. P. Blackmur, *Henry Adams*, ed. Veronica A. Makowsky (New York: Harcourt, Brace, Jovanovich, 1980), 6; hereafter cited in my text as HA.

13 See Fredric Jameson, "The Politics of Theory," NGC, no. 33 (1984), 53–66; and "Postmodernism, or The Cultural Logic of Late Capitalism," NLR, 146 (1984), 53–93.

14 *The Political Unconscious: Narrative as a Socially Symbolic Act* (Ithaca: Cornell Univ. Press, 1981), esp. chap. one.

15 See Immanuel Kant, *The Critique of Pure Reason*, trans. Norman Kemp Smith (New York: St. Martin's Press, 1965), 20.

16 For some discussion of this figure, see Bové, *Intellectuals in Power* (New York: Columbia Univ. Press, 1986), esp. chap. one.

17 See *On the Genealogy of Morals*, trans. Walter Kaufman (New York: Vintage Books, 1969), 16; and *Intellectuals in Power*, 14f.

18 See *Intellectuals in Power*, chap. six.

19 R. P. Blackmur, "A Critic's Job of Work," *Language as Gesture* (New York: Columbia Univ. Press, 1981), 372; hereafter cited in my text as LG.

20 I want to thank Don Pease for talking over this issue with me and helping me to a clearer understanding of the necessity of unsentimental conflict in Blackmur's writing.

21 Henry Adams, *The History of the United States of America During the Administrations of Thomas Jefferson* (New York: The Library of America, 1986), cf. 96f.

22 *The History of the United States*, 81.

23 Bryce took Adams's anonymous novel as the text for an essay defending democracy. See "Some Aspects of American Public Life," *Fortnightly Review*, 38 (1880), 634ff; see too, Ernest Samuels, *Henry Adams: The Middle Years* (Cambridge: Harvard Univ. Press, 1958), 88f. "Democracy" is reprinted in *Adams: Democracy, Esther, Mont Saint Michel and Chartres, and The Education of Henry Adams* (New York: The Library of America).

24 Adams, *The Education*, 1057–58; hereafter cited as EHA.

9 Paul de Man

1 I shall cite this essay, parenthetically, from the following: Paul de Man, "The Rhetoric of Temporality," in *Blindness and Insight*, 2nd ed., Introduction, Wlad Godzich (Minneapolis: Univ. of Minnesota Press, 1983), 187–228.

2 *Critical Writings 1953–1978*, ed. Lindsay Waters (Minneapolis: Univ. of Minnesota Press, 1989), lvi.

3 In *The Romance of Interpretation: Visionary Criticism from Pater to de Man* (New York: Columbia Univ. Press, 1985), 220.

4 *Critical Genealogies: Historical Situations for Postmodern Literary Studies* (New York: Columbia Univ. Press, 1987), 24, 196.

5 *Visionary Compacts: American Renaissance Writings in Cultural Context* (Madison: Univ. of Wisconsin Press, 1987), 168.

6 *Critical Writings*, lvi.

7 *Ursprung des deutschen Trauerspiels* (Frankfurt am Main: Suhrkampf, 1963); trans. John Osborne, intro. George Steiner (London: New Left Books, 1977).

8 *Critical Writings*, lvi.

9 Ibid., lvii.

10 Ibid., lvi.

11 For some further sense of how one might carry out this reading, see de Man's "Semiology and Rhetoric," *Allegories of Reading* (New Haven: Yale Univ. Press, 1979), 3–20.

12 "Allegories of Reading Paul de Man," in *Reading de Man Reading*, ed. Lindsay Waters and Wlad Godzich (Minneapolis: Univ. of Minnesota Press, 1989), 105.

13 "The Lesson of Paul de Man," *Yale French Studies*, no. 69 (1985).

14 Edward W. Said, *Beginnings: Intention and Method* (New York: Basic Books, 1975), esp. 83–84.

15 *Beginnings*, p. 84.

16 Michael Hays, "As If Spellbound by Magical Curves," paper given at Dartmouth College, Spring 1989.

17 See my discussion of this problem in *Ezra Pound's Cantos. Intellectuals in Power* (New York: Columbia Univ. Press, 1986), 3–9.

18 "Allegories of Reading Paul de Man," 119; the quotation from de Man occurs in *Allegories of Reading*. On the use of the word "excuse" Jacobs advises we see de Man's final chapter in *Allegories of Reading*, "Excuses." On the use of the "rhetorical question," Jacobs advises we see de Man's opening chapter, "Semiology and Rhetoric." The necessity to allegorize her own irony seems, despite her brilliant self-consciousness, to indicate some nostalgia for symbolism in the master's student.

19 One need not mention the names of specific critics to be understood here. The recent debates and exchanges of letters in the columns of journals and reviews make clear the differences between the students who learn and go on and the ephebes who can only echo and track the master.

20 See *Intellectuals in Power*, 3–9, esp. on "Canto XIII."

21 I have elsewhere written about the confluence of these two traditions and so I won't repeat myself on that level here. See "The Metaphysics of Textuality: Marx's *Eighteenth Brumaire* and Nietzsche's *Use and Abuse of History*," *The Dalhousie Review*, 64 (1984), 401–22.

22 See *Language as Gesture: Essays in Poetry* (New York: Columbia Univ. Press, Morningside Edition, 1981), 13ff.; originally published 1952 by Harcourt, Brace.

23 *Diacritics*, 2 (1972), 44–53; reprinted in *Allegories of Reading*, 79–102; I shall quote from this reprinted edition.

24 Ibid., 79–102.

25 Ibid., 80.

26 Ibid., 80.

27 Ibid., 81.

28 Ibid., 81.

29 Ibid., 82.

30 See ibid., 101–2.

31 Paul de Man, "The Resistance to Theory," in *The Resistance to Theory*, foreword by Wlad Godzich (Minneapolis: Univ. of Minnesota Press, 1986), 19.

32 See Paul A. Bové, *Destructive Poetics* (New York: Columbia Univ. Press, 1980), 92–130.

33 *The Resistance to Theory*, xviii.

10   *Dante, Gramsci, and Cultural Criticism*

1 For a theoretical sense of this problematic which has been very important to criticism's discussion of modernity, see Edward W. Said, *Beginnings: Intention and Method* (New York: Basic Books, 1975).

2 *Gramsci's Cultural Writings*, ed. David Forgacs and Geoffrey Nowell-Smith, trans. William Boelhower (Cambridge: Harvard Univ. Press, 1985), 151, 156. Hereafter cited parenthetically by page number in my text.

3 Benedetto Croce, *The Poetry of Dante*, trans. Douglas Ainslie (London: George Allen and Unwin, Ltd., 1922), 90–91.

4 Antonio Gramsci, *Letters from Prison*, ed. Lynne Lawner (New York: Harper Colophon Books, 1973), 210. Hereafter cited parenthetically by page in my text.

5 Lawner points this out in her note 7 to page 212.

6 "Gramsci's 'little discovery': Gramsci's Interpretation of Canto X of Dante's *Inferno*," *boundary* 2, 14, no. 3 (1986), 87, "A Special Issue: The Legacy of Antonio Gramsci," ed. Joseph A. Buttigieg.

7 Since I have treated Auerbach at length elsewhere, I will focus on Eliot in this essay. See Paul A. Bové, *Intellectuals in Power* (New York: Columbia Univ. Press, 1986), 196–203.

8 *Selected Essays: New Edition* (New York: Harcourt, Brace, & World, 1964), 200. Hereafter cited parenthetically by page in my text.

9 Gramsci struggles to align Cavalcante's anguish with other classical images of suffering such as Timanthes' veiled portrait of Agamemnon at the moment of Iphigenia's sacrifice. This is a move that typically aligns his with traditional conservative idealistic humanists. See, for example, the similar gesture in Charles Altieri, *Act and Quality* (Amherst: Univ. of Massachusetts Press, 1981).

10 On this structure of relation, taken psychoanalytically, see Harold Bloom, *The Anxiety of Influence* (New York: Oxford Univ. Press, 1973).

11 See Daniel T. O'Hara, *The Romance of Interpretation* (New York: Columbia Univ. Press, 1985).

12 See Paul de Man, "The Rhetoric of Temporality," in *Blindness and Insight*, 2nd. ed. (Minneapolis: Univ. of Minnesota Press, 1983), 187– 228, and Paul A. Bové, "Paul de Man: Some Notes on the Critic's Search for Authority Against Consensus." *Criticism*, 32 Spring (1990), 149–61.

13 See *The Romance of Interpretation*, 1–9.

14 Fredric Jameson, *The Political Unconscious* (Ithaca: Cornell Univ. Press, 1981), 225.

15 R. P. Blackmur, "The Critic's Job of Work." In *Language as Gesture* (New York: Columbia Univ. Press, 1981), 372.

16 See Daniel O'Hara, *Lionel Trilling* (Madison: Univ. of Wisconsin Press, 1988) for the best working out of the dialectics of such imagination.

17 *The Poetry of Dante*, 117–18.

18 Dante, *The Inferno*, trans. Charles S. Singleton (Princeton: Princeton Univ. Press, 1980), 103.

19 *The Poetry of Dante*, 120.

11 Madness, Medicine, and the State

1 Michel Foucault, *Folie et déraison: histoire de la folie à l'âge classique* (Paris: Librarie Plon, 1961); *Madness and Civilization* (New York: Random House, Inc., 1965); hereafter cited parenthetically in my text as MC.

2 2nd. ed. With an afterword by and an interview with Michel Foucault (Chicago: Univ. of Chicago Press, 1983); hereafter cited in my text as SH.

3 Michel Serres, *La Communication* (Paris: Les Éditions de Minuit, 1968), 178f.

4 *The Birth of the Clinic: An Archaeology of Medical Perception*, trans. A. M. Sheridan Smith (New York: Random House, Inc., 1973); published as *Naissance de la Clinique* (Paris: Presses Universitaires de France, 1963).

5 Trans. anonymous (New York: Random House, Inc., 1973).

6 I include myself in that list. See Paul A. Bové, "Power and Freedom," *October*, 53 (1990), 78–92.

7 I capitalize these terms in the way that Richard Rorty capitalizes the latter, to specify their existence as organized institutional disciplines of knowledge with, as such, their own interests, histories, discourses, and prejudices. See Richard Rorty, *Philosophy and the Mirror of Nature* (Princeton: Princeton Univ. Press, 1979).

8 I have argued this case before in relation to both Philosophers and Historians. For the former, see my discussion of Charles Taylor in the preface to Gilles Deleuze, *Foucault*, trans. Sean Hand (Minneapolis: Univ. of Minnesota Press, 1988), vii–xix; for the latter, see *Intellectuals in Power* (New York: Columbia Univ. Press, 1986), *passim*.

9 *Foucault* (Berkeley: Univ. of California Press, 1987); first published by Fontana Press, London, 1985. Merquior, a Brazilian, according to the publication notes, did his Ph.D. in sociology with Ernest Gellner at the London School of Economics; hereafter cited in my text as M.

10 "Foucault, Structuralism and the End of History," *Journal of Modern History*, 51 (1979), 451–503.

11 For an interesting example of this from a friendly philosophical reader, see Nancy Fraser *Unruly Practices* (Minneapolis: Univ. of Minnesota Press, 1989), 18–23, 35–38. See also my reading of Taylor in the preface in Deleuze, *Foucault* for a closer demonstration of the tactics I mention here.

12 Here Merquior relies on Foucault's famous essay responding to George Steiner, although he confuses the reference in his own note. See Foucault's first response to Steiner, "Monstrosities in Criticism," trans. Robert J. Matthews, *Diacritics*, 1 (1971), 57–60. Steiner's reply to Foucault's response was "Steiner Responds to Foucault," *Diacritics*, 1 (1971), 59. Foucault's final remarks were "Foucault Responds 2," *Diacritics*, 1 (1971), 60.

13 Georges Canguilhem, *On the Normal and the Pathological*, trans. Carolyn R. Fawcett with editorial collaboration of Robert S. Cohen and an introduction by Michel Foucault (Dordrecht, Holland and Boston: D. Reidel Publishing Company, 1978); originally published as *Le Normal et la pathologique* (Paris: Presses Universitaires, 1966); originally published in part as the author's thesis, Strasbourg, 1943. See also my essay "The Rationality of Disciplines: The Abstract Understanding of Stephen Toulmin," *After Foucault*, ed. Jonathan Arac (New Brunswick: Rutgers Univ. Press, 1988), 42–70.

14 *Hegel: Texts and Commentary*, trans. and ed. by Walter Kaufman (Garden City, N.Y.: Doubleday Anchor Book, 1966), 24, 26. Emphases in this quotation are mine.

15 I realize I am withholding serious discussion of an entire range of problems here. Not only the relations between Kant and Hegel and Hegel and Foucault, but also the problem of modernity and of Hegel's system's role in constructing modern disciplines and the state. For some sense of the complexities at hand, see Wlad Godzich's as yet unpublished paper, "Thirty Years' Struggle for Theory."

16 Jacques Derrida, "Cogito and the History of Madness," *Writing and Difference*, trans. Alan Bass (Chicago: Univ. of Chicago Press, 1978); originally published in France as *L'écriture et la différance* (Paris: Editions du Seuil, 1967).

17 Of course, Erich Auerbach has authored the major study on the "figural" tradition

and so it need not be redescribed in this context. "Figura," trans. Ralph Mann-heim, *Scenes from the Drama of European Literature* (Minneapolis: Univ. of Minnesota Press, 1984), 11–78; first published in *Neue Dantestudien* (Istanbul, 1944).

18 One might say in passing that "theory" should be seen as the recuperation of figure but within the problematic of language.

19 Foucault's Kantian obsession with "finitude" in the early sixties can be traced in part in *Intellectuals in Power*.

20 See Claude Lefort, *Democracy and Political Theory*, trans. David Macey (Minneapolis: Univ. of Minnesota Press, 1988), esp. 183–210.

21 Ibid., 55.

22 *The Birth of the Clinic*, 29.

23 Edward W. Said, *Orientalism* (New York: Pantheon Press, 1978).

24 "A Genealogy of Modern Racism," *Prophesy Deliverance! An Afro-American Revolutionary Christianity* (Philadelphia: The Westminster Press, 1982), 47–68.

25 "Correcting Kant: Bakhtin and Intercultural Interactions," *boundary 2*, 18 (1991), 16.

Index

......

Paul A. Bové is Professor of English at the University of Pittsburgh and Editor of *boundary* 2. He is the author of *Intellectuals in
Power*, *In the Wake of Theory*, and *Destructive Politics*.

Library of Congress Cataloging-in-Publication Data
Bové, Paul A., 1949–
Mastering discourse : the politics of intellectual culture / Paul
Bové.
Includes bibliographical references and index.
ISBN 0-8223-1232-8. — ISBN 0-8223-1245-X (pbk.)
1. Criticism.   2. Discourse analysis.   3. Philosophy, Modern.
I. Title.
PN98.S6B68   1992
801'.95—dc20   91-41256 CIP